Karl-Heinz Heddergott

New
Football Manual

Limpert

In collaboration with Inter Nationes, Bonn-Bad Godesberg

© 1976 by Limpert Verlag GmbH, Bad Homburg, v.d.H.
Translation: Mark Fair, Cologne
Cover design: Wulf Weiß, Frankfurt am Main
Illustrations: Karl-Heinz Grindler, Stuttgart
Distributed by: Soccer Books, Inc.
            A Division of CYSA
            908 Industrial Ave.
            Palo Alto, CA 94303

TABLE OF CONTENTS

1. INTRODUCTION

The "New Football Manual" has no intention of categorically denying and rejecting everything that is "old" and has proved itself; far rather "new" means constructive change in the sense of adapting teaching methods to fit the trends in the development of present-day football as well as to fit the player of today who after all, is responsible for what is taking place on the field of play. The game and the player are taken as the root of the teaching method. The "homo ludens" occupies the centre of the stage. He represents both the challenge and the target of the system of teaching. Both the game itself and the player have become more substantial and intensive with regard to what is demanded. They are perpetually placing the value of the teaching system in question and under permanent pressure. And this is a good thing to ensure that there is no stagnation and that contact to further development is not lost – above all, when success manages to obscure the process of development.

The development of the game and the increased demand on performance mean that every change must be observed and examined concerning its progressiveness in order to ensure that one adopts the proper approach both with regard to the form and extent of training and guidance of the players.

In top performance football nowadays, goals mean more than merely ascertaining who has won or lost. The game is motivated beyond victory or defeat. The desire to win has grown and as a result the provoking "might" of a massed defence is increasingly growing in importance. Every ball is fought for harder and more grimly.

This represents at one and the same time a problem and a challenge for the attack. It must try and score goals in spite of this in order to maintain the beauty and attractiveness of the game of football and to further enhance its educational value.

The urge of the individual to achieve greater freedom of decision, to have the chance of codetermination and co-responsibility – is also expressed in the game. The game requires lightning-fast decision-making and a responsible attitude in solving tactical tasks. Knowledge and tactical maturity govern the proper playing behaviour in *every single* team position.

All this must be reflected in the teaching of the game. He who – in the free world of he game –, is supposed to play creatively and constructively, gladly sharing decision-making and responsibility, should not – en route to this target – be restricted by stereo-typed instruction, so-called patent solutions, long-winded preambles or catalogues of traits of movement, which alone owing to their abundance, cannot possibly be realised. The reproduction of "old hat" will not get you anywhere. The only way to encourage and foster an active and re-active style of play is to tackle the stress of real live situations purposefully – at all times – which contain both main technical and tactical aspects.

Competition itself continues to govern the range of exercises and training and the method of teaching is in each case orientated to the player as a particular type of performer with his specific likes, traits and attributes.

2. THE FUNDAMENTS GOVERNING PERFORMANCE IN FOOTBALL

2.1. THE PLAYER AND THE GAME

The permanent striving towards achieving top performance and improving upon this is linked to the term "sport". Each branch of sport fosters this in a different manner. As a consequence, for the most part you select your form of sport according to your own constitutional disposition; it enables you to feel at ease, you find it enjoyable because your ability makes it possible for you to produce the movements and behaviour required by the game. The pleasure produced by success stimulates the activity and the effort to attempt improve one's personal best performance. The demands on performance which the game of football makes, are extremely differentiated, alone owing to the various positions in the team with their specific field of duties within the framework of team performance.

The most significant inherent traits of the football player as a particular performance type are:

1. senso-motoric variability, i. e., manifold and multifareous talent with regard to movement and adaptability (e. g. controlled speed);
2. speed of reaction;
3. ability to make contact (social reference);
4. strength of nerve;
5. the power of making up one's mind and rapidly taking decisions.

In addition to this of course, there are special features which have made it possible say, for a Wolfgang Overath or a Günter Netzer to play the role of schemer or motor in midfield, which have allowed Gerd Müller to become a dangerous goalgetter or Berti Vogts to become an outstanding defender (see Chapter on Special Training for the Team Positions). These basic traits or constitutional suitability characterise the footballer. They govern his playing behaviour as well as his expectations in training. He is pre-programmed in such a way that he can respond to the many stress situations which crop up during a match with skill and dexterity, determination and purposiveness, with imperturbability and composure. It goes without saying that these basic characteristics are to be found more in the one person than in another. It regularly happens that a coach feels he would dearly like to be able to combine two types of player!

The utmost ability to concentrate and adjust oneself, in order to make rapid action possible, is called for at a comprehensive and complex level to ensure play of the highest standard. Every movement is the chosen response to a complex range of impressions obtained from the immediate and not so immediate surroundings of the player involved in a particular situation. The purposive selection of just how to react calls for a certain type of intellectual-mental orientation. A good player must not allow himself to become burdened or confused by the stress brought on by any given situation.

Within this range of impressions and ever-changing conflict situations, the player finds the challenge accorded him and in tackling it, the experience of success or failure. The joy of success after overcoming perpetually new and different difficulties or possibly alternatively, disappointment brought on by failure activate the whole range of emotions and provide the suspense experienced during a game. In this field of tensions of ever-changing conflict situations and an emotional barometer gyrating between success and failure, the player hopes to prove himself. Here, he is experiencing himself, here, he finds his fulfilment.

2.2. THE CONSCIOUSNESS AND WILL TO PERFORM WELL

To perform well means to make use of all available qualities purposively and successfully in the accomplishment of certain tasks. The magnitude of the performance always depends upon the nature and intensity of the forces employed. Thus experience reveals that many a highly gifted player, who finds he is able to achieve things all too easily, nevertheless, appears to be colourless and unsatisfied with regard to his overall performance because the necessary desire to make an effort and the strength of will are missing. These types of players have never learned to really make an effort because during training they normally task themselves too little. Each player must learn to appraise his own performance capacity self-critically in order to work on improving his own overall performance consciously and purposefully. The English principle "Teach the player to train himself" is a target deserving priority and one which should be aimed at far most intensively by us as well. This demand and approach to more activity and responsibility on the part of the players in building up their own performance strengthens their consciousness to perform well. The prior condition for this though is a cooperative relationship between the coach and the players. The player must be aware of the performance requirements and the principles governing performance for a high standard of play. In top-class football, only the player with whom you can mull over and discuss training problems and tactical concepts, can possibly hope to assert and establish himself.

Tactical maturity and conscious playing behaviour based on a thorough knowledge of the general tactics of attacking and defending play are important criteria for the quality of a player – especially with regard to the present-day performance requirements.

2.3. CONDITIONING

By condition we mean the physical state achieved as a result of training efforts geared to suit competitive requirements. It is the physical prerequisite to ensure that all competitive demands can be met. The kind of training is governed by the requirements specific to competition and by the character of the player as a particular performance type. The effectiveness of conditioning must express itself in any case in an improved game with the ball and in improved behaviour during competition itself. The game of football, possessing as it does a whole range of possibilities of movements, has laws of its own. There are no constantly recurring series of movements such as the pre-programmed movements in the field of athletics or gymnastics. In the game of football, each movement is part of behaviour which is governed by a given situation. There is no situation which is identical to another, and the player must time and again adopt a new approach and adjust himself to the behaviour of opponents and team-mates. Movement is always only a part of the perpetually complex playing behaviour in each new situation. Thus condition is the speed, stamina and endurance which have been trained for the game. The player must also discover elements of the game in conditioning in order to address his constitutional character and mentality. He must be able to feel that these training forms have actual relevance to the game in order to arouse pleasure, spontaneous willingness and open-mindedness while he is engaged in them. The features of fitness training must be adapted to suit the specific requirements of the game of football and the constitutional orientation of the players on the basis of the latest scientific findings in training instruction. The ball is the piece of equipment which the footballer has chosen; therefore it should also be at the centre of things during fitness training.

2.3.1. Speed

The very term speed is extremely complex and differentiated in the game of football. The player who is the faster one over a sprint course, is not necessarily also the faster player during a game or in his approach to a game. The inborn ability, which is to be found in the intellectual-mental sphere of perception and recognition, of being able to recognise almost unpredictable situations and to act or react quickly is an extremely decisive factor governing speed in the game. The English say about such a player "he reads the game", that means, he can sum up the situation quickly, interpret and assess the many intentions of his team-mates and opponents and respond to them with a constructive approach (anticipation). The player always moves, whether on or off the ball, under the influence and the challenging pressure of surroundings which adapts themselves to the course he takes. His running during a game is more arhythmic, variable, i. e., the player runs, above all when he's on the ball, with short, varying steps and changing tempo, in order to be ready at all times to surprisingly change the direction he is running in. Thus running becomes a tactical means. The ability to sprint and the power to be quick off the mark are expressed in running free. making space, on the way to the ball, when forcing the ball towards the opposing goal, when bursting through or spurting past the opponent, or similarly when the defender reacts to the fast running behaviour adopted by an opposing forward. or when intercepting a pass, when taking advantage of a split-second chance or pursuing an attacking forward who is about to burst through, etc. Above all, the surprise, rapid change in running tempo, the change from subdued and moderate running only then to suddenly burst into top speed, is of supreme tactical significance. Thus, the good footballer must have two gears available in his "box". Sometimes even top players make the mistake of running into the opposing defence at full pelt with the ball so that when the opposing players skillfully block the ball they topple head over heels. It can also be observed frequently that players approach the opposing defence at high speed whilst controlling the ball too far away from their bodies; they tend to push the ball too far forward and consequently lose it because they are no longer in a position to shield it and control it.

Sprinting ability has to be brought into harmony with skill and ball-playing ability. The running speed and playing skill determine the playing rhythm of a player. This makes it clear that any increase in meàsurable running speed has to be geared and coordinated to the game on the ball. Speed as an important factor of condition is essentially effective in a complex relationship in the game of football and must be considered in this integrative connection. Its components are elasticity, the ability to sprint and accelerate, skill and manouevrability, speed of action and reaction coupled with discernment and perspicuity allowing the player to do the right thing amidst the greatest stress produced by a competitive situation and finally the kind of speed which allows behaviour to unfold sub-consciously and outside the normal time of reaction. Thus in the game of football in particular speed is not just simply speed.

2.3.2. Stamina

A football match lasts 45 minutes each way as a rule and as a result of the intensity of movement involved it makes high — and as the game progresses — ever higher demands on the circulation's capacity. Seen tactically, the game generally calls for prolonged sprinting ability in many situations. For instance, when Berti Vogts, as defender, pursues an opponent, gets the ball away from him, then counter attacks and heads for the opposing goal going at top speed with the ball, and then finishes the move off with a cross or a shot at goal and then rushes back at full speed to take up his position in defence. Forwards, who continually take part in attacking play at high speed, who head for the opposing goal and who immediately drop back to play a defending role the moment the ball is lost, who take up pursuit of their opponent and run back in order to participate in defending their own goal, are only capable of fulfilling this tactical role thanks to well-trained organic strength and stamina. As the game progresses, such challenges and demands occur with ever greater frequency.

In building up performance in football, we must not simply refer to standard values but we must perpetually be comparing these with the latest scientific recognitions and coordinating them. It must be observed here that forms of training practised in other sports should not be blindly copied and that footballers cannot be treated like light or heavy athletes. These basic scientific recognitions must be interpreted in footballing terms before they are applied.

Thus the acceptable methods of training designed for the special development of organic strength, interval training and the continuous demand on stamina are made possible taking into account all the basic features, by means of technical and tactical training forms of competition. The footballer does not require a running track! He regards this monotonous occupation as an imposition.

It kills all spontaneous activity and pleasure and is in direct contrast to the character of the footballer as well as the specific requirements of the game (see Chapter on Conditioning).

2.3.3. Strength

The footballer's deployment of strength must always be linked to discernment and skill. For the footballer in particular, who must always adapt himself to the most varied situations employing a whole range of technical attributes, the properly dosed application of strength, steered by the sensitivity of his nerves, has a decisive role to play. The build-up of strength during training is thus the prior condition for a well-adjusted coordinated performance. This special deployment of strength is taxed in particular as the game progresses according to the external conditions, the state of the pitch, the climatic conditions as well as just how difficult and tough the game turns out to be.

The strength required for being quick off the mark and jumping to head the ball as well as the powerful header itself, the strength required for the shot and the supporting strength of the standing leg, as well as the strength of the arms required to break a player's fall gently in the case of "diving headers" represent a number of the main occasions when the footballer must deploy strength. During the heat of the battle, these demands are repeated with ever-changing targets. As the game of football is not played without bodily contact but instead tough tackles increasingly test the players, overall athletic training of the whole body is essential. *Skill in tackling is not enough on its own; only when it can be applied in conjunction with the proper strength does it become an important tactical means.* When watching Arsenal of London during training, I was able to observe how in particular tackling, hard but fair jostling, was consciously practised everyday. The dynamic and powerful brand of football as played in England has its roots not only in the combative and purposive attitude towards competition but also the necessary pre-requisites of will are *the result of strength which is engendered in youngsters.* The essential basis is provided in the schools which are responsible for sport for the young. The promising 15-year old youngster, who has selected the profession of footballer, uses light dumb-bells and medicine balls for half an hour every day. It is interesting to observe the dedication with which these youngsters apply themselves. Primarily, such exercises were designed to develop the muscles of the leg, rump and arm. As a result, additional impulses towards growth were provided here, both consciously and thoughtfully. In our clubs, they first – if at all – concern themselves with strength training when it is too late and when it can no longer have any influence upon growth. Getting accustomed to the training load at an early age is of great importance whereby of course, the load factor must always be in relation to the general development and the available potential. The kind of load is isotonic, i. e., it takes place in series of movements, which are provided as variably and interestingly as possible for the footballer, with thoughtful movement features. Thanks to the frequency of these drills, a circular effect is achieved. The load period should be, in the case of daily training, three times a week before the season and twice a week during the season, lasting for half an hour. The load possibilities are as follows:

1. overcoming one's own body weight (jumping and press-up exercises), using the ball as the apparatus;
2. overcoming one's own body weight against the resistance of a partner (pushing and pulling exercises, attempting to wrest the medicine ball from one another, etc.);
3. overcoming foreign bodies, whose weight should be from a fifth to a third of one's bodily weight so that forced breathing is avoided when jumping, leaning, hopping, lifting or bending.

In the intervals between each exercise unit, which should last one to two minutes, stretching exercises and playing the ball after thoughtful strength training represent a welcome and important counter-balance. In so-called strength training as well, a uniform sequence of training should be avoided, in that the load factors are varied and the form made more relaxed through the introduction of play. *Strength training has not the purpose of producing a mass of muscle which only serves to get in one's way, but is supposed to create the prior conditions for the manifold demands made on the deployment of strength in competition. Strength training is orientated to playing skill.* And last but not least, a strong muscle structure also acts prophylactically by reducing the proneness to injuries of the joints (Dr. Schneider, Cologne).

2.4. FORM

The word form is interpreted as meaning the mental driving forces, the feelings and emotions which influence the performance. Experience has shown that the spiritual, physical and mental forces and components governing performance are linked together in an integrative relationship. Conditional strength and skill as well as the will to aim methodically at the achievement of targets, in order to be successful during the game, require *the thrust provided by positive mental orientation* of feelings and emotions. This internal vitality and balance of the emotions first serves to stimulate the approach to the game, it finds expression in the enthusiasm for one's own capabilities and lends itself to kindling the "fire" of the other players. The feeling of strength and ability determine *the consciousness of performance.* The success of mastering a challenge posed by a given situation during the game provides evidence of ability. The heady feeling of pleasure at one's success and of overcoming obstacles and difficulties is related to this. The pleasure at one's success is all the more intense, the more difficult the situation to be overcome and your opponents were. On the other hand, failures can lead to the emotional barometer sinking and seriously affect the stimulating *emotive balance, self-confidence* and *self-security.*

The experience of success and the *self-affirmation of ability* do not always lead to a positive influence on the performance behaviour. It happens quite frequently that following strenuous efforts, a team finally manage to score a goal, only then to clearly lose their vitality as a direct consequence of this pleasure at their success and their opponents are able to equalise with their next move. Similarly, initial failures can mobilise forces within a team which remind them finally of what they are actually capable of in playing terms and the initial lack of success is transformed into success. Teams which, following an impressive performance and holding a seemingly safe lead, lose some of their vitality and allow their opponents, which they had clearly dominated up until that point, to take over the initiative, in fact place themselves in a difficult position as a consequence. And this can often lead to throwing the match away or indeed even losing it. This leads to the conclusion that the game calls for the *utmost concentration and vitality* at any given moment, if optimal performance is to be achieved, quite immaterial of whether a defensive or an offensive game is being played. Each game engenders a certain field of tension produced through the relative strength of the teams involved and the motivations relating to the outcome of the match. Within this field of tension, fresh conflict situations arise which also challenge emotional balance and mental stability.

Most sides, when playing away from home, adopt the tactics of attempting to unsettle the emotional balance of the home team. Home sides are of course favoured in front of their own fans and depend on fulfilling the high expectations of success placed in them by scoring a goal quickly. They are pre-programmed correspondingly. The longer the opponent succeeds in delaying this quickly sought after scoring success by means of a clever, massed defensive game, the more the home side enter a clear conflict situation, which results in many players revealing nervousness and a lack of wits, something which is enhanced by the attitude of the disappointed spectators. The ensuing confusion and instability and the resultant relaxing of the defence provide the opponent, whose tactics succeed, with the best chances of counter attacking. Given similar playing qualities, the team which have the best chances of success are those who can quickly compensate for any rise or fall of the emotional barometer and above all, do not permit themselves to be influenced by externalities. *Composure, concentration* and *purposefulness* along with *undisturbed confidence in one's own capabilities* are vital prerequisites in successfully asserting oneself.

Special skill must be shown by the coach in his guidance in mobilising and conserving the full performance strength of his team throughout a whole championship series. This calls for *intensive and concentrated work on the part of the coach* in preparing and adjusting his team to meet their next opponent and to draw up and formulate anew the eternal theme "football" under the aspect of the new game and all the special features connected with it. In the course of a championship season, fluctuations in form can often be determined in the case of sides which have landed in a complacent middle-of-the-table position. They are *undermotivated,* they are not spurred on by the fear of the drop nor by the chance of winning the championship.

Form is thus always subject to fluctuations. There are manifold reasons for this and they can be recognised before they really become acute by a good, experienced coach and combatted by means of the appropriate counter-measures. However, there are also losses in form which have to be overcome, without there being any plausible reason for their existence. Their causes are hidden far deeper and frequently cannot be identified properly.

The training set-up of course, bears great influence on form. Here too, the coach has to work out new points to concentrate on together with his players − at all times relating to the further development of the game – and he must understand how to arouse *open-mindedness, interest, the readiness to collaborate of one's own accord and pleasure in the projected effort.*

2.5. TRAINING

Training is an educational process in which the player spontaneously comes to terms with the highest competitive loads through the deployment of all his personal powers, in order to achieve his maximum possible performance capacity in competition by means of adapting and improving the functioning and structure of the organism. One of the most important tasks facing the coach is *guiding his players to an active training performance.* Here in particular, competition is the best instructor!

The game is the sphere of free creation of movement. Every situation calls for free, creative, but at the same time adjusted behaviour with regard to movement. Nobody is there to help and no instruction manual can embrace all the many requirements and possible solutions. The player must take the responsibility upon himself to come to grips with the given match situation and the behaviour of his team-mates and opponents, with the target of ensuring that his side keep possession of the ball in order to score goals.

The demand for independent, constructive behaviour in the interests of one's own team becomes stronger as the match wears on. As the pace increases, inevitably more and more inter-relating changes of *position, duties* and *initiative result*. The elements contained in the challenge also become more complex.

These facts governing the development of the future game must also be taken into account during training. They call for *greater activity and an independent and co-responsive approach to training by the players* in the building up of their own performance. Training is not authoritarian drill, the coach is not a drill instructor, far rather he skillfully directs proceedings in order to bring out the best with regard to the individual gifts and capabilities of the individual players.

The approach to performance cannot be commandeered nor passively brought about by means of patent solutions and stereotyped notions on the part of the coach but instead can only be developed through coming to grips independently and actively with training forms as closely as possible representing competitive conditions. *The player has to build up his behaviour with regard both to movement and the game by means of his own creative force.* Only in this way can *imagination with regard to movement, intuition for the game, and a love of making decisions and showing resolution be developed.*

This training target calls for increased personal involvement on the part of the coach, he becomes the team-mate of each of the players. Each player must be aware that the coach is concerned about him and clearly recognises his capacities. On no account should a player be allowed to disappear from sight or be overlooked within the training community – instead he must be constantly aware of the significance of his individual capabilities for the performance of the team. This raises his *self-estimation* and increases his *readiness to perform.*

In this way too, the essential *confidential relationship which the coach must have with each of his players is consolidated.* No one should be allowed to feel he is at a disadvantage or is being disregarded because the coach has granted his "stars" a special position with regard to the way they are treated. Consulting and discussing the tasks lying ahead in a game and the approach to performance with the individual players strengthens their performance consciousness and the position of the coach. *Thus training should not simply be interpreted as physical preparation of the players for competition but at the same time it should aim at improving and consolidating intellectual-mental fundamentals (strength of will, purposefulness, a self-assertive playing approach, self-confidence and finally pleasure in one's own capabilities).*

The law of economics governing the clever distribution and challenging of all personnel to the greatest possible advantage which also applies in training, demands from the coach

1. methodical,
2. biological and psychological basic knowledge,

in order to aid each player as a specific type, in his effort to come to terms with the highest demands on performance as posed by competition. *On no account should training be regarded as bothersome or be regarded as a punishment for a lost match or be used as a threat should a game be lost.* This can only serve to distort the real purpose and the result would be a reluctance to perform bringing with it all the negative effects of a reduction in performance and the destruction of the basis of trust between the coach and the players.

The extent of training is the load demanded within a given period of time. It is based on

1. the degree of performance,
2. the target of performance,
3. the prior competitive load,
4. the differentiated biological basic qualities of the players, their ability and their age.

Training forms designed to simulate competition as much as possible have the advantage that the necessary leeway can be provided for differentiated load. Above all, the older player should exert himself more frequently but with reduced intensity commensurate to his age and with longer intervals between exertion sequences.

Training is a manifold and varying challenge for all physical and intellectual-mental forces, designed to simulate competition as much as possible. The mature competitive performance itself is developed on the basis of good training preparation only as a result of the frequency of competitive participation and in spite of all the motivations missing in training such as rivalry, the drive for success, spectator influence, etc.

2.6. TECHNIQUE

Technique means the skill of being able to control the ball even during the tightest situation during play, in order to keep possession of the ball with the object of getting it in the opposing net. There is no other form of sport in which there is such a manifold range of technical demands on movement as in football. The more intensively the defence reacts against attacking play, all the more skill on the ball is called for. As a consequence, technique – an important factor in proficiency can only be built up under stress situations simulating competition as much as possible. The player has to learn amidst the pressure brought on by a range of impressions as a result of the differentiated playing behaviour of many opponents and team-mates, to maintain possession of and assert himself on the ball. Thus concentration and vigilance are more or less widely scattered and not only directed at the ball. The type of pass and the point in time when it is made and each individual action when in possession of the ball are different and dependent on the situation. The Brazilians are able to show their great superiority in this respect. Not their system, which is more than simple and dictated by the hot, climatic conditions in Brazil, provides the reason for their strength but the superiority of their individual skill of being able to assert themselves in the tightest possible space and under great pressure. Hereby, they often differ greatly from the technical schoolbook clichees in their technical execution. This superiority has been built up since a very early age during games "in the backstreets". The traits which they learned there provide the orientation for their methodology. *Our* methodology has to compensate for these missing "wasteground pitches". For this reason, the path towards the aim of enhanced skill on the ball leads by way of playing the game itself rather than via stereotyped and alien sets of movements.

2.7. TACTICS

Tactics represent the systematic use in any competition of all the forces and means at one's disposal designed to register success against the opponent. This subject comprises individual, group and team tactics, individual and group behaviour as well as the inter-relationship of all parts of the team in order to achieve the best possible efficiency in both attack and defence. Tactically-clever playing behaviour is not merely restricted to the basic tasks which a player has to fulfil within the scope of his position in the attack or in the defence, but he must also be able, according to the given situation, to defend as a forward and to attack as a defender.

This important requirement posed by progressive football, sets each player the task of involving himself above and beyond the task corresponding to his talent and inclination. Every player, whether a forward or defender must understand both sides of the game and must be able to adapt himself quickly from thoughtful activity in attack to a defensive reaction or vice versa. A player can only hope to improve conscious, tactically-clever playing behaviour and lead it to maturity, if he first comes to terms with certain match tasks in order to find and put into practice possible solutions on his own accord.

The experience thus gained is supplemented with additional suggestions on the part of the coach. In actual match practice, they are further expanded and consolidated whereby the tactical consciousness of performance develops itself. In addition, the joint analysis of a match, match consultations and the discussion of tactical possibilities widens the horizon and encourages tactical capacity of thinking. Of prime significance for the development of tactical match behaviour is not theoretical dicussion however, but far rather the challenge made to and the activation of the players as a result of practical competitive tasks.

2.8. FAIRNESS

The hard, manly battle for the contested object and the efforts of both teams to succeed, mobilise and foster all the forces and performance factors we have mentioned so far. However, good performance is unthinkable without the realisation of the term fairness. Despite all efforts made to attain success, the performance designed to lead to this success is only then complete when play is fair and carried out in accordance with the rules as well as the unwritten laws of sporting conduct, not because of any fear of punishment but based on a clean, sporting attitude and conviction and respect for the performance of your opponent.

Fighting strength does not mean the brutal and reckless struggle to attain success instead fighting strength means making full use of the means of playing artistry, i. e. playing skill, clever, tactical and fair behaviour with controlled and thoughtful deployment of strength of mind, in order to achieve the best performance.

3. SPECIAL FEATURES OF YOUTH TRAINING

Playing with a ball is an enjoyable pleasure at any age on account of the range of possibilities of free movement that it provides. The "free range" possibilities of movement available in earliest childhood have a fundamental and essential influence on the further development of motorial ability. The child in its development requires *stimulation and impulses for movement* which are provided when frolicking around in free play. The more possibility there is to romp around to one's heart's content on playgrounds and waste areas, the better it is for biological and special motorial development. Such essential free playing areas are increasingly less available. Above all, in the big towns and those areas which have been taken over and built up by the planners usually restrict the possibility of movement. Normally, ball games are forbidden. However, by means of playing freely, children are able to develop the fundaments of skill, manoeuvrability and motorial adaptability which decisively influence the diversity of their mobility in their future development. Every talent needs challenging surroundings in order to be able to develop; and each person develops within the bounds of his capacities. *Everyone plays and is able to achieve something within the bounds of his possibilities* but not everyone is *equally talented and capable of learning.* As a consequence, our efforts are not solely aimed at top performance, but just as much as the less talented player in lower performance categories, who makes the effort to achieve his own personal best performance. The pleasure of overcoming difficulties, which a football match gives rise to in diverse ways as it progresses, does not depend on great talent but upon willingness to make the effort. The game of football with its surprising succession of conflicts and testing situations and the uncertainty with regard to their outcome, provides the boy engaged in the game with adventure, hazard, the taste of success and failure in a never-ending series. The player gains both experience and pleasure in perpetually coming to grips with his opponent for possession of the ball and to score goals. Such expectations from the game have to be recognised and taken into account if we intend to improve and refine boys' playing behaviour. In the exercise and training forms too, the youngster must be able to recognise his game. The aim of instruction work must be to guide youngsters to genuine enjoyment of their game as soon as possible. The path towards this target leads through a varied range of exercise and training forms orientated towards the game.
At which age can you begin playing football and when can you begin with training directed at improving fitness, technique and tactics? The chance to play

uninhibitedly on wasteground represents an important basis for the development of footballing talent. Merely by contesting for possession of the ball and by scoring goals, a whole range of adjusted and skilled movements crop up.

The fact that more free spaces are available for play in rural districts is surely an important reason why more boys from small rural clubs are to be found in the select sides of the provincial associations and also of the German Football Association at schoolboy level. The talented players from these districts have been able to play and develop freely and of course, are also less subject to influences distracting their attention from football than promising youngsters in the towns. In fact, the importance of playgrounds cannot be stressed often enough – where youngsters at the earliest possible age, before they undergo systematic training with a club, have the chance to romp and play around to their heart's content. *The diversity of the challenge to movement in free play provides the best basis for further development in the performance-fostering environment provided by the club. The principal aim* in the training of all age and performance categories *is the improvement of competitive behaviour.* The instruction of the youngest is primarily orientated towards developing playing skill.

The question pertaining to magnitude of load and extent of load is secondary. The physical load in a football match is no "compulsory load" which has been established in advance and remains equal throughout, but instead there is the chance to recover after every effort. This non-determined relationship between effort and recuperation provides effective stimulation for improving the performance of the circulation and makes it possible for everyone to dose the extent of the load in such a way that there need be no misgivings about overloading or even exhaustion in the case of a normally motivated game, as is to be found in the case of youngsters. The youngster instinctively senses when he needs a break. This is evident in the case of unorganised back street or waste patch games where boys can go on playing football for hours with never-lessening enthusiasm.

Every boy will arrive at his own particular game within an age-group.

Individual playing behaviour depends on his talent and his inherent traits with regard to suitability, the level of his biological development and the experience he already possesses of playing the game. His behaviour is his expression of the challenge raised by the simple playing motivation to score the most goals against the resistance of the opposing side. This playing motivation is extremely simple but most intensive in its challenging character so that with regard *to the very youngest, straightforward rivalry is the prime feature of their behaviour.* Enjoyment of the game holds pride of place and is always the driving force for their eagerness. Here, it does not really matter at all about the technical means used to play the ball. Everyone involves himself using his particular means in his own way, feels that he belongs to his team and takes part in fulfilling the common target, which with all the experiences of success and failure leads to the *playing experience.*

3.1. ACCLIMATISATION (UP TO 8 YEARS)

The enthusiastic youngster, who wants to play in the E youth groups of the clubs, brings certain expectations and notions with him. *He wants to play football* and emulate his heroes. We put them into small, easily supervised groups and teams, in which they have to get used to *the playing environment and* its *complex challenges*. Thanks to the reduced range of impressions produced by the small group, they are able to come to terms with events of *their* own accord. Usually, it is a case of a game in which one boy plays against the rest.
Space cannot be tactically made use of nor is a team-mate sought for as a partner in combining. The target itself is alone clear: the realisation that the ball belongs in the opponent's net. They have *their game* and *their playing experience.*
Any attempt to school this age group employing the performance conceptions and standards of the adult in order to produce systematic technical and tactical qualities, would not only be too much for the boys but would also spoil their enjoyment of the game because their expectations and notions would not be fulfilled.
The basic form is the game itself! The demands on movement are so diverse and call for adapting oneself time and time again so that *the aim of the initial instruction* is to develop *this quality and that of familiarization.* Through coming to terms with simple stress situations in their mini-games, even the smallest develop certain empirical values and *adjustment processes,* which along with the further development towards differentiation and the ability to recognise playing coherences, lead to more conscious learning and playing behaviour.

3.2. GROUNDWORK (8–12 YEARS)

Stepped-up conscious learning and playing behaviour is possible and can be systematically schooled at this stage of development. Biological development facilitates the understanding of general tactical means of behaviour and the favourable motorial ability to adapt almost invites the development of technical accomplishments and playing skill. Youngsters in this age are avid for knowledge and want to learn. Thus for this very reason, they require good guidance in order to build up and consolidate the basis of technique, tactics and also general physical invigoration. The youngsters start to seek their playing partner and they take over certain functions within the group. Initially, however, they are very uncritical with regard to the appraisal of their own performance, something which alters decisively at the end of this phase of development. Experiences of success and failure are also more intensively processed when this point is finally reached.
The methodical approach with regard to the game in particular is of great importance in this phase which is so decisive for future development. Technical

development must on no account be isolated from the game and restricted to mere instruction in movement. The pass with the inside of the foot or the outside for example, should not be regarded abstractly and taught as an individual movement but in its form of application as a means of interlinking, which again should end up with a shot at goal. The how, when and where in passing the ball always depends on the movement of team-mates and opponents in a given playing situation. The direction, distance and proper dosing of the passing move vary in a similar manner. Whether the inner or outer side of the foot is used to play the ball or whether over a greater distance, the full, inner or outer instep is used, is determined by the situation and also by the free decision of the youngster depending on how he believes he can best solve the challenge posed by the situation.

The situation raises the challenge *of coming to terms with the environment and senso-motorial adjustment. Skill in movement should* be arrived at *under the stress of more and more new situations, with an ever-changing wealth of impressions from the playing environment. The development of psychical adaptability in particular is of great importance at this age, in order to reduce the disturbing feelings of agitation which occur, which express themselves in nervous, precipitous, uncontrolled and insecure playing behaviour.* Self-confidence, thoughtfulness and playing ability are developed during this favourable age for learning.

The fundaments of general tactics, such as running into the open space and covering, how to react during tackles, dribbling and shielding the ball, should all be present as conscious means of playing behaviour when the end of this age-group is reached. Experience has demonstrated that with regard to running into the open space that using the method of the "three against one" game in a restricted area pointing out both the free and the covered space is something which cannot easily be passed on. On the other hand, youngsters can far more easily comprehend what being covered and as a consequence running into the open space means, when they have to try and move away from the close covering and guarding of an opponent who is covering the man, in order to bring themselves into the game.

The development of strength must proceed alongside the development of playing skill. Here, the ball serves as the apparatus in overcoming one's own bodily weight. Partner exercises too, which foster the deployment of strength against the resistance of an opponent are effective on account of the rivalry they engender and are also fun. At the end of this important phase of development, the youngster must be able to control his own weight when jumping or, when he dives for the ball, catch himself with his arms and be able to assert himself powerfully in tackles. The target of this phase of learning must be the development of *the basis for dynamically powerful playing skill.*

3.3. THE YEARS OF PERFORMANCE (12–16 YEARS)

What is meant here by the years of performance is that the groundwork and the factors of the performance capacity have already been stamped out and are available and that these qualities are also fostered in competition, orientated to winning points and becoming champions, in relation to the overall biological and sporting development. During this period of development we discover extremely large differences between the actual calendar age and biological development and similar extremes between the traits of behaviour and specific ability for playing football. *A global generalisation of behaviour as typical for this age does not correspond to reality.*

The pronounced differentiation in the degree of development and performance necessitates classification into appropriate lower or higher categories of performance, as is already taking place in the case of a number of provincial associations belonging to the German Football Association, where down-gradings of youngsters who have failed to develop as anticipated are recommended by the sports doctor. Similarly, a youngster who is capable of a better-than-average performance should be given the chance to play in a higher category that is commensurate with his performance, thus ensuring sufficient stimulation.

In the upper performance sphere we find youngsters of vastly differing size; however, physical size as a feature of development is not the sole criterion for accelerated development. Smaller player types too, reveal superior features of development compared to their contemporaries, which express themselves in an extremely harmonic and strongly developed muscular system and certainly a strong organism and correspondingly stronger and more dynamic playing behaviour. In addition, with reference to the motorial development, there is no need to talk about a poor coordination performance either with regard to the players who are large in stature or those who are small in stature in this upper performance category. We are aware that no disharmonies exist with regard to the physical and organic development (Hollmann and others).

This period of development is no close season. However, there should be lengthy intervals between systematic, permanent loads owing to the fact that the nervous system requires a longer period to recuperate and regulate the circulation and the pulse frequency. It has already been pointed out that the game of football creates practically ideal possibilities to impose load on each player effectively according to his capacity and without the danger of overdoing it.

In the case of a harmonic premature development of physical performance traits, it is observed with regard to the majority of youngsters that their intellectual-mental development does not correspond to their physical one. Above all, they are psychically unstable and extremely irregular in their performance behaviour. This is revealed principally in the case of matches when there is some special motivation and when a series of failures has to be digested during a game. Certainly, a stabilisation of the psychical performance behaviour could be achieved here through more frequently having to come to grips with particularly motivated stress situations, as English schoolboy teams have proved. More mature and mentally more stable playing behaviour can be achieved not only through systematic training but rather by means of competition orientated to this target.

All technical and tactical prerequisites must be present in this upper playing category by the time a boy is 16. These youngsters are separated from the capable adult only by the strength and dynamism accounted for by the gap in development. It goes without saying that all performance factors should be built up through simulating competition as closely as possible, whereby the demands of training should be directed to this target, with increased tempo and games under particular stress conditions, such as playing against superior numbers. Not only playing artistry and playing skill but also a conscious deployment of physical strength as well as controlled, fair hardness ensure that the boy can assert himself on the ball, are all important targets in the instruction of this age and performance group.

3.4. THE YEARS OF TOP PERFORMANCE (FROM THE AGE OF 16)

The consolidation of the performance groundwork previously established takes place in this age group. A training load devised to support and foster the natural biological development must create the prior conditions for ensuring that the youth can smoothly join the ranks of senior football. The young talent between 16 and 18 should aim at this target and receive the corresponding training and competition load.

The youngster in this age should train daily, thrice a week together with his team-mates and on the other days by himself, according to a programme of his own within the scope of his scholastic and professional possibilities. The process of learning how to preoccupy oneself and act independently in particular, is of especial importance for the development of responsible, self-confident and thoughtful performance behaviour.

Of course, there are also pronounced differences in development among the 16 to 18-year olds, which just as strongly cause their performance capacity to vary. However, the outstanding talents of this age group, whose performance capabilities are liked with a biological development which is premature with regard to their actual calendar age, require a strong and challenging performance environment to ensure further progress.

The capacities and training load of each boy must be supervised in close collaboration between the responsible trainer and an experienced sports doctor. The supervisory and advisory work of the doctor is not merely restricted to the circulation or to taking care of acute injuries, but also to discovering possible pus-focuses in the area of the head, which are regularly the hidden cause for proneness to injury and a general decrease in performance.

The properly dosed and systematic deployment of youngsters in the first senior team, providing that this possesses the necessary playing strength and can lay claim to being sportingly clean, does not place too high a demand on a physically strongly developed talent but represents, as examples in the case of other nations show, an appropriate challenge for the youngster and encouragement for him. If the gifted young player plays in a weak team, this results in a false and distorted picture of one's own abilities, which is expressed in the overestimation of one's performance.

Teams which completely dominate play and win their matches easily are also not in a position to develop further and in their case, the yardstick for the strength of performance aimed at is effaced. This leads to the conclusion that proper organisation should provide the possibility to group together talented players and strong teams in order to build them up in a competitive series where strong performance is called for. Similarly, the playing time for the 16 to 18-year olds should generally last 45 minutes each way and in the case of the younger age-groups too, it should be lengthened by 5 minutes per half. The highest proficiency can only be reached within the framework of a competitive system which is a highly demanding one. *Competition and training only then stand in an effective inter-relationship to one another when high demands on performance during competition also set the standard for a correspondingly high and complex training load.* This training load is not only aimed at coming to terms with and adjusting oneself physiologically to the diversity of the challenges posed by competition but equally applies to the intellectual-mental sphere. The teaching target is not the analysed movement, but competitive behaviour with a constantly new movement, adjusting itself to the situation, under the stress of different competition situations.

Training for youngsters can and must simulate real competition as much as possible. But only through constantly asserting oneself in the field of tension as provided by competition with a balanced relationship of forces can fantasy of movement and competitive behaviour be formed with the necessary, dynamically forceful and combatively strong accentuation.

3.5. SUMMARY

The "special features" of training youngsters are governed by the different suitability and ability characteristics of the youngsters at individual age and development stages:

1. The higher possible load imposition with regard to the individual level of development. The game provides an optimal but "compatible" load at one and the same time.

2. No overall judgement of the performance capacity and performance behaviour with specific reference to the phase of development. In each phase we find pronounced differentiation, which calls for a methodical adjustment to the constitutional differences. The game provides the challenge to each player to strive for success using the means at his disposal.

3. Guidance to the highest performance capacity via a system of competition with a balanced performance standard and competition-orientated training load. Each boy needs an environment commensurate with his capabilities – without being over or understretched. Supervision by the trainer and the sports doctor.

4. Match and competition-orientated exercise and training forms correspond to the expectations of the youngsters, encourage them, as they are geared to competition, in a diversity of ways, arouse pleasure and interest for this very reason and lead to teaching success more rapidly. *Steer clear of stereotyped, constructed forms of exercise, not directed at a youngster's interest.*

4. TACTICS IN GENERAL

4.1. ATTACKING PLAY

The target in a game of football is the opponent's goal. Striving towards this target time and time again, against the organised resistance of the opponent, is the most important task facing a team and the overall behaviour all the players in the team must be directed towards fulfilling this task as frequently as possible.

The ball is the object to be relentlessly pursued. Wherever it is, there is a struggle to gain possession of it. All effort is directed at securing possession of the ball, asserting oneself on ball and making headway with it, until it crashes into the opposing net, or at least the attack is rounded off with an attempt at scoring. This urge to score must be the driving force for collected playing behaviour, aimed at success. This applies to all the players, beginning with the goalkeeper. The speedy and directed attacking move started by the goalkeeper, the rapid change from defensive into attacking actions, good and thoughtful team-play, indeed every move aimed at the opponent's goal is borne and governed by this urge to score goals. Thus each player tries as hard as he can to secure possession of the ball and to make use of it thoughtfully.

When the game is played properly, the defender must also seek the chance to move up in attack and to round off his surprise attacking move with a shot at goal or a well-directed pass.

Attacking play should be regarded as a complete entity, beginning with gaining possession and ending with a shot at goal. On no account should it exhaust itself in a passing sequence which fails to be productive.

Let us not forget here either the effect thoughtful attacking play has on the public; that with the obvious will of all the players to assert themselves on the ball and to score, the expectations of the spectators are also fulfilled. Each conflict situation on the ball, especially in front of goal, arouses new excitement, unrest and uncertainty regarding its possible outcome. The spectator identifies himself minute for minute with the players, unfolds his own playing behaviour in his thoughts, whereby he experiences and expresses the whole range of emotions from enthusiastic jubilation to the deepest disappointment and bitter sorrow, in his own way. The attraction of football has its roots here. All coaches and footballers must make the effort to maintain this fascination.

Only the diligence and competitive urge of the players and exciting scenes in front of goal following fast moves which simply eat up the ground en route to goal can positively influence enthusiastic spectators intently following play. This in turn is reflected back on to the field of play. This genuine inter-relationship between the players and spectators creates the proper sporting competitive atmosphere, so desired by the fans, which spurs on the players on the field of play to sparkle and open their box of tricks.

4.1.1. The Shot at Goal

Every player is aware from his own experience just how important it is not simply just to create but also to take chances, even if subsequently the ball should be off-target or a goal is prevented by skilful defensive work. Nothing can depress the elation of an attacking team more than when chances there for the taking are not taken. The playing harmony of a team begins to fall to pieces, their self-confidence disappears and the result is that the initiative is gradually handed over to the other side.

The shot at goal is the fulfilment of thoughtful attacking play. The culmination of initiative, decisiveness, purposiveness, will and determination.

It is important for a trainer to ensure that he always includes these factors determined by the very idea of the game when guiding his side. No training session should be held in which the taking of scoring chances under competitive conditions is not practised as an essential point. In doing so, all the possibilities of creating and taking advantage of scoring chances must be taken into account and brought home to all the players by repeated practice in a free, thoughtful form. British teams remain shining examples for us in this respect.

4.1.2. Interpassing

A common attempt by a team to register success over an opponent, whilst acting together as a community in which individual playing behaviour is adjusted and subjugated to the whole. The quest for success initially presupposes the *determined willingness of all players* to assist during the course of a match in an alert and concentrated manner in putting the ball into the back of the opponent's net as often as possible. The *will of the individual player* is directed to maintaining possession of the ball and to asserting himself against the defensive efforts of the opposing side and to keeping possession of the ball for a longer period throughout the match than the opposition.

Good interpassing is thus fostered by the unselfish desire to assist, a genuine brand of comradeship put into actual practice and realising the joint intention and target "all for one and one for all".

A team which is playing well is a homogeneous *performance community*. The players fit in with one another, they supplement one another in their playing and interhuman disposition. Individual consciousness and the feeling of solidarity join them together harmonically, i. e. the self-confident, responsible, constructive playing behaviour of the individual is aimed at achieving the common aim — striving for success by means of the best possible team performance.

30

4.1.3. The Significance of Systems

The smooth integration and coordination of the various human and playing traits of the individual types of players results in the order, the system of a team. The essential significance of playing systems ist to be found herein. Playing systems are frequently referred to as if they were a mathematical formula and one could be inclined to believe that the game corresponded to a mathematical problem.

But luckily the game cannot in fact, be evaluated clearly and precisely along mathematical lines. This would put an end to its attraction and excitement. Reactions and patterns of behaviour cannot be calculated for the simple reason that there are so many unpredictable conflicts with which the player must come to terms during the course of a game. Free decision, the free, creative formation of his playing behaviour, his genius – all these qualities are what makes it so fascinating both for himself and the spectator. The excitement and fascination of a game of football after all, can be traced to this uncertainty of human behaviour. Notwithstanding all considerations of a tactical nature, such as in the case of the question relating to playing systems, the basic idea of the game is and remains the yardstick and basis for discussion: the struggle to gain possession of the ball at all times, wherever the ball may be and to score goals and secure success!

The target then is success – in a match, in a series of matches, to win the championship, or in a more modest way: to win the battle against relegation, to justify the outside chance top in a field of fancied teams, to progress further in a tournament, as represented for instance, by the World Cup or an Olympic tournament. World Cups in particular, in which the best teams in world football compare their strength and the thought of prestige raises the desire for success to an unusually high level, have already provided us with a number of model systems in which "defensiv might" was in the foreground. Let us for instance, consider at this stage, the "retreating defence", the 4–2–4 of the Brazilians, or recall the massed defensive block, which the English set up in their goal area launching fast counter-attacks, in which each player took part providing an element of surprise which helped lead to the winning of the World Cup.

System as a word means an orderly entity, a systematically arranged association of parts, which stand in a logical relation to one another. In the case of our own sphere of interest, the game of football, we define the term system as a logical organisation of the available types of players in order to facilitate a thoughtful, success-orientated ability to manoeuvre in attack and in defence.

This best possible capacity for action calls for a) an organised distribution of forces covering the depth and the width of the field of play and b) the distribution of tasks according to the special basis qualities of the players. A system in our sense is no stereotyped, rigid order, but far rather a basic order, a framework, within which each player, having the freedom of responsibility and decision, can and should evolve his individual basic capacities in the interests of the team.

Originality and playing genius, harmoniously adjusted individual characteristics and the playing ability of the players in a fast and flowing interchange of attacking and defending duties enliven the system and govern the potential ability of a team.

The "coat" – in other words, the system – must fit, the player must feel comfortable in it. He must sense that the task he has been asked to fulfil suits him perfectly. The player must be convinced that the concept is indeed the right one. If he has been properly programmed in advance, then both his playing spirit and willingness to exert himself will be spurred on. Realisation of the clear relationships within the framework of the system results in the growth of self-confidence, responsible and thoughtful action. Against the background of this systematic basic order, a player is capable of unfolding all his playing ability in the interests of the team.

The coach of course, must himself be fully aware of what he wants. His will and his targets are expressed in clever reasoning and equally clear instructions, which must impress and convince each player. The essential points must be brought home one by one in a concentrated and watertight form and the most important points regarding individual behaviour discussed jointly!

The systematic framework set out by the coach must then be practised in preparatory training in a clear and intensive manner. Consciousness of one's ability, the will to perform well and last but not least, potential ability can only be built up by actually practising on the pitch.

The coach has to be keenly perceptive to be able to recognise the basic qualities of his players. Numbered among these basic qualities, we have technical and tactical ability as well as mental-intellectual traits, mental stability, the ability to make contact, adaptability, strength of will and tenacity, imperturbability and thoughtfulness, in short, the overall manner in which a player should deploy his playing capabilities. These are especially important critera when it comes to signing on new players, if the coach wants to ensure the realisation of his concepts regarding the system.

Simply grouping together the best-known players does not always guarantee the best team. Not every player is able to digest mentally a change of environment or higher demands on performance in a select team.

The building up of a side, the fitting together of a system is no mere problem of addition nor can it be solved according to the cookbook recipe principle "Take . . .". Instead it represents a genuine task of management concerned with guiding the individual players to their utmost potential ability within the framework of the system.

The players expect the coach to have a strong, convincing personality. They want to be managed commensurately and not authoritatively led by the nose nor have their favour courted. Management means posing a challenge and making demands through a range of tasks which corresponds to the characteristics of the players as well as the development of the game and last but not least, the general trend of the times as well.

An important aim of management is thus to motivate the players towards active cooperation in that the coach calls on the players to develop and put forward their own conceptions as well. The coach's suggestions should foster the development of the players' own thoughts and consequently their awareness of performance and co-responsibility for their own potential ability within the framework of the playing system.

A comparative study of the WM system with the systems practised at present, which depends on the basic qualities of the individual players and the effect of their special traits on the capacity of action in attack and defence, clearly reveals that the WM system too, was never simply a rigid, stereotyped delegation of tasks, as people far too often suggest nowadays without properly considering the matter. The WM system was also played in a variable manner.

Mercurial inter-changing and fluent position changing by the strikers, between the inside-forwards and the strikers or through a full-back rushing upfield whilst an inside-forward covers up for him, were of course, obvious features of the WM system as well as its variations.

The provoking "might of the defence" always represented a challenge for the attack *to attempt score goals in spite of it.* This provocative polarity between defence and attack will continue to govern the game decisively in future. It goes without saying that thinking in commercial terms, as well as the public's high expectations regarding success and considerations of prestige, which for instance, are very closely associated with international matches, to a large extent govern the overall playing conception and the playing behaviour of the players in particular.

Resulting from all this, there is the responsible task for coaches, players and all those in authority, regardless of the overheated field of tension produced, to strive for and realise the beauty of the game, something of course, which the original playing conception strives to achieve. It is a good thing that this tendency is discernible in the case of the top teams in the National League. A bumper gate depends on the ability and class of a team and not on tactical manipulations, which renounce the features of good football! Football in England remains a great example in this respect as well.

Thus it becomes evident that it is not juggling around with figures in a system which in the end determines good and successful football, but rather the attitude, willingness and ability of the players. Who does not recall with enthusiasm the playing strength and the balance of attacking and defending forces of teams of the past such as FC Schalke 04, FC Kaiserslautern, 1. FC Nürnberg, BV Borussia Dortmund, VfB Stuttgart, 1. FC Saarbrücken, etc.?

The 1954 World Cup side built up by Sepp Herberger presents a convincing example of the balanced distribution of the types of players within the framework of a system which surprisingly enough greatly resembled the 4–3–3 system practised today: in the attack there were three forceful strikers in the shape of Helmut Rahn, Otmar Walter and Hans Schäfer, behind them, Max Morlock who came out of midfield like a modern "fourth striker" would do. Fritz Walter revealed genius in directing the game in midfield, mainly assisted by his club-mate, Horst Eckel – always industrious and with great staying-power. Karl Mai, the left half turned out to be a considerable support for the three defensive pillars Liebrich, Posipal and Kohlmeyer, thanks to his defensive attributes.

In the WM system, the two half-backs took it in turns to play offensively. While the one took part in attack, the other dropped back for safety's sake, ready to defend. The inside-forwards operated in a similar fashion. The inside-forwards and half-backs were in fact allied types. In the case of the inside-forwards, the attacking qualities had priority whilst the defensive qualities enjoyed the priority in the case of the half-backs. The present-day midfield player is a combination of the inside-forward and the half-back. He must combine attacking and defending qualities.

The means and characteristics of the attacking game have experienced a more intensive and play-determining accentuation, with the further development of the game. These higher requirements are a direct result of having to come to grips with a numerically reinforced defence and more consequent and definitely harder playing behaviour in defence.

The present-day game with its surprising fast and flowing changes of attacking and defending tasks for all the players, requires faster action and reaction both with regard to mental flexibility as well as movement both on and off the ball. Improved physical readiness and mental stability are fundamental requirements in order to come to terms with such increased demands. Present-day football has become more intensive with regard to all features governing performance:

1. Breaking away from an opponent more rapidly, more surprisingly and more effectively. Maintaining command of the situation whilst seeking the open space and making use of the ball.
2. More skilful behaviour in tackles. Being able to assert yourself on the ball and making headway in the tightest of situations.
3. Dribbling, tying up your opponent or putting him out of action with a pass.
4. The wing as an important area of attack with forwards in front of goal who are ready to shoot and who are strong in the air. Return passes instead of crosses. Shots from long range.
5. A surprise shifting of the area of attack.
6. Thanks to the "free man", a possible break upfield by defenders, which has a surprise effect (following a successful defensive action), without risk, with an effective conclusion.
7. Mercurial, dangerous strikers who can penetrate or shoot at goal from the back thanks to their dangerousness and mobility.

The significance of a system is to be found in the systematic distribution of the available players in the area of play according to their basic qualities in order to achieve the best possible capacity of action in defence and attack. You cannot copy model systems blindly. You must have the types of players who fit into this "coat".

In the basic order of a system, the game is ultimately characterised by playing ability and the harmonic balance and mutual understanding of the players.

General tactical knowledge, the ability to assert oneself on and make headway with the ball, as well as the physical attributes of all the players govern a team's potential capacity.

However, success depends to no small extent on the whims of footballing fortune. Performance is thus always the essential thing. Success can only be aimed at employing the utmost potential capacity but it cannot be guaranteed. In the long run, success is achieved by the diligent. You can and you may lose a match, but you cannot and may not play badly! This would be the case if you were to re-sign yourself prematurely, to give up and not be ready and willing to fight against any possible playing failure using all the strength and concentration at your disposal.

Encouraging and stimulating successes, which continually feed one's stock of enthusiasm and playing disposition must time and time again be fought for and won during the course of a match. Success can only be achieved by dint of steadfast industry. This so often applies in particular to those types of players who have been granted playing genius by nature, who have never had to work to achieve their standard of ability through sheer hard work and by stretching themselves to the utmost.

4.1.4. The Game off the Ball

We want to retain possession of the ball until it lands up in the opposing net! This task contains a diversity of challenges.

The attacking game begins in the very moment when the ball is won back by your side. The speedy reversal of defensive actions into attacking ones helps ascertain the success of attacking play. "Reversing" means covering the area leading to the opposing goal by means of a surprising, fast movement using the width and depth of the field. Completed defensive measure in fact should initiate the counter-attack as quickly as possible to attempt exclude any possible pursuit or defensive action on the part of the opposing forwards and to steal time from the opposing defence in their effort to get organised effectively.

Even during the opponent's attack, the speed of reversing can be enhanced by ensuring that a forward stays as far upfield in a striking position as possible, orientated towards the final defensive player. In this way, it is possible to start the counter-attack from a deep-lying position (see Fig. 1). The players who are not directly involved in defence, prepare the beginning of the attacking move in their heads. On no account should they wander around aimlessly behind the opposing attack but instead ensure that they have plenty of space to operate in, in that they keep themselves and consequently their opponents out of it.

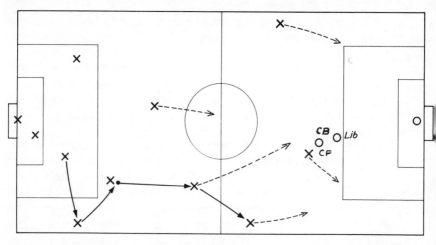

Figure 1

Effective running into the open space, the moment you gain possession of the ball must thus be planned. The important prerequisite for launching a fast counter-attack and effectively gaining territorial advantage is remaining vigilent and ensuring proper orientation to the whole playing area.

What must I observe? What kind of mental preparation is necessary? Where your own attack is developing, or where the ball can come from and how it can come!

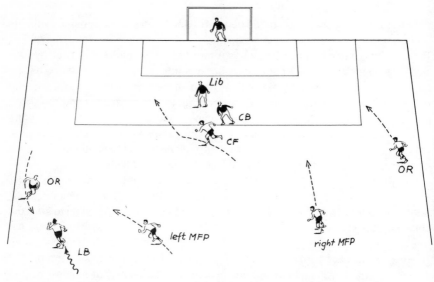

Figure 2

How I can seek the open space, how I can offer my support, namely

1. move towards the man on the ball (offer support at short range),
2. stay away providing that there is numerical superiority on the ball (the centre-forward stays away for instance, and keeps the final defensive player occupied, whilst the second striker approaches the player in possession; or the attack takes place over the left wing, the winger and the second striker offer their services at short range, the centre-forward moves up into a forward striking position, the right midfield player stays on his side of attack (see Fig. 2).

Running into the open space is an important factor in the game off the ball. The term is self-explanatory although the explanation is somewhat superficial: to elude the defensive readiness of the opponent by running into an unoccupied space. This explanation, however, still leaves the question of just "how" open; the very clarity and reason contained in the significance of seeking the open space in the interests of good inter-passing lead to a certain amount of carelessness and superficiality when it comes to its practical execution, even in the case of many of our top players. A feature of overall tactics which is self-understood, something relegated to being a platitude, something which we are all aware of, slowly but surely slips from our awareness with regard to its comprehensive importance for fluent inter-actions. Underestimation of what is "self-understood" often can be the cause for thoughtless, careless and even slipshod playing behaviour. In the end effect, a good playing performance by the individual and by the team is based on the careful and thoughtful application of these "self-understood" tactical platitudes.

The intelligent use of playing space calls for the highest concentration and vigilance regarding the behaviour of team-mates and opponents, as well as thoughtfulness and brilliant playing genius. Moving away from and shaking off an opponent no matter how closely he may be marking you, is the decisive important task for good inter-action en route to the opponent's goal.

Just what are the important features of seeking the open space properly and effectively?

1. Vigilance, orientation, mental preparation, the choice of a free space where I shall be able to most effectively make a contribution towards the game, after appraising the overall situation.
2. The surprise burst of speed, the sudden change of pace.
3. Irritating the opponent by means of a deception and running for the (surging forward in one direction – one, two steps – and then running for the open space in the opposite direction). It should be observed here that one deceptive movement is enough, for feinting a second time can irritate the man on the ball and result in a bad pass.
4. Make use of the effect of surprise. Make use of speed to widen the gap between yourself and your opponent so that the ball can be played freely and without hindrance.

Let us point out the most important features of running into the open space by means of an example:

Pele, the famous Brazilian forward, was being marked so well and closely during a match against a Saar select that initially he had no chance of getting the ball. However, all of a sudden, when his team-mate in possession of the ball was on the point of passing, he surprised his opponent with an explosive surge forward – of some two or three metres – in the direction of the opposing goal, only in the same moment, to run towards his team-mate just as explosively in the opposite direction. This manouevre was so effective that he was able to take possession of the ball a good ten metres from his direct opponent.

In other words: Seeking the open space properly depends on waiting for the right moment, when it is evident that a team-mate on the ball can pass it to you and then making use of a surprise, sudden burst of speed, combined with a deceptive movement! This major feature of inter-linking good play off the ball, has to be practised and brought home time and time again under competitive conditions.

En route to the ball, on the other hand, I must look around and orientate myself regarding the behaviour I should adopt once on the ball: whether I

1. meet the ball, and in doing so face up to the opponent quickly, look round and play the ball;
2. pass the ball immediately without bringing it under control, running to take up a new position together *with* the pass;
3. hold the ball, dribble with it and then play the ball, when I am certain that my pass will reach a team-mate either running into the open space or proferring himself;
4. dribble up to the opponent and then carry out a "one-two" movement with the aid of a supporting team-mate or pretend to execute the one-two movement with the aid of a team-mate and then forge ahead with the ball;
5. attempt to penetrate in order to unleash a scoring shot of my own accord.

The aim of seeking the open space is not only simply to bring oneself and the ball into the game but additionally through this move, I can succeed in tying up one or more players on the opposing side thus enabling team-mates to find the open space. Seeking the open space, above all, when it is carried out surprisingly and rapidly, is well worth-while and effectively serves good, successful inter-action. The surprise move to find the open space in an imaginative and territorially-advantageous manner provides the man on the ball with alternatives regarding his further behaviour. It must always be the target of inter-passing both on and off the ball to create such possibilities so that as a result of the range of alternatives open, the opponent remains uncertain about what the player on the ball intends realising. Seeking the open space is thus not simply a task for the individual player instead it is executed jointly by all the players who are not on the ball. The player on the ball should never be left without support. At least one, but better still, two players should offer their support at close range, in other words, they should move up with the man in possession.

When the other players move in the direction of the attack and out on the wings, they provide the player in possession with an alternative to the short pass, in other words, to execute surprise defence-splitting passes.

Thus seeking the open space means providing the player in possession with various possibilities for passing the ball or of course, facilitating a solo effort and a breakthrough. When a dangerous centre-forward rapidly seeks the open space, this for instance, provides openings for a "second spearhead" who can dribble and penetrate strongly or for advancing midfield players or defenders coming from behind.

The confusing inter-switching of the strikers, the varied and variable exploitation of attacking space by means of imaginative, thoughtful movements, offering support and moving away create the prior condition for alternative and surprise action, something which also proves its worth when up against a reinforced defence.

How often do we observe, even in the case of top sides, that the winger is passed the ball or he is sent racing after a through pass and there is no one either in front or behind him offering their support so that a direct confrontation is the only course left open to him. In other words, there is no alternative course. The team-mate moving up in support, in anticipation of a possible pass facilitates a choice which enables him to act more effectively when tackled by a defender in that he now either passes the ball, triggers off a one-two sequence or pretends to pass the ball, surges on of his own accord and attempts to break through.

Setting up a one-two passing movement, during which play both on and off the ball occurs in rapid succession, is a particularly effective means of attack on account of the surprise alternatives it provides. Either the player running at an angle against the "wall" is put through by means of a short, square pass or the square pass is surprisingly put through to another area of attack or the player who passed the ball and who has moved up in support himself goes through with the pass and pierces the opposing defensive area.

4.1.5. Behaviour on the Ball

The player on the ball is responsible for ensuring that his side retains possession and that the opposing goal is reached. Mental preparation, concentrated attention upon the playing environment, the vigilant observation of the behaviour of team-mates and opponents create the prior condition for secure and thoughtful playing behaviour on the ball. Concentrated and consciencious self-orientation, overseeing and reading possible competitive situations in the immediate vicinity and the overall match picture are numbered among the attributes of good players. Such alertness in no way restricts freedom of action in that one may decide upon a single course of action, for the good player is prepared to react by means of an entirely different approach in the very moment he is executing an action should a new, unforeseen situation crop up. Such lightning-fast, adjusted playing behaviour, reacting to opposing defensive measures and suddenly-changed challenges within the competitive environment is one of the most important basic qualities of good playing behaviour. This feature of fast and constructive playing behaviour clearly shows how speed in *football* depends upon rapid assessment and perception of the situation and is therefore governed and controlled by the intellectual-mental sphere.

There are competitive situations which are comparable with regard to the intensity they engender with experiencing moments of the greatest danger, whereby substantial reserves are mobilised, the player "overgrows himself" and executes constructive actions in spite of the stress, actions which often lie beyond the bounds of consciousness. Above all, scenes in the penalty area, in which attacking and defensive play clash with one another in a decisive phase, in which the attacking player fulfils or dashes the high expectations of the onlookers, place especially high demands upon the mental robustness and strength of will of the players involved in this most precarious situation. In addition, when victory or defeat for a player denotes material gain or loss or other higher aims, the pressure brought on by the responsibility that has to be borne turns into a real test. Not every player can master such a stepped-up demand and indeed this often leads to players making mistakes or even failing completely.

There are also the cases where a player changes his club. Previously, in familiar surroundings he felt at ease and was able to score goals. Frequently though, he is unable to do as well with his new club. Conscious of the expectations set in him, he loses his carefree manner of play. He appears hectic, careless and uncertain. His failure becomes a disappointing experience for him. He finds himself under psychical pressure. This frustration can only be removed by means of understanding and patient work in conjunction with the coach and helpful teammates.

It is obvious here too, that football is not merely composed of automatic movements but that the effectiveness of the art of playing depends upon the intellectual-mental characteristics. A mistake in front of the opponent's goal in failing to take a chance is usually not attributable to a false notion of how to act but to a lack of strong nerves and speedy comprehension and exploitation of the chances in the tense atmosphere of the penalty box. Such traits though, govern the dangerousness in front of goal of a Gerd Müller. To a large extent, they are inherent and a gift of nature.

Behaviour on the ball can only be improved in training under the stress of competitive situations, which also make strong demands on one's intellectual-mental adaptability, such as games involving an inferior against a superior number of players. Constructive behaviour, which is adapted to fit the competitive environment with its fast and furious changing situations, can be optimally enhanced by means of such forms of training. Other main features of technical and tactical basic behaviour alter the contents of the training whilst the form of organisation remains the same. Such main training features should not be interpreted as "mere behaviour" or behaviour stereotypes but always as a target to be aimed at. Any better possibility of behaviour, which proffers itself in the solution of a situation, should be recognised and taken advantage of. Thus every player has the free responsibility of how he is to decide about the further development of a playing move. In any case, the player must make the effort to bring his behaviour on the ball to a successful conclusion, i. e. to assert himself on the ball and to attempt break through to reach the target.

The overall tactical behaviour with regard to getting possession of the ball, demands that the player who has created space for himself and is ready to have the ball played to him runs towards the ball passed to him and orientates himself as to how team-mates and opponents are behaving. Just how he himself will behave from then on in possession depends on this:

1. Bring the ball under control, smoothly meet and move with it, face up to your opponent, look around and pass the ball. When meeting and moving with the ball shield it from your opponent, securing it with your body. Never allow a ball destined for you to pass by and then run after it or allow high balls to bounce first.

2. If your opponent is threatingly near, pass the ball on without first getting it under control or allow it to rebound to the player who passed it and then run into a new position (the possibility of a "one-two" movement).

3. Hold the ball and dribble with it, pass it only when it is certain that the pass will reach a team-mate who has gained the open space or who can offer his support.

4. Dribble towards your opponent and set up a one-two movement with the help of a team-mate in support or simulate the one-two movement but instead go through on your own. The one-two movement you set up facilitates an effective switch of the attacking area.

5. Penetrate the opposing defence in order to conclude your attacking move with a shot at goal.

However, there are situations which do not require running into the open space but instead, a team-mate is drawn on to the ball by means of a pass in order to entice the opponent out of his defensive area. A further variation of the one-two movement can be carried out by this means — one which is exemplarily practised by Franz Beckenbauer with Gerd Müller acting as the "wall".

It goes without saying that behaviour on the ball depends on individual traits. Such traits have their effect upon a player as he carries out the tasks he has been set in his given position within a team, a position which makes demands upon behaviour corresponding to his attributes. Thus e. g., the playing behaviour of a Libuda or Grabowski is marked by tricky dribbling, and in the case of Wolfgang Overath or Günter Netzer, their precise, field-bridging passes are the outstanding features of their method of playing. Above all, it must be pointed out that players occupying the same positions who possess the same basic qualities, develop different technical features which consequently contradict any standard conception with regard to technical behaviour in the game of football. These very special features govern the effectiveness of a player's playing behaviour. They are the starting-point for every methodical means of improving his performance capacity. The present tendency in the development of football of having a reinforced organised defence fosters *dribbling* as an important tactical individual variation within the attack of a side. The following tactical possibilities of application can be discerned:

1. dribbling in midfield, holding the ball, in order to dribble team-mates "free" and to look for chances to pass the ball;
2. field-bridging dribbling in conjunction with fast inter-switching strikers, in order to – with a whole range of alternatives available – surprisingly attempt the breakthrough or to conclude your attacking move with a one-two movement (Beckenbauer-Müller);
3. tricky dribbling with the intention of breaking through, as we know it on the wing from Libuda, Grabowski and Held;
4. dribbling at high speed with the aim of gaining ground and of bringing the move to a conclusion, with as little risk as possible (shot at goal, a cross or a pass), "driving" the ball on as we have become accustomed to seeing it executed by defenders surging forward in exemplary fashion (Beckenbauer, Vogts, Cullmann).

Dribbling must in any case, serve a purpose and be in the interests of your side.

4.2. DEFENSIVE PLAY

The target of the defending team is to win back possession the ball as quickly as possible in order to unleash an attack oneself in order to try and score goals. In attempting to win back the ball from the opposing side as soon as you have lost possession of it yourself, you are also fulfilling the task of preventing goals. if possession is lost then the whole team should immediately revert to defence. Attacking play which makes proper use of space and a deep-set formation can easily switch quickly to effective defensive measures.

The tactical means of defence are:

1. the immediate pursuit and combatting of the opponent in possession,
2. delaying the opposing attack in midfield,
3. organising your defence in front of goal,
4. challenging, marking and tackling the opponent on the ball and
5. speedily reverting to attack.

The playing concept calls for scoring goals. Possession of the ball is the prime requirement for achieving this aim. It is equally clear though, that once possession of the ball has been lost, you must immediately revert to defence. The player who loses the ball or whoever is nearest the opposing player in possession, pursues him and challenges him. He can separate him from the ball and take possession with a great chance of counter-attacking himself, return the ball to a team-mate or force the opponent to undertake a premature and uncontrolled pass. It is important therefore that the opposing attack is nipped in the bud as early as possible. If you concentrate on not allowing the other side to come into the game at all, this has a demoralising effect upon them, which is particularly depressing in front of their own crowd. Prevent goals by going after the opposition immediately the moment you have lost the ball!

If it is not possible to separate the opponent from the ball by immediate pursuit then he must be prevented in midfield from quickly carrying out a successful attacking move so that he is forced to pass the ball square as much as possible. By doing so, your defence gains time to get itself organised in front of its own goal. It should be observed when employing such delaying tactics in midfield that the defender should not challenge or tackle the opposing player too soon for fear that he is outplayed far from his own goal or outmanouevred by means of a one-two movement. The defender gradually moves back maintaining a gap which makes it impossible for his opponent to spurt past him or try a one-two movement. He challenges him in front of the defensive block that is to say, before he is in position for a proper shot at goal. He provokes his opponent and waits patiently until the attempts to break through and then the defender reacts and moves in to intercept. His team-mates are ready to stop any attempted pass.

4.2.1. Defensive Organisation in front of Goal

The area in front of goal is the most important defensive area. The playing area in fact, is shaped like a funnel. The defence makes use of this funnel effect, it digs itself in and makes the attempt to keep the opponent's playing space as narrow as possible.

The best possible set-up for the defenders in front of goal is achieved by means of man-to-man marking. Each attacking forward is marked by an opposing player who is similar in his playing characteristics. In front of goal it is essential that each defensive player is aware who he is up against. Only if there is clarity regarding the set-up is it possible to combat effectively confusing interchanging of position above all, by attacking players who can dribble strongly.

Covering the space means that each defensive player guards a zone of the defensive area and combats the opponent who intrudes into his zone. This method of covering requires types of players who are able to adapt to fast changing situations and who are sufficiently alert to digest what is happening in the zone of attack as well as variable attacking behaviour. Typical "man-to-man" types find they are unable to cope here and feel ill at ease and uncertain owing to the fact that they lack the suitable traits.

The argument that zone defence is more economical than the strength – sapping pursuit of constantly interchanging forwards, is correct, but what is the most economical is not always the most successful method of defence, as many examples can show. Tussles between similarly-matched opponents during a match help enhance good football, attractions which are lost when covering the space is employed.

The tactical disadvantage too, should not be disregarded. It can easily happen that when strong dribblers capable of piercing a defence begin to interchange confusion results and the defenders find themselves having to constantly adapt themselves to the play of different forwards. Thus there is the danger that no one really knows who is supposed to be covering whom. Such breaks in action and uncertainties make it possible for forwards with strong dribbling capacities to pierce a defence easily. Man-to-man covering provides the best system and in my view, is to be preferred to zone defence.

Most sides organise their defence with a "free man", the "libero". He is a playing personality with experience who exudes confidence and who plays in a consciencious, reliable manner. He covers the area behind his team-mates in front of him who are covering their men, "takes over" should an opponent get past one of his team-mates, or challenges an opposing forward who has worked himself "free" before he can reach the point where he can shoot and takes part in surprise attacking moves whilst his fellow-players cover up for him.

Man-to-man cover is carried out in an elastic manner. In proximity to the ball, the opponent is covered "closely", the further away the ball is, the more the defenders take up a deep-set formation in the defending area; but not too far away so as to be able to take up their positions in time should the ball suddenly be swung elsewhere.

To organise a defence effectively, it is important that the wingers too, take part in it. They should go after the opposing defenders who are counter-attacking, possibly adopt a "delaying" position in midfield, drop back into the defensive area and often cover up for a defender who has moved up into attack.

4.2.2. Positioning, Marking and Combatting the Opponent

To combat the opposing forward directly, the defensive player has to follow the game intently and alertly. He takes up position to the side behind his opponent – on the side nearest the ball, i. e. on the side from where a pass can reach his opponent. He studies his direct opponent and adjusts himself to his special traits. Should e. g. the opponent be a tricky dribbler, then the defender must try to prevent him reaching the ball in the first place. He attempts to intercept the pass. The next occasion for an effective interception would be to get to the ball at the same time as his opponent and to stop him from controlling the ball properly. If he observes that he cannot get to the ball before or at the same time as his opponent then he must keep at range and allow his opponent to advance. Thus e. g., the defender in this situation allows the attacking winger to advance and by

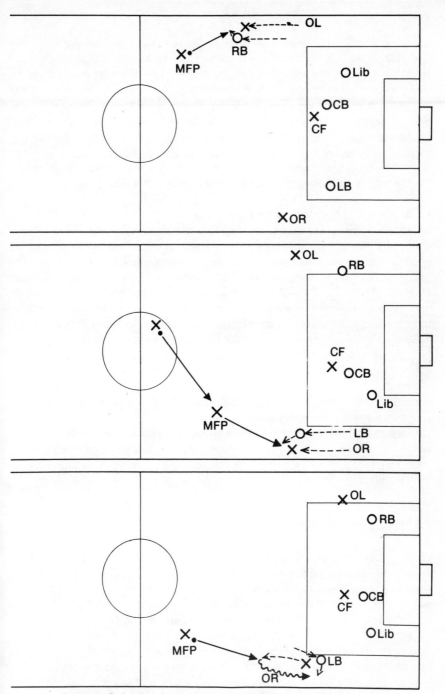

Figure 3 *Defensive Behaviour and Positioning of the Defence*

adopting a position on the "inner line" prevents the winger from cutting inside and making for goal by the shortest route. The defender is able to take the ball away from him on the touchline (sliding tackle). The defender must on no account allow himself to be provoked by the winger as he slowly dribbles forward, he must not intercept too soon, but instead he must for his part allow the opponent to make the move and then react to it. The good defender gives himself the chance to deprive his opponent of the ball and wins possession for his side through thoughtful behaviour and not through blind recklessness. Good defenders know that you should not allow a high ball to bounce and that if possible the ball should never be passed square near one's own goal.

4.2.3. Reverting to Attack (Counter-Attacking)
Defensive play is successful when it results in starting up an attacking move of your own. The quicker this reverse into attack can take place, the greater the chance is of piercing the opponent's unorganised and wide-open defence. The prior condition for starting an attack successfully is to quickly open up, occupy and exploit territory. If the goalkeeper for instance, has caught the ball then the defenders should immediately make for the touchline so that the keeper can pass the ball to one of them to start up a new attacking move over the wing. Counter-attacking through a defender moving forward with the ball is particularly effective when an opposing attacking move, carried out with a great deal of effort, has been halted. All those responsible, the coach and the players should influence the development of the game in the direction that a reinforced defence should revert to an equally reinforced attack and that goal-scoring should be regarded as a really attractive aim.
Only when defenders join in the attack threateningly and forwards take over defensive functions in order to regain possession of the ball, does football experience a positive and constructive development, becoming more than ever before an attractive team game.

4.3. EXCURSUS: REVIEW OF MEXICO

World football championships when the world elite pit their strength against one another reveal the trend in development of the game of football and cause systems and tactical means which were successfully practised there to be copied avidly here, there and everywhere. The particular climatic conditions in Mexico forced European teams to revert from their customary style of tempo football, possible in their climes and generally reduce the pace. What was almost an outbreak of panic at the start of the championships regarding the fear of playing too fast and thus investing too much strength not only led to the pace of a game being considerably slowed up but many players also revealed a pronounced lack of concentration and vitality and a consequent capacity of performance which was below their usual standard. As far as the Brazilians and the other South American teams were concerned the climate was nothing out of the ordinary for they are accustomed to playing under far more unfavourable climatic conditions. The European teams' adjustment to the climatic conditions called for certain tactical means and attitudes within the playing system. The available resources had to be deployed in such a way that a deep-set and space-exploiting formation was operated in attack in order to pull back the instant possession was lost, with a defensive block made up of eight or even nine players into the funnel-like defensive area in front of one' own goal, delaying the opposing attack in the process. Strength-consuming pursuing and tracking down of the opponent in possession, which in our view is still the principal means of defensive play, was not often seen. All teams, with the exception of the German side, had been programmed in advance to adopt the more economical zone defence which meant in fact, they had renounced a definite system, which is only achieved by direct man-to-man cover of the opposing strikers. You could in fact gain the impression that a number of sides fell victim to tactical experiments under the unfavourable climatic conditions, for which they did not even possess the necessary types of players not to mention an adequate, solid basis of experience. This was shown above all, by the often seemingly helpless defensive play of the Bulgarians – programmed to covering the space – in their match against the Peruvians, who were artistic on the ball and also tricky as well as in their match against the German side. The Bulgarians often stood around in defence uncertain as to who should face up to whom and take on whom when confronted with the surprising, fast, frequently unpredictable, attacking play of the South Americans. Such breaks in action were sufficient for good dribblers, which of course, the South Americans are, to take advantage of their opponent's weakness. Good technical players and dribblers who are strong on the break must be combatted by not allowing them to get possession of the ball in the first place, or alternatively they must be effectively intercepted in the moment they are trying to control the ball. The German side were optimally prepared with the balanced relationship of consistent man-to-man cover of the opposing strikers, a flexible means of cover in midfield and the free defender defending the zone, and consequently also successful.

Covering the zone calls on the defenders, particularly when they are up against tricky forwards who switch positions a lot, to be able to face up to various types of players. When such forwards move from one zone to another, they are free for a moment and can collect a pass – something which can easily lead to disorder and uncertainty and can be extremely dangerous when speedy technically-gifted players who are fast on the break and goal-getting dribblers are concerned. What we generally understand as a change of pace, holding the ball in your own ranks only then to unleash surprise attacks suddenly in order to gain ground and seek success, was especially accentuated in Mexico and was in fact, a consequence of the hot climate and the altitude. The actual range of pace employed varied from somniferous and delaying walking "pace" to lightning-fast and mercurial attacking play. This balance between the delaying game in attack as well as ultra-fast and very sudden attacking moves is a tactical necessity for reasons of economy in hot regions, but it is something which we should not try to emulate in this form, above all, with the accent on slowing up the game. It simply does not correspond to our conceptions of good football – not to mention the expectations of the spectators.

In our climate, no player would ever dare to walk with the ball or get involved in fiddle-faddling or pushing the ball back and forward aimlessly without gaining ground, without expecting to hear the whistles of the crowd. Changing pace is also a natural tactical means in the course of an attacking movement for us as well; but in contrast to Mexico it takes place at an overall higher speed.

Qualities which belong to the tradition and character of the Brazilian players and team, e. g. the method of deploying their resources, had also to be adopted in part by European sides in Mexico as well. If you examine the Brazilian method of playing and their system in an effort to find the secret of their success then you arrive at the conclusion that their system as far as the concept goes, was very simple indeed: Eight, sometimes with Pelé, nine players formed the defensive block covering the zone. The then obtained possession of the ball and suddenly, deploying their resources well, they created space for themselves and attacked in a deep and wide formation, whereby their superior, individual ability was instrumental for their success. They made the attempt to hold the ball in their own ranks under all circumstances, employing the simplest of means, and made use of the simplest of passes, which, when they could not be played forward, were pushed back, in order to ensure that possession was retained.

Their individual ability which of course, has evolved on the beach or wasteground endowed them with great self-confidence and provided the impression that they had no difficulties whatsoever regarding technique. Even in the most precarious situations they were able to pass the ball with a kind of selective instinct to the player who had taken up the most favourable free position for continuing the attack.

Very often the build-up took place over the right wing and they had no trouble at all in completing the attack initiated on the right on the other wing with a wide sweep of the ball. It was also worthy of note that each player, whether a forward or a defender, was extremely dangerous in front of goal and that each one possessed the athletic strength and the nerve to round off an attacking move with thunderous shots at goal. The ability to dribble, employing confusing changes of speed and deceptive movements, was something which each player was superbly equipped with, quite immaterial of whether it concerned the skilful holding of the ball before passing it, or within a tackle, advancing with the ball to gain as much ground as possible at high speed, or – and this was especially worthy of note, when penetrating the massed defence in front of the opponent's goal. It is unforgettable how Tostao in the game Brazil versus England, following several bouts of harmless dilly-dallying in front of the English penalty area, suddenly burst past two, three English players suddenly and explosively, into the penalty area, to see Pelé, in spite of the very limited space and the pressure he was under, standing at an angle behind him, and passed the ball to him. Pelé pretended to shoot and passed the ball to the right where he had seen Jairzinho, who ran on to it and crashed it into the back of the net. The Brazilians provided a parallel to this goal in the final when the defender (!) Carlos Alberto scored number four for his side.

Natural ability enables the Brazilians to act in a confusingly fast, unpredictable manner to an extraordinary extent, something which can be attributed to systematic awareness but also to intuition, improvisation and subconsciousness. Their playing genius and their fantasy of movement appears to be practically inexhaustible.

Such imaginative, adjusted behaviour is not the result of practising with stereotyped forms of drill, instead it has grown organically. Hundreds of talented youngsters, who are trying to join the Brazilian clubs, to a great extent, in the hope of securing their social existence through becoming a footballer, possess, apart from their great ability, match experience and maturity of movement which they have gained in the "free games" on the sandy beach of Copacabana or elsewhere, where they play football from morning till night. These basic qualities are fostered and developed in the case of those talented youngsters who are selected by the clubs in an improved, and more intensely demanding playing environment.

If one analyses the successes of the Brazilian brand of football then one comes across features which are particular traits of progressive development in football, but which are specially accentuated and distinctive in their case:

1. Reinforced attack from out of a reinforced defence making optimal use of space.
2. Surprise switching of the zone of attack; wing play.
3. Surprise switching of the playing pace.
4. Rational use of conditional resources employing delaying tempo, surprise and explosive increase of pace as well as switching position, tasks and initiative, especially with regard to the positions making demands on the resources.

Traits which govern their special playing behaviour must be added to this:

1. Match-dominating, superior individual ability, always a threat in a scoring position.
2. Technique as a natural prerequisite for solving all tactical requirements at any tempo during interpassing.
3. Skill, manoeuvrability, speed of action and reaction to realise surprise, lightning-fast sequences of movement as well as adapting to the opponent's intentions of movement.

4. The combination of methodically conscious, intuitive, freely improvised and subconscious playing behaviour, predestined through great natural talent.
5. Natural talent and resultant superior ability as the prior conditions for self-confidence and purposiveness.
6. A highly pronounced national consciousness as the basis for strength of will and fighting spirit.

Their enjoyment of the game when playing the ball or facing the opposition frequently bubbles over and is governed by a feeling of natural talent which enables them to master in a split-second even the most unpredictable of situations and the diversity of surprisingly changing demands on movement which are constantly recurring. Their pronounced drive towards individual technical brilliance results from this.

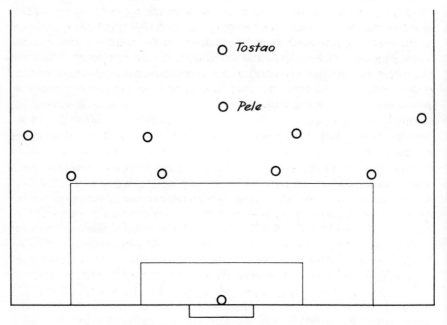

Figure 4 *The Brazilian defensive formation*

If you examine the organisation of their defence, then it is evident that two chains of four players are drawn up one behind the other. In the goal funnel they form a closely-knit net, in which they attempt to halt the progress of their opponent, whose ability and playing skill incidentally are considerably tested in the extremely narrow area available to them. They are greatly assisted by their superior speed of reaction, something which nature has bestowed on them and the routine in zone defence, the only possible method they could employ, which has grown up in their hot climate.

The midfield players and the *wingers* are included in the organisation of the defence. Apart from possessing the features of proper strikers, they also have the ability to defend. Inter-changing and tasks on the wing are governed by the laws of economy, for the important and necessary game on the wing which is so essential against a reinforced defence would take too much out of a winger physically, who continually found himself forced to attempt strength-consuming dribbling and rapid sprints, particularly under hot climatic conditions.

In midfield, in front of the front chain of four players, Pelé would operate, and Tostao would occupy a forward striking position as far as possible. Both were very fast, tricky and dangerous and tied up opponents through their positioning and their play, and they facilitate the speedy reverting to attack, begun from a deep-lying position as soon as the opposing attacking move had been stopped. Initially they attempted to bridge the midfield rapidly in order to attempt pierce an incompletely organised defence with their counter-attacks. But if the other side were able to reform their defence quickly, they advanced thoughtfully, slowly but surely, at times by means of harmless and even apparently unconcentrated shilly-shallying, only then to attack the opposition suddenly, explosively, surprisingly and confusingly fast, employing constantly changing of position.

In possession of the ball, they would attack with six players, taking advantage of the available space. Tostao would operate up front – strong in dribbling and a constant threat in front of goal, Pelé would lurk behind him as the second striker, equally peerless on the ball and with tremendous firing power. In midfield, Gerson would direct operations, assisted by Clodoaldo, and on the wings, the wingers and the defenders would take it in turns to advance forward. A chain of four covered the attack at the back. With regard to the system, the team was harmonically balanced. Each and every player possessed the talent and the features which ensured that the "suit" fitted. Within the framework of this system, their individual, superior ability on the ball, their astounding self-confidence and their often effervescent enjoyment of the game were the actual key to their success. It should be observed that a number of national league teams in Germany have attempted to play and copy this 4-4-2 system, at least as so-called "away tactics", the way the Brazilians are used to doing representing as it does the best set-up in defence and attack given their climatic conditions. However, something which is determined by the climate in Brazil and is a sensible method of playing with regard to the natural talent of the players, cannot be emulated without hesitation under our conditions! As a consequence, many established players used to "covering the man" have come to grief because they were expected to revert to covering the zone overnight. For this reason, many players who, according to their talents, have adapted themselves to man-to-man covering from the time they were youths, find they cannot fit into the system their

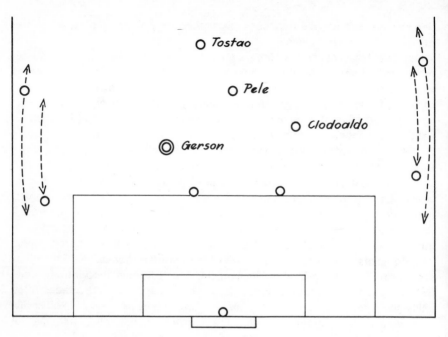

Figure 5 *Attacking formation of the Brazilians*

coach has devised for them. They feel ill-at-case and cannot reproduce their best game.

The English also played with two rows of four in defence and in Hurst and Lee they possessed two athletic and strong attacking strikers who were strong on the break and extremely dangerous in front of goal. With Ball on the right and Peters on the left side of the front row of four, the English had types of players who possessed excellent defensive qualities, but who were equally good forwards both in build-up and in taking chances. In the centre of the defensive zone, Mullery and Bobby Charlton covered at the front whilst Bobby Moore operated behind Mullery and Labone at the back of Charlton. The English attack was given its edge and its pace controlled by Bobby Charlton, who was indefatigably supported by Ball and Mullery. They were able to force the game over the wings, making use of a clever distribution of labour, with always another player attacking up the wing or surprisingly appearing on the other wing to wait for a possible cross to continue the *attack and round it off*.

Both backs, Newton on the right and Cooper on the left, continually took part in the attack on the overlap, whereby Newton received the necessary cover from Ball and Mullery, and Cooper mainly from Peters. The English did not field typical wingers but it can always be said of them that skilled dribbling and goal-get-

Defensive formation of the English

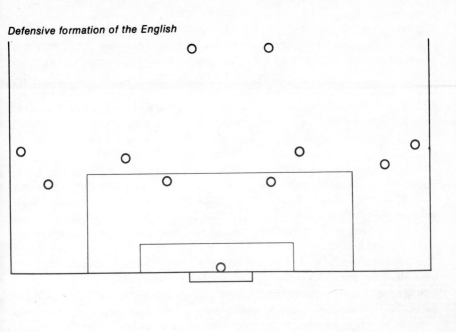

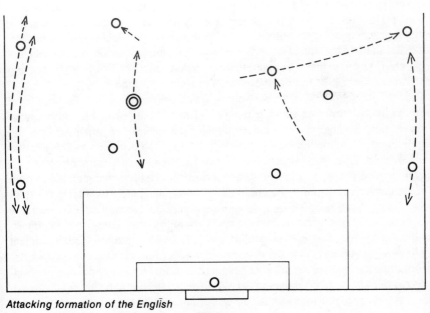

Attacking formation of the English

Figure 6

ting ability are numbered among their characteristic playing attributes and that having to play up the wing or from the wing presented no real difficulties to any of the players. As an example for their successful attacking play over both wings let us mention the two goals which the English scored against the German side: In the case of the first goal, Hurst crossed from the right, Peters had followed up and pushed the ball into the German net. In the case of the second, the right-back Newton overlapped and finished off the move with a sharp cross, which Mullery who suddenly appeared from nowhere in front of the German goal hit home.

The crosses were of particular relevance here: they were put across very hard, low waist-height, at the most chest-height, in front of goal. The forward lurking in front of goal "exploded" at lightning pace on to the ball and hit or nodded it home. This took into account the fact that balls lobbed into the penalty area could far too easily be parried by world-class keepers and defenders who were strong in the air.

The English played their concept in a very disciplined and purposeful manner, whereby their zone defence turned out to their Achilles' heel.

The German team played in their customary 4-3-3 formation with Schnellinger as libero. The midfield players, Uwe Seeler as second spearhead, Wolfgang Overath as the dynamo and Franz Beckenbauer as the defensive midfield player, pulled back into the defensive area for the organisation of the defence and helped form a defensive block composed of seven players. When the opposing defenders moved up in support, the wingers also dropped back to play a defensive role. The functions in the defence were clearly split up: the libero as the last line of defence in front of the keeper covered the zone, the backs and the centre-back faced up to the opposing strikers "man-to-man", the three midfield players operated in front of them, containing the opposing defence in midfield, covering their men right up to the defensive area in front of the goal.

In attack, our team possessed well-balanced playing material and distribution of forces: in the foremost striking position, Gerd Müller, with his phenomenal goal-getting ability, was the most effective player with regard to taking the chances which came his way, not just with respect to our team but also to the whole World Cup tournament. As a result of this known goal-scoring ability, every evasive action he undertook meant he was constantly tying up the opposing defence. Consequently he created the prerequisites for the attacking effectiveness of Uwe Seeler whose goal-getting ability is governed by his exemplary never-say-die fighting spirit. Playing one behind the other, they dovetailed perfectly. A mobile and dangerous striker always draws the attention and important defensive resources of the opposing side towards him, which of course, facilitates matters for all the other players advancing on goal from the rear both with regard to penetrating and finishing off. Whether for instance, he helps a "solo effort" in finishing off a move or ties up an opponent by acting as a "wall", making a one-two movement possible.

Wolfgang Overath was the schemer and with his passes, played short or long and with great precision, the dynamo in midfield. Within the basic system, Franz Beckenbauer played the defensive midfield role but, however, thanks to his brilliant capacity to dribble, to participate in one-two movements in the narrowest possible space and to shoot, he proved to be another dangerous factor in the attack. When Franz Beckenbauer moved forward, it was a case of "red alert" for the opposing defence. If the player he was covering did not follow him then this player had to be covered by either Uwe Seeler or Wolfgang Overath in order to ensure that in the event of counter-attacks by the other side, no attacking player was left to operate freely in midfield, thus providing cover for the attacking defensive midfield player. He himself of course, in the event of losing possession of the ball, had to set off in pursuit of his opponent at once and join up again with the defensive system.

Midfield players are free to decide on just how to set up an attacking move and when doing so they must not allow themselves to feel handicapped by the fact that have the task of covering an opponent, but they are also to a considerable degree responsible for fulfilling their defensive duties, which they must carry out jointly and with mutual understanding and support for one another.

The surprise attacking surges by defensive players were a pleasing sign of progressive development in Mexico as well against the otherwise so dominant "defensive might" of all the teams. The superior number of defenders and the "free man" make it possible for defenders to move forward alternately when the situation is ripe and sufficient space is created. Such lightning-fast counter-attacking, immediately turning defence into attack by dint of territory-bridging dribbling, is particularly effective when the opponent has just been stopped following exhausting attacking moves.

A defender must move up into attack without risk, without unnecessary tussles or obvious and "telegraphed" square passes and round off his move in such a way that the attacking defensive player can hurry back to take up his position in defence.

The further reinforcing of the defence is an inevitable result of the ever greater quest for success. The development could then be described as threatingly negative and destructive if a team were programmed to defence without or with only very little attacking initiative. The reinforced defence should be regarded as a means to regain possession of the ball in order to be able to attack just as strongly by means of counter-attacking defensive forces and score goals.

A positive and constructive relationship between the defensive and attacking game was displayed in exemplary fashion by our team in Mexico in spite of the difficult climatic conditions, in as much as, within the reinforced defence, even the "libero" was potentially a goal-getter.

This positive development of the game helps to foster as this development proceeds of the type of player, who fulfils his basic task within the framework of a system which corresponds to his talent and inclination and in addition as a de-

German defensive formation

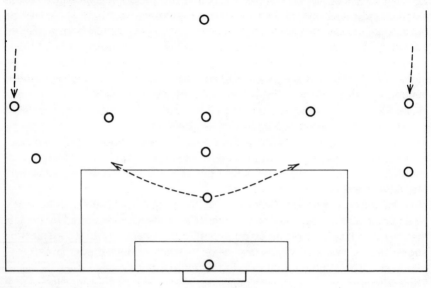

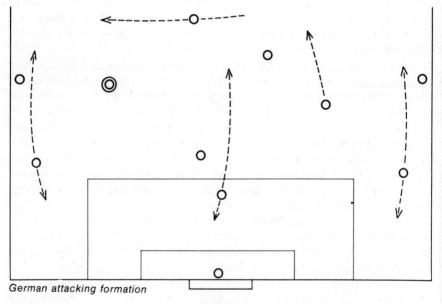

German attacking formation

Figure 7

fensive player is equipped with all the prerequisites of an attacking player, and as an attacking player not only goes after and follows the opponent in possession but is also capable of facing up to, marking and successfully combatting an opposing player within the defensive zone.

The positive development of the game of football can be traced to this expansion ot the range of action and tasks of each player as well as the callenge in properly coming to terms with this development during training.

4.4. EXCURSUS: OBSERVATION AND EVALUATION OF THE 1974 WORLD CUP

The World Cup in Mexico created particularly difficult conditions, as a result of the climate and altitude, for European teams and these had to be overcome. The physiological adjustment, the rationalisation and economisation of the available means as well as the psychological preparation of their readiness to perform, above all, the retention of concentration, attentiveness and strength of will, made particularly high demands on the coaches and players.

The environment in which the games in the World Cup in the Federal Republic were held created the best possible conditions for the world elite in football to exploit their potential ability fully. In addition, it could be expected that the positive process of development, which mainly is characterised through attacking defensive players and defending strikers with a wide field of operations would continue. The 1974 World Cup, like its predecessors in 1966 and 1970, clearly revealed that the might of a reinforced defence – provoking the attacking game – had gained further ground, both in respect to more intensive and more skilful individual behaviour or in the collective action of a number of players in combatting the opposing striker in possession or with regard to compact marshalling of the defence and its increasing stability in front of goal. The decisive question of how the means of the attacking game have developed further must be raised here, which possibilities and means have still to be developed in order to make attacking play potentially more dangerous with regard to scoring goals through further purposive training measures, in spite of the reinforced defence.

The good coach lives from observation. Watching, analysing and recognising competitive behaviour as it progresses in its development, is an essential prior condition for bringing training measures and methods up to date. The coach finds himself in a constant process of learning, he researches for reasons, the why and wherefore of playing behaviour, in order to sharpen his dissecting and analytical field of vision. The coach must constantly be questioning his own actions. By means of healthy self-criticism he is able to consolidate his position or, if necessary, to realign his thoughts and actions governing the game. A coach, who wishes to guide others towards the utmost proficiency and who has taken on great responsibility through having this target in mind, must himself be thoroughly committed to performance and be constantly on the look out for new re-cognitions. The guiding principle should of course always be the original play-ing notion: scoring goals!

The 1974 World Cup was, as could have been anticipated, dominated by Euro-pean sides, although Europe and South America can continue to learn from one another. The game of the future will be governed to a large extent by skill (the ability of the individual player to alter his movements surprisingly and quickly according to the needs of the situation as well as being able to carry out equally surprising changes of pace and direction) and also by stamina. Playing skill is, as this World Cup tournament also proved, the domain of the South Americans. However, European football can also produce players in the South American mould with respect to skill. A major step forward has been made. It was again amazing to behold how the Brazilian players were able to assert themselves and maintain possession even in the tightest of situations with great skill of move-ment and technical perfection. They "sneaked" their way through the opposing defensive rows with speedy and safe passing moves and by skilfully shielding the ball. However, their game had slowed down and they required too much time and they used up too much concentration in tight situations, and as a result squan-dered scoring chances. Running without the ball to gain ground, which really strengthens the position of the player in possession, as he can choose the alter-native between passing, going it alone and breaking through, was lacking in the play of the Brazilians. Their playing skill, admirable as it may be, lacked success-determining effectivity without European stamina which provides for a consequent overall dynamisation of the positions with all the players covering considerable distances. The comparison of South American and European football confirmed the basic principle that playing artistry must be coupled with fighting strength. An essential component of such fighting strength is a capacity for stamina in competition.

Tactical Aspects
Defensive Play
Defensive play begins immediately after losing possession of the ball through chasing after and tracking down the player initiating the attack (see Chapter on Defensive Play). As we were able to read there this is nothing new. However, ra-pid switching from defence to attack or vice versa and the ensuing pressure im-mediately felt by the players initiating the attack have become more intense. The strikers immediately drop back into midfield and narrow the area of attack to-gether with the midfield players. The player in possession is placed under strong pressure in this way both with regard to time and space. This possibility of nar-rowing the area of attack can be arrived at by setting up a deep attacking forma-tion when putting the goal area under siege. This deep-set formation in attack is not only important regarding the goal-getting potentiality of the attack, as will be

demonstrated later. The "inner line" law – that the opposing attack must be in front of you, that is to say, that you stand closer to your own goal than the opponent in possession, also applies to the defensive behaviour ot the strikers, wherever the opponent gains possession and initiates an attack. Only one forward can stay up front in order to tie up two defenders. All the others must, as soon as possession is lost, run back to be nearer their own goal than the opposing attacker is. Ultra-fast reverting from attack to defence is one of the most vital initial defensive measures for the further organisation of a stable and effective defence. The practice of putting the opposition under strong pressure right from the onset of an attack, which of course, demands a large measure of physical fitness, could be observed in the case of all European teams and continues to govern the trend in development of this partial aspect of defensive behaviour. Once the target of gaining repossession of the ball quickly is achieved then ultra-fast counter-attacking against the opposing defence, which is open at the onset of the attack, is essential.

The organisation of the defence and tactical interaction varied. Admittedly, the concentration of eight or nine players in the goal-scoring zone was a characteristic feature of all teams and systems; however, covering the zone and covering the man once again rivalled one another during this tournament. Man-to-man cover clearly emerged the victor from this clash of tactical systems. Its advantage over zone defence has already been mentioned elsewhere. A resourceful and dynamic player with a wide radius of action, e. g. Johann Cruyff, was only faced with problems, when he was pitted against an equally resourceful, mobile, fast-reacting and strong-willed player with fighting strength, who could adapt himself more and more to his wiles as the game wore on (Vogts versus Cruyff). Each experience of success enhances the fighting morale of the marking defender and that of his opponent begins to reel. The match preparation too, can be more thoughtfully carried out regarding the application of ways and means through which the opponent, whose game has been analysed, can successfully be combatted. In this way, the defender can be sent onto the field well prepared and with increased self-confidence. It was definitely a major advantage for Johann Cruyff and his team that they came up against teams which had adopted zone defending in the First Final Round matches. Cruyff was able to use all his ability to reveal his brilliance unrestrictedly and raise his playing mood to the point of euphoria.

The zone defence was the weak point in the Brazilian defence as well. In the case of fast diagonal changes of position, combined with "taking over the ball", their defence was often confused and vulnerable. The same could be said about the Yugoslavians, the Poles and other teams which covered the zone. The method of covering the zone cannot be recommended at all when close to goal, where attentiveness and concentration are most strongly challenged on account of the abundance of moments of danger for if the defenders do not pursue interchanging strikers they cook their own goose.

Close to goal, each defensive player must keep tags on his opponent and be aware how he has to combat him. Order in defence, particularly in the goal area where all the decisions and tensions take place, prevents the confusion of concentration and fosters thoughtful attentiveness.

Attacking Play
Every good attacking move begins with a well-organised, stable and consequently secure defence which radiates confidence. Such security in defence acts as a stimulant and sets the will to attack and all the other inner driving forces into motion, which cause an attacking move to be full of elan but at the same time thoughtfully carried out and directed. The development of even more massed defensive behaviour which resulted during the World Cup, with ultra-fast reversing by the spearheads, pursuit, closing the gap, challenging and combatting the opponent the moment he began an attack in order to regain possession of the ball, all meant that reversing defence into attack had to take place even more rapidly. This called for all the players seeking the open space even more rapidly using the depth and width of the field in order to create as many possibilities for passing as possible when the attacking move began.

The provoking confrontation of defence and attack increases the pace of playing behaviour. The more intensive pressure seen both from the point of view of room to move and time to move also increases the demand made on the basic performances capacities in the intellectual-mental sphere. The demand made on more rapid decisiveness and action requires increased powers of attentiveness and concentration and calls for alert anticipation and thought. However, the state of agitation which has a far greater influence as a result of the increased stress must be controlled in order to be able to master coordination disturbances and slackening of movement. Increased speed of action, triggered off by situations under pressure, calls for greater mental preparedness and psychical stability. The player interprets this pressure as a threat, he feels under great stress. His powers of perception and attention are concentrated on the point of this threat, his immediate playing surroundings. The result is a series of short and back passes, the ball and the responsibility are passed on to the nearest player. The capacity to read and overlook the situation by means of wide (peripheral) attentiveness is unable to cope with the increased stress produced by this challenge, decisions governing behaviour lack determination.

As a result of this changed influence on the character of the challenge, the player experiences the game more intensively. The standard of demand called for grows and more than ever before requires alert observation and analysis of the development of play in all the sub-sectors of the complex performance challenge. Evaluation of the analysis creates the prior condition for the fixation and more conscious experiencing of performance targets in training as well as their realisation and effectivity for increasing performance in competition.

The targets are thus clearly discernible:

1. The expansion of techno-motorial skill. A player who possesses good technique is one who can realise additional possibilities and alterations of movement in a playing situation which surprise and confuse the opponent, beyond the technical basic conceptions of a particular movement; a player who possesses a further potential spectrum of movement, in other words, fantasy of movement. The success of techno-motorial behaviour in a competitive situation greatly depends on the ability of the player to digest mentally and physically the range of impressions from his surroundings, to interpret them rapidly and to decide upon what is the tactically best solution in a fraction of a second. Frequently the situation changes so surprisingly and suddenly that it occurs at the same instant as an intended movement which is on the point of being executed. Good technical players have the ability to transform the nervous process already being activated into new movements corresponding to the change in the environment. Technique is after all the unascertainable multitude and variety of possibilities of movement on the ball.

Treating competition with its increased standard of play and the resultant intensification of the challenge it poses, in an original and inventive manner as well as both thoughtfully and purposively, should also govern the teaching method during drill and training. The skill of movement and coordinating capacity in tight situations, as they more or less occur all the time in football, depends on the potential capacity of the sphere of perception and attentiveness as well as psychical stability.

This basic fact makes it evident that the most effective teaching environment is created by playing situations. The selected playing tasks contain instruction targets which each player makes the effort to solve employing means and possibilities of his own. In the process the decisions governing his movements are triggered off by the results of what he has perceived. The player must learn to interpret situations with all their impressions and to overcome what he is confronted with both mentally and psychically. His ever active and spontaneous commitment towards seeking and finding solutions is enhanced and the experience of success more strongly motivated. The 1974 World Cup clearly revealed that essentially each individual player is faced with the challenge, immaterial of whatever position he might play in, of improving his skill i. e. the ability to demonstrate surprise changes of movement in every situation with regard to creativity, pace and direction. The player must not allow his opponent to work out his movements. However, this is then the case when he employs rigid sets of movements and stereotyped approaches.

2. The organisation of attacking play reveals an increasing dynamisation of positions. This not only signifies the switching of positions by the spearheads up front but also interchanging between themselves, the midfield players and the back line of defence. E. g. the Polish centre-forward Szarmach changed positions with Deyna, one of the midfield players. Gut, the right back overlapped

down the right wing. Szarmach switched to take up the right-back position in order to cover up for the attacking defender. This change of position and function was even more perceptible in the case of Johann Cruyff. But let us also cast our minds on the two defenders in the German national team: Paul Breitner who was continually going forward and attacking dangerously or Berti Vogts, who was faced with the task of marking and combatting Cruyff in the final and who attacked the Dutch goal, when his opponent had pulled himself back thus forcing Cruyff to cover him.

Equally effective was the sporadic and consequently surprise moving forward of Franz Beckenbauer, the libero, through midfield in an effort to score goals. In doing so, he created a number of alternatives in that he a) exploited the strikers seeking the open space diagonally and as an alternative to passing the ball, shot at goal himself or b) with Müller as the lethal spearhead he set up and played the one-two movement, c) passed to Müller and ran through as he passed thus inviting the square pass, only for Müller to turn in the direction of attack and go through on his own or d) Müller, with Beckenbauer acting in the same way, passed the ball to a third player who unleashed a shot at goal.

Here you can discern how important on the one hand seeking the open space is in order to support the man on the ball, who dribbles with the ball and shoots at goal instead of passing it; but on the other, the short pass to the man who is already covered in order to be able to be able to set up dangerous one-two passing movements with all their variations.

The wide-sweeping interchanging of positions was especially characteristic of the European teams which were able to assert themselves in this tournament. The Federal Republic's side were certainly more adept than all the others in exploiting wide radii of action in their running.

Covering wide areas with and without the ball and the surprise switching of the areas of attack (switching from one wing to the other) at high speed, as well as going after and pursuing opposing forwards as a means of defence, requires a high degree of anaerobic stamina capacity (speed stamina). Deceptive dribbling capable of piercing the defence (techno-motorial skill on the ball) alternating with rapid, directed series of passes, allied to a high stamina capacity have emerged as the most important means of realising tactical aims.

3. The increased demands on condition call for overall physical fitness. Properly informing the players about the targets of fitness training arouses their spontaneous readiness to cooperate, above all when the training exercises relate to competition. The footballer's fitness training should not simply be restricted to an application of the recognised general training methods instead if these are going to be practically and effectively exploited they require an interpretation which has been adapted to suit both competitive requirements in football and the physically different types of players.

Strength, speed, variability of movement and stamina must all be trained in accordance with their match application.

Here is an example for the methodical adaptation on the part of the trainer to the player's approach in practice: meeting and moving with the ball is the object of the exercise.

"Meet the ball and move it past your opponent in the direction of attack. Head towards goal". The coach is watching closely and observes: the player moves towards the ball, the opponent follows him. The player shields the ball when meeting it and moves square with it, but not past his opponent in the direction of attack. The coach interrupts the training session at this point: "You are able to control the ball well (praise), but you are not gaining ground in the direction of attack. Spurt past your opponent and head for goal."

The coach watches how the move is now carried out: The player makes the attempt to sprint past his opponent using a surprise burst of speed. His opponent keeps up with him along the "inner line" and forces the player out to the side. The coach interrupts the session and suggests a further task: "Sprint as you have been doing, drawing your opponent with you. After a short burst of speed turn in the opposite direction and then head towards goal."

The coach watches closely and observes the following: The player draws his opponent with him during his burst of speed, he turns and surprisingly moves away from his opponent and heads for goal. His opponent has been shaken off. Success and the teaching target have been achieved. Rapid turning and moving off with the necessary purposiveness can be a main aspect in playing behaviour and is something which should be patiently practised further.

In terms of fitness the fast burst of speed with the ball, skill and manoeuvrability as well as speedy reactions on the part of the defensive player are all practised simulating competition as much as possible by means of this technical-tactical task of man-to-man play. Important! There must be breaks in order to eliminate the factor of exhaustion as much as possible. This applies to the overall training sphere embracing speed, skill and coordination.

The high demands made on physical performance which in fact increase as one progresses necessitate a periodical control of performance by a sports doctor at set intervals.

Systems and their Composition

Under system, we understand the functional integration of types of players with the aim of achieving the utmost effectivity in the joint execution of attacking and defensive reactions.

Observation of the teams participating in the World Cup tournament was thus concentrated on:

1. The organisation and the means of the defensive and attacking game,
2. the types of players and their means in their technical-tactical ability to succeed and
3. the tactical-functional integration, above all of dominating player personalities.

It is interesting to observe that the three top teams played in the same basic order: the goalkeeper, a "libero", with three defenders in front of him, three midfield players and three strikers. The Dutch and West German sides played man-to-man against the opposing strikers and with a "libero" defending the zone. The Poles showed a preference for zone defence and played with a "libero", who operated more as a "sweeper" and who only very seldom moved up to take part in attack. This took place when there were free kicks close to the penalty box: two Polish players moved out to the left and right of the defensive wall away from the ball. Their running forward suggested that the ball would be played in the direction of the goal; however, the ball was played back diagonally where Gorgon was lurking, waiting to demonstrate his shooting power.

Italy, Yugoslavia, Scotland, Sweden, Argentina and Brazil played with a 4:4:2 system. In the case of these teams as well, only the basic order was the same. There were differences in their functioning, which were attributable to different dominating types of players or, above all in the case of the South Americans, to their racial characteristics.

Types of players, in other words, the characterisation of special traits, by means of which players distinguish themselves in their playing behaviour, as help in orientation for observing the game and the tactical preparation of players to oppose them. In other words, we are concerned here with determining the traits of players and their integrating effect upon the performance of a team.

You can talk about typical defenders, whose primary behaviour is governed by inherent traits and qualities which facilitate their prompt reacting to attacking moves. No defender is the same as another. E. g. Breitner normally moves in on his opponent when the opponent is in possession and has turned towards him. Berti Vogts on the other hand, attempts to deprive his opponent of the ball at the very latest when the opponent is attempting to meet it. If we watch the Italian defender Fachetti then we have a quite different type of defender, in physical terms alone. This large athletic figure incorporates more the centre-back type. In his case in particular it was shown that when up against a fast, mercurial winger such as the Pole Lato, whom he pursued when he switched from the right to the left wing, he finds himself in considerable difficulty. The defender, who is not only quick off the mark, but who also possesses a high degree of adjustable mobility and manoeuvrability, has decisive advantages when it comes to facing tricky opponents. If, in addition, he is able to apply his motorial variability to lethal attacking behaviour then he exemplarily points to the future by dint of these qualities.

Most players in the "libero" position concentrated on their task as organiser and stabilising factor in defence in that they adopted the duties of the "sweeper" and many in fact did not participate in attack. Starting with the match against Yugoslavia, Franz Beckenbauer turned on an exemplary display in this position. He fought with great determination, employing the utmost concentration and vitality. As a result, he stabilised the defence, and was a real source of stimulation for his fellows. Exploiting his outstanding technical qualities, he participated in attack, often surprising the opposition. Strong in dribbling, he quickly bridged midfield in order to shoot at goal as quickly as possible and then returned to take up his position equally rapidly. The "libero" can only fulfil his responsibility in the execution of his defensive duties; he cannot fulfil a second role as the brains in midfield.

This important task and the responsibility which goes with it has to be delegated to another player personality who is equipped with all the necessary attributes. This player also requires a possibility to display his skills, the confirmation of the successful application of his means. The attack profits from his ability to read the game, his genius, his precise passes – both short and long and his urge to get the ball in the opposing net.

We recognise just how important it is that two outstanding player personalities understand one another both as persons and tactically and are integrated into a team, fully aware of the responsible fulfillment of their basic tactical duties. If the stronger personality of the two forces the other out of his responsible role then the player who has been repressed has his effect neutralised. Another outstanding playing personality was the Swede Edström, whose height alone makes him particularly suitable for the game in the air. Together with Sandberg he formed a dangerous attacking duo in the Swedish 4:4:2 system. The majority of the Swedish attacks were built up to be finished off by Edström in the air; he either headed the ball towards goal himself or nodded it down to the inrushing Sandberg.

The most interesting player personality with regard to the diversity of his spectrum of movement, his surprise burst of speed full of deceptive manoeuvres, but also with regard to his wide range of tactical-functional means of application, was Johann Cruyff. He cleverly directed the attention of opponents away from his own initiatives and intentions through gesticulating and directing proceedings while moving about. His area of action was the whole pitch: he was in a striking position as goalscorer, played on both wings and crossed dangerously, operated as motor in midfield and occupied all defensive positions in order to allow the defender in question to move up in attack.

Gadocha, the Polish outside-left had an equally wide spectrum of playing possibilities. He played on the left wing, was equally dangerous on the right, appeared in midfield, scored from the most forward position, took the corners from both sides and helped strengthen the defence. His motorial speed and skill made him strong in dribbling. He combined these technical advantages with thoughtfulness and untiring deployment of his qualities.

Gerd Müller, the world champions' centre-forward was a true phenomenon when it came to the most important quality that a centre-forward should possess, namely being able to score goals. His special traits are to be found first of all in the mental and psychical sphere: a high degree of attentiveness and concentration, the ability to read goal-scoring situations rapidly, decisiveness and speed of thought, drive and purposiveness and above all, psychical stability. In the tightest situations under pressure, he experiences no inhibitions but instead he regards them as a challenge and cooly makes a self-confident, thoughtful decision which is reflected in his actions. He sees the corner of the goal that is free. By means of this self-confidence and inner composure he is able to apply his inherent motorial speed effectively.

Systems are moulded, with regard to their tactical effectiveness, with regard to the presentation of the performance picture of individual ability, above all by the special playing qualities of the player personalities. Similar systems are only similar in their basic order, the number of players required for the organisation of the defence and attack. Teams which played a similar system, as for instance, the Polish, Dutch and West German team revealed marked differences in the method of their playing style. In midfield, the Poles did not possess a player who could be immediately recognised as the creative dynamo. The impulse sometimes came from Deyna, sometimes from Kasperczak or from Maszcyk, but both Gadocha, the outside-left, and Szarmach, the centre-forward appeared in midfield while the midfield player moved over to the wing or into a forward striking position in attack. There was not a single midfield schemer instead every player could take over in midfield and every player was prepared to run and subjugate himself. Their game was characterised by constructive running, breakthroughs created by strong dribbling, and rapid, short passing sequences, making pronounced use of the attack over the wings. (Lato and Gadocha either playing together or switching on both wings) Above all, crosses and corners had been carefully prepared to exploit them fully: five players took up formation on the far side of the penalty box, as seen from the player on the ball. Four players ran towards the ball, one remained standing at a distance to take advantage of the long corner (Deyna or Szarmach).

The Dutch side was composed of players from two clubs who are arch-rivals in the Dutch championship. They began the tournament without bearing the tag of favourites and were consequently not under pressure, and following a series of brilliant initial successes they moulded together to form an astonishingly self-confident and homogeneous unit and rapidly qualified as an almost certain claimant to the champions' crown. Hard and uncompromising in their defensive operations, strong in maintaining possession of the ball, they held the ball in their own ranks employing fast and safe passing sequences. Surprise spurts without the ball permitted dangerous passes deep into the area of attack. Equally surprising dashes with the ball (e. g. Cruyff moved up to the opposing defence and then suddenly made use of his speed off the mark put the opposing defence under pressure. Strong shots at goal from outside the penalty area were also numbered among their goal-getting repertoire (van Hanegem).

The special feature of their tactical attacking concept was that their centre-forward Cruyff – whose manifold talents have already been described – moved out of the spearhead position for one of the midfield players, above all, van Hanegem and Neeskens, or even the centre-back or libero to move up into it in order to finish off attacking moves or crosses they themselves had instigated; if Cruyff dribbled up the wing then the winger would move into the middle in front of goal to wait for his cross. Instead of crossing the ball he often played it back to van Hanegem or Jansen who then hit the ball above the heads of the massed defence. Cruyff was without doubt, the most conspicuous member of the Dutch team and the one who most impressed his stamp upon their game, however, the opposition's attention was equally directed at Neeskens who not only possessed the means of a midfield schemer but also the lethalness of a Gerd Müller.

The offside trap was an additional tactical feature. The manner in which the defenders moved up in one line and their moving forward in order to place the opposing forwards "offside" was clearly something which had been practised to perfection. Here, however, the question regarding the purpose of the offside rule is raised and whether placing the opponent "offside" in such a way, when there was no intention of exploiting this offside position, actually promotes the attraction of the game. Professional behaviour does not always serve the constructive development of the game and should not be copied thoughtlessly.

The German team, playing at home as well as holding the European championship, were the number 1 favourites. The public's high expectations of success had to be psychically assimilated with every match. Each opponent was in a position to play unconcernedly to prevent the German team's expectations of success. The team grew into a real community in the course of the tournament which self-confidently justified their role of favourites, playing and battling towards the projected target. Maier, was a reliable goalkeeper and the backbone of the team. A further stabilising factor in defence was Franz Beckenbauer who was optimally supplemented in his effectiveness as a libero covering the zone by the defenders Vogts and Breitner, covering the man, as well as Schwarzenbeck at centre-back. The discernible reliability of the goalkeeper and the good harmony and strength of performance of the defenders had a mutually stimulating effect. The midfield was made up of Overath, the schemer with Bonhof, an athletic player, quick off the mark, fast to react and act who played the defensive role and the athletic, Hoeness also fast off the mark, strong in running and penetration, in the offensive role. Hoeness operated over a wide field of action: switching with the wingers he attacked over both wings, he functioned as spearhead if Müller had dropped back to reinforce the defence or he supported the defence himself in order to exploit his strength in running from out of a deep attacking position once in possession.

Both wingers, Grabowski and Hölzenbein presented problems for the opposing defence with their tricky dribbling and their wide field of action from wing to wing. Skilful dribblers who reveal ever changing variations of movement and speed, allied with the determination to push into and pierce the opposing defensive block and then have the necessary strength of nerve to round the move off lethally, exemplarily possess the criteria for the attacking qualities of the winger, qualities which we cannot do without, whatever the system. Together with these

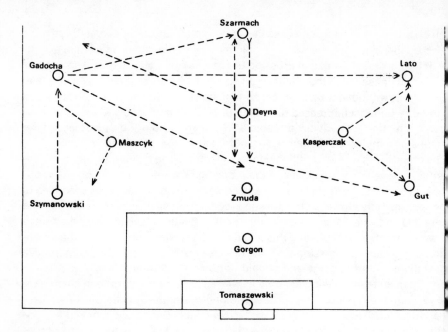

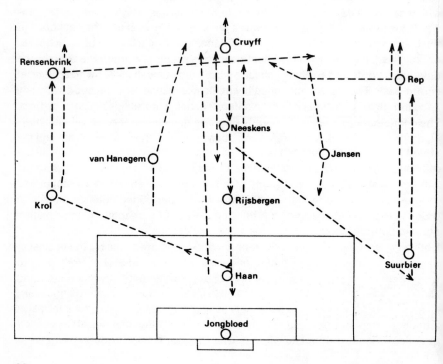

qualities of attacking behaviour they combine important qualifications needed to carry out defensive duties: high anaerobic stamina capacity (speed stamina), the ability to go after and pursue the opponent, to link up with the defensive block, to display clever tactics when directly engaged in fending off an opposing attacking player, fast counter-attacking in that the winger himself gets off or, on the other hand, he "sends" the defender on his way and covers up for him (economisation).

All the positions in the Federal Republic of Germany's team were filled exemplarily and thanks to a dynamisation of the positions over the width of the field as well as a functional breadth in attack and defence, it was able to set standards for the future.

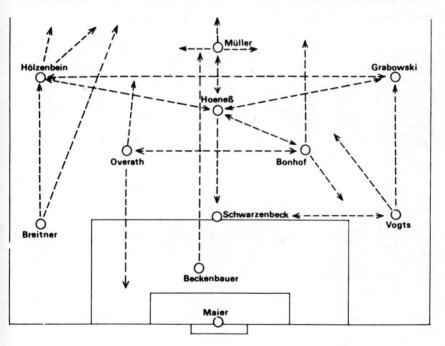

The analysis of teams and types of players who were outstanding during the 1974 World Cup can be summed up in the following main points:

1. Reinforced, restrictive defensive behaviour. Eight and nine players organise the defence in front of goal.
2. An increase of the techno-motorial playing skill, creativity, variations of movement, direction and pace.
3. A dynamisation of positions, an expansion of the tactical width of functioning and the areas of action.

4. An improvement of the basic physical requirements with regard to the demands of competition. Transposing the recognitions of scientific training theory into actual competitive requirements.
5. More active training: informing the player more adequately about training targets and measures.

Learning by means of coming to grips with competitive situations. Improved perception and recognition of the possibilities of using and applying an increased number of technical and tactical means during the complexity of a match. Competition provides the best environment for learning!
More pronounced individual consideration of mental and psychical dispositions as the basis for performance behaviour which is stable during competition.

5. MATCH-ORIENTED METHOD OF TEACHING FOOTBALL

The game is the sphere of free creation of movement and free decision achieved through individual behaviour within a common task and target. The progressive development of the game in particular increasingly calls for the free, constructive decision, thoughtful, responsible playing behaviour, sparkling genius and fantasy of movement. The defensive game poses a challenge here with its reinforced structure and more intensive individual behaviour resisting attacking play. The playing area has become narrower and subject to more pressure as far as the attacking game is concerned, especially in front of goal. The object is to shake off the attentions of the reinforced defence, to maintain control and assert oneself en route to the opponent's goal and nevertheless to be able to score. No matter which player is concerned, the challenge to his playing qualities has become greater and more intensive. Vitality and involvement have increased, the game demands concentrated attention, faster action and reaction, more systematic and also more forceful behaviour. Under the stress of this explosive field of tension with its range and diversity of new conflicts, the player performs his movements, a different one for each new situation.

"Controlling the ball in every competitive situation" as we have defined the term "technique" so far, is always a movement depending on and adapted to a given situation; it does not merely represent a simple execution of movement but instead is performed throughout the game and requires a high degree of mental concentration and nervous vitality. Success in a competitive situation depends on the ability of a player to assimilate the range of impressions from his environment, to read them rapidly and to be able to decide on the tactically best solution. Thus technique is always being in the position to control the ball as a means of a movement representing part of behaviour under the pressure of every new competitive situation.

The task and target of instruction is to develop proper competitive behaviour i. e. to develop the ability to come out on top of the range of impressions during a competitive situation and to assert oneself on the ball. It becomes apparent that the path leading towards this target depends on the frequency with which the player can come to grips with competitive situations, during which he experiences and registers possibilities of behaviour on the ball.

Practising the main points of technique should be carried out as practice under the complex challenge of genuine playing situations.

The match situation poses a challenge to technical behaviour, whereby the player has to decide by himself just how to execute the type of movement, whether for instance, he wants to use the inside or the outside of the foot. There is no such thing in actual competition of acting simply according to the golden rule of technique, instead the movement carried out corresponds to the situation and traits of the player in question. One player prefers to solve the situation on the ball with the inside, the other prefers the outside.

This recognition of the essence of the game and playing behaviour finds its expression in a method of practice geared to competition. We introduce youngsters to the game and provide them with technical problems to be solved within the framework of very simple playing situations. They find the association when practising technique in match play and not outside the game in abstract, constructed stereotyped forms of training. An isolated, formal form of practice does not pose sufficiently complex demands to be able to play "between the lines of the coaching manual", in order to develop fantasy of movement and to be able to do the right thing according to the given situation. The technical tasks posed should be discussed regarding their forms of application. The talk relating to the target is related to play and the target conception which is of such importance for the person practising and his practice, understandable and clear.

If for instance, we consider "stopping the ball", then this actually does not mean stopping the ball at all but rather bringing the ball under control fluently – uninterrupted by any actual stopping of it – during interpassing, with the intention of getting it into the opposing net. The ball is brought under control during the movement in order to switch over fluently to the next phase of play, dribbling or a pass. When practising the instep shot, the target conception is directed to its forms of application such as a shot at goal, a cross or a pass over a long distance. Heading the ball is something which we also practise relating to the game either as a header at goal, the nodding home of crosses or as part of interpassing with a final header towards goal.

Practice should not only be restricted to practising technical tasks, instead the objective should be directed as often as possible the final target of every playing move, namely goal-scoring. As a result, thoughtful, lethal playing behaviour is built up. This method of practice relating to match-play and goal-scoring arouses open-mindedness, interest, willingness to learn and leads faster and more economically towards success in learning. The basic form is thus the game itself! Forms of practice relating to the game, allow the youngsters to associate themselves with their game and they thus correspond to the expectations of the boys. As a result, learning the material becomes easier and makes more sense as far as the person practising is concerned.

Which path should we follow? Playing and practice sequences must be suited to the given standard of performance of the players. Thus for instance, playing "two versus one" with one goal can be a task both for beginners and top-class players. The difference in the degree of difficulty is first of all to be found in the pace, then in the greater skill and differentiated, tactical playing behaviour. At every age, we find good and interior players, and each one solves the problem set him according to his talent potential and his available capabilities. Thus it can be maintained, that everyone is capable of playing but that not everyone is capable of learning to the same extent. The degree of ability to learn depends on the talent and the disposition regarding movement which differs from individual to individual. It is in fact often necessary to differentiate the performance requirement within a practice group, to raise the requirement in the case of some players, to reduce it in the case of others or even to take the bounds of their ability to learn into account. If we suppose that everyone, whether more gifted or less enjoys playing football then we must not make excessive demands or too low ones either, in order to ensure that the emotional barometer remains high and that the willingness to play and learn which is allied to it, is not placed in jeopardy. The game accepts everyone. The challenges posed by the game and a playing task are accepted by everyone, and every individual plays and behaves in the way that his basic qualities allow.

The individual teaching and learning phases are as follows:

1. The coach demonstrates the exercise, he determines the target of the exercise and the form of organisation.
2. The player seeks for and discovers possibilities of how to solve the exercise; he actively comes to terms with the posed task and collects experience of his own within the playing experience.
3. Correction and active information, comparison with the model player.

By means of alternative questions ("Is your stance on the ball or a movement like this or like that?") attention should be drawn to important aspects of movement behaviour so that the player who is practising can himself actively build up his target. The information should not be a hindrance but merely contain the most important movement characteristics. In doing so, it is essential to recognise the special features of a player and to develop them. Thus, the coach demonstrates the exercise, determines and defines the aim of the exercise and lays down the form of organisation. For example: "Let's take freekicks with the full instep". Heinz and Rolf take it in turns to shoot at Willi in goal. Each of them has ten attempts. Who can score the most goals? The youngsters experience the challenge contained in this form of play and also observe in the process that they must lock the ankle, must "keep it stiff", or also where and how they have to hit the ball in order to execute a hard and directed shot successfully. The coach watches closely and in doing so becomes a team-mate of each of the practising players. He recognises serious mistakes as well the fact that individual differences in movement in the case of different boys are not actually mistakes providing that they are able to reach the target employing their own particular means. The individual development of movement and the method of finding a solution to a situation often contradict the stereotyped teachings regarding a technical sequence of movement. Thus the right technique is the one which finds an optimal answer to the situation.

Striving towards stereotyped notions restricts free and creative movement behaviour, fantasy of movement. The player should learn through the overall task and complex challenge to adapt himself purposively to the stress produced by the range of impressions in his playing environment, in order to secure possession of the ball for himself and his side.

During the first stage in learning, the player experiences, in coming to grips with the task, how he can best solve it according to his own conception and on the basis of his individual motorial disposition. He gleans this first of all from what he has himself experienced.

The findings collected during this first stage duly receive their confirmation in the second stage. The further information is directed towards the mistakes which the coach observed and is actively rounded off by the players themselves who ask questions about movement characteristic to be improved, on the basis of observation and recognition. Thus players themselves set up the target for their further practice. Such information must not be complicated nor must it be allowed to restrict the development of freely creative formation of movement. The coach must observe that in the case of a number of mistakes regarding movement only one, or possibly at the most two pieces of information should be imparted.

The coach observes e. g. that several youngsters are shooting the ball over the bar when kicking with the instep. A number of mistakes could be at the root of the trouble here: 1. They are taking up position behind, instead of next to the ball. 2. The body is bent back, instead of over the ball. 3. As a result of 1 and 2 the player is "scooping" the ball, instead of hitting it fully with the outstretched foot in order to keep it low. The trainer asks the alternative question: "Is the standing leg next to or behind the ball?" He demonstrates the proper way of kicking the ball a number of times with the standing leg next to the ball. The players watch closely and make the observation: "The standing leg is *next to* the ball". The trainer then allows the practice session to continue. It should also be observed here that when one mistake has been corrected, others automatically correct themselves as well.

Information should be restricted to the bare essentials! By means of precise setting of the task (Let's shoot the ball at goal keeping it low!) the player thus gains informations from out of his own experience. He gains more knowledge by observing closely when a correction is suggested. This active information is more intensive than a range of patent solutions in the form of a catalogue of movement characteristics recited by the trainer, which are made up of an analysis of a stereotyped movement conception and which cannot be transposed into movement by the players on account of the host of information which cannot be assimilated.

The extension and refining of playing behaviour should have reached a climax in the case of talented player by the time they are fifteen or sixteen-year old; this should be consolidated over the next few years in the shape of increasing athletic strength. Stepped-up demand of course, always depends upon the available talent and the standard of performance already achieved. The trainer has to form a clear picture of the learning and development potential of his players.

The learning phase of expansion and consolidation of competitive behaviour embraces: 1. increasing the tempo, 2. greater technical strength and the improvement of playing skill under competitive conditions, 3. extended tactical aspects of individual, group and team play.

Thus e. g. increasing the march-oriented challenge in the case of the instep kick can be achieved in that those who are practising pass the ball while under pressure from an opponent at high speed over a long distance to a team-mate running into the open space at speed or attempt to score against a reinforced defence (one versus two or two versus four, for instance).

In addition, when a minority are interpassing against a superior number of two or three players, new aspects should constantly be worked out (using the space and running clear, covering and regaining possession, the one-two movement, behaviour in tackles, dribbling and attempting the breakthrough, bringing volleys under control, heading, rapidly aiming towards the target of the attack, etc.), in order to improve playing skill and overall tactical competitive behaviour.

At every stage of learning, the game itself with all its complex challenges occupies the centre of attention. The path leads from the simplest playing forms to the most difficult and most differentiated forms of competition. Everyone plays the game, but it depends on his potential ability how well he plays and to what extent his play can be improved.

5.1. INSTEP KICK

Playing the ball with the instep has also increased in significance as the game has developed. Consider for instance, the surprise switch in the area of attack when for instance, a one-two movement is begun on the left wing and the midfield player sweeps the short, square pass from the winger far over on to the other wing, where perhaps, the defender on the overlap picks up the ball and finishes off the attacking move.

Forceful attacking over the wings, as an answer to the reinforced defence, requires skilful crossing, whether "soft" or "hard". The rapid and straight forward bridging of midfield, the thoughtful start of the attack by the defenders, and as the highlight and conclusion of the attacking move, the shot at goal, whether it results from interpassing or takes the form of a freekick, are all important forms of application for the instep kick. Above all, when you are shooting from a considerable distance, when the strikers have darted about effectively in such a way that the goalkeeper's attention has been drawn to their movements and a possible pass, a hard and well-directed shot with the instep can be very effective.

Note
The range of exercises is governed by the game itself and takes into account all possibilities of applying the instep kick.

The coach observes the individual teaching and learning phases:
1. He demonstrates the exercise and determines the object of the exercise and the form of organisation.
2. The youngsters set about coming to grips with the problem and initially attempt to successfully solve it using their own means. Under the pressure of this playing exercise they learn how to adapt their behaviour and collect experience with regard to movement.
3. The trainer observes them and registers certain special features and also basic mistakes. Correction, further information and building up of the guiding principle take place actively through demonstration and posing an alternative question (should the stance, position or movement be this way or that?).

Take heed!
The information must not impose a burden but should be restricted to the most essential characteristics of movement (see Chapter on Method of Teaching Football).

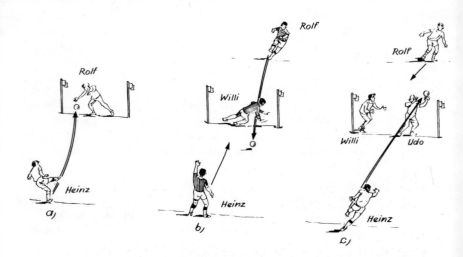

Figure 8 *Shooting at goal using the instep*

Game to practise the instep kick

1. Heinz against Rolf in goal. They change after ten shots. Who can score the most goals?
2. Heinz shoots from the one side, Rolf from the other at Willi's goal. They take it in turn. After ten shots, the keeper is changed.
3. Two against two. Heinz and Rolf against Willi and Udo. Both sides take it in turn to shoot. Each player shoots ten times, then Heinz and Rolf go in goal. Who can score the most and which side can score the most goals?

To be observed
Do we stand next to, in front of or behind the ball? What is the position of the foot adopt? What is the position of the upper part of the body when the ball is kept low and when it is vollied?

To be recognised
Stance next to the ball! The foot is stretched out and kept firm! In the case of a low shot, the upper part of the body is bent over the ball, in the case of the volley, it leans back!

Figure 9 *Shot at goal with the inside and outside instep*

Procedure as in Figure 8/c. The corners of the goal are also shot at. With the right inner instep at the left corner of the goal – as seen by the player shooting the ball – and with the outer instep at the right corner of the goal. Shoot low, half-volley, on the turn.

To be observed
What is the position of the foot
1. when taking an inner instep kick, 2. an outer instep kick?
What is the stance on the ball? Next to the ball or to the side behind the ball?

To be recognised
The foot is stretched out and firm, turned slightly outwards in the case of the inner instep shot, inwards in the case of the outer instep shot. The position is to the side, behind the ball.

Figure 10 *Dribbling then shooting*

Procedure as before. Dribble towards a given line and then shoot at goal from different points along the line (full, inner and outer instep).

To be observed

What is the stance on the ball in the case of a low shot?

To be recognised

When shooting when moving at speed be half a step in front of the ball!

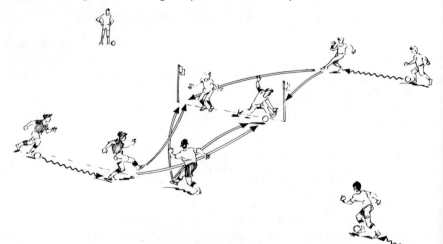

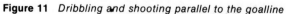

Figure 11 *Dribbling and shooting parallel to the goalline*

1. on the turn, 2. across the standing leg, 3. from the other side with the outer instep.
Procedure as before.

To be observed
What is the stance when shooting on the turn? And when shooting across the standing leg and the outer instep shot?

To be recognised
When shooting on the turn, place the standing leg in the direction of the shot. When shooting across the standing leg as well as when shooting with the outer instep, we remain in the direction we are running in.

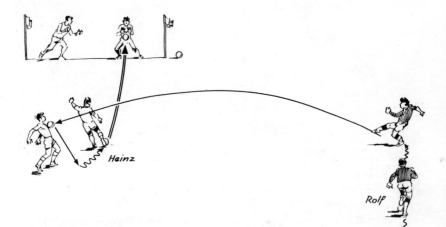

Heinz

Rolf

Figure 12 *Dribbling away from goal and shooting on the half turn*

Figure 13 *Crossing with the inner instep*

Procedure as before. *Note:* Change point of shot and shooting angle.
Procedur as before. Rolf executes five crosses with the dead ball and five after dribbling with it. Heinz brings the ball under control and shoots from a predetermined distanze. Rolf and Heinz switch, then there is a switch between the field and the goal players.

Extension
Crosses at highest possible speed.
Converting the crosses 1. with two touches at the ball 2. directly.

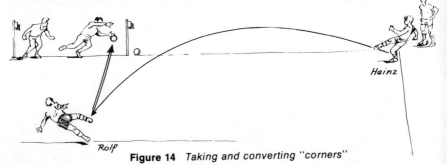

Figure 14 *Taking and converting "corners"*

Procedure as in Figure 13. First Heinz takes ten corners, five of which are "soft" and five "hard". Rolf attempts to convert them. Then they change as under Figure 13.

To be observed
What is the stance on the ball? 1. Close to the ball or 2. Away from the ball, to the side behind it?
How should the foot make contact with the ball? 1. Full-face, or 2. does the foot graze the pitch (in the case of the "soft" or "chipped" ball)?

To be recognised
Stand at an angle behind the ball. In the case of the "soft" or "chipped" instep shot, the tip of the foot grazes the ground laterally, with the playing leg almost crossing the standing leg in the process.

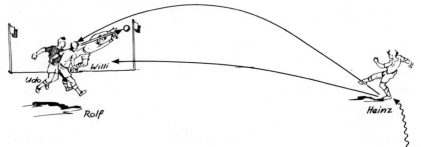

Figure 15 *Converting freekicks with the head*

Procedure as before. Willi is in goal and Udo marks Rolf. Heinz takes the free-kicks. 1. hard-hit shots with the inner instep, 2. "chipped", balls which come in softly, 3. "sliced" swerving balls. Each type of shot is repeated five times and then the players switch round.

Note

In the case of sliced balls we differentiate between 1. balls which are met fully with the instep, inner or outer instep away from the ball's centre point and 2. balls which are "scooped" with the inner instep with the tip of the foot stretched out whereby the inner instep hits under the ball laterally (see Figure 16).

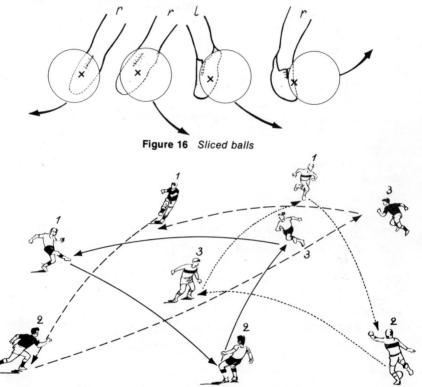

Figure 16 *Sliced balls*

Figure 17 *Interpassing over a lengthy distance*

Link up with one another over a wide area in groups of three, four or five. The ball should run in a certain sequence, from one to two to three then back to one. Keep your distance (30 to 40 metres)!
1. Slow warming up tempo.
2. Moving with the ball using a sudden spurt (running clear).
3. The pass is carried out at high speed whilst dribbling and is destined for the team-mate running clear at speed.

According to the situation low or high interpassing with the full, inner or outer instep.

Figure 18 *Two balls are passed among a group of seven*

One begins with his pass to two, four to five.
1. Slow running tempo but fast pass.
2. Call for ball by running clear.
3. High tempo (compare with Point 3 of Figure 17) with two touches of the ball.

Note
Always be ready for the ball and watch for the next player. Where will the ball come from, where should I pass it and where do I run to when I pass it?

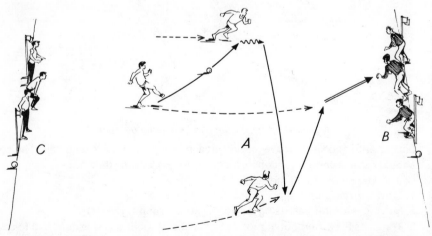

Figure 19 *Long pass with the inner and outer instep rounded off with a shot at goal*

Three teams (A, B and C) take it in turns to attack. B and C are in the goals. Team A begins and attacks in the direction of B's goal. Following the shot at goal, B attacks C's goal and C attacks A's goal, etc. Each team has a ball of its own.

Extension
As under Figures 17 and 18.

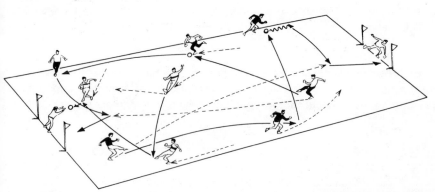

Figure 20 *Three groups of three or groups of four link up at a distance between two goals*

Each group forms a team. The teams attack back and forth, from one end to the other with neutral goalkeepers in the goals. Considerable distances between the players should be maintained. Which team has scored the most goals after ten attacks?

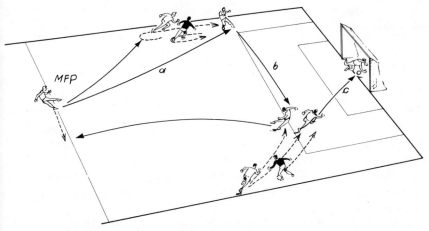

Figure 21 *Long passes between a midfield player and the wingers*

A midfield player as schemer provides two strikers with long passes. They run clear of the opponent covering the man. Keep a fair distance apart!

a) Each pass is returned to the midfield player who has sought the open space. The defence also links up with him or switch between attack and defence, when the defence is in possession of the ball.
b) The strikers pass to one another, then play the ball back to the midfield player.
c) Play at one goal (maintain distance!). The keeper's clearances go to the mid-field player.

Note
The midfield player passes to the forwards who are running clear. The forwards must assert themselves on the ball and free themselves from their opponent's pressure in order to put through the long pass to the midfield player!

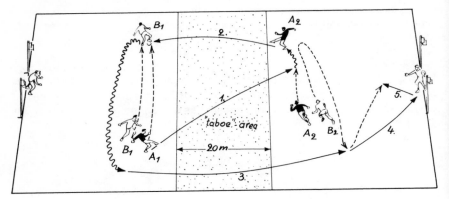

Figure 22 *Two against two maintaining a clear distance*

1. Without goals, there is an area of "forbidden territory" between the two play-ers of each team, which they are not allowed to enter. A1 plays against B1on the one side of the free area, A2 against B2 on the other side. This gives us "one versus one" on the ball and running clear and getting away from the op-ponent. The pass to the team-mate who is running clear takes place under pressure.
2. The shot at goal takes place after the long pass. Each player remains in pos-session until his opponent wins the ball.

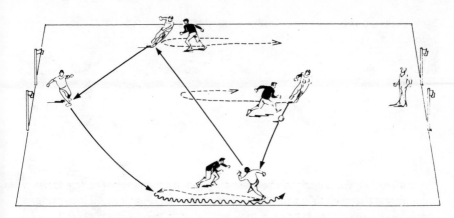

Figure 23 *Three against three or four against four maintaining a considerable distance, moving back and forth between two target points (midfield player or goalkeeper)*

Each team plays from target point to target point until deprived of the ball by the opposing side.
1. How often can each team reach the target points in a determined time, or,
2. which teams can score the most goals?

Note
Ensure that you cover the man to be sure that the ball is passed under pressure from an opponent. In the course of an attack, each player must have touched the ball at least once, before it can be passed to the midfield player or shot at goal. This exercise calls for great intensity of movement; as a result, one of the players whose side is in possession can switch with the target points.

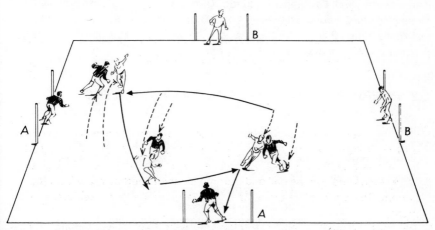

Figure 24 *Three against three (four against four) with four goals*

Five players make up a team. Each team must have two players in the two goals, who can switch with the players on the field as they want to.
What must be taken into account here?
Sudden change of the attacking area and the direction of attack with long passes. Make use of space!

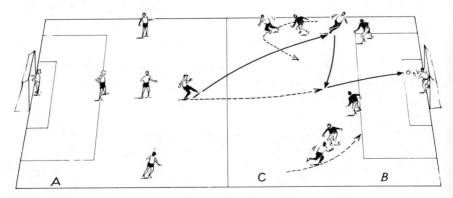

Figure 25 *Three teams alternating in attack and defence*

Main Aspects
Play over the wings, surprisingly switching from the one wing to the other. All types of crosses, shots at goal from outside the penalty box. Passing over a long distance.

Procedure
Three teams (A, B, C) comprised of four (five, six) players: a midfield player and three strikers. C begins attacking, A and B organise the defence in front of the two goals. When B wards off C's attacking move, B attacks against A. When B is warded off, A then attacks against C, etc.

5.2. INTERPASSING WITH THE INNER AND OUTER FOOT

Note
When interpassing using short combination sequences, the given situation calls for certain movement behaviour. The player himself has to decide whether the pass should be made with the inner or outer side of the foot. During the course of the game there is no such thing as playing "only" with the inside or "only" with the outside. As a consequence, the methodical approach to the game ensures that both possibilities are taken into account and practised along side one another.

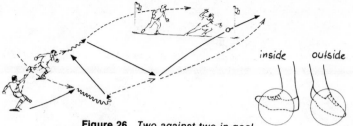

Figure 26 *Two against two in goal*

Play round the goal. Thus the ball is always in play. Goals can be scored from either side. Use the inside and outside when shooting at goal. After five minutes of play, the fielders switch with those in goal.

To be observed
When the pass is executed with the inside should the tip of the foot point to the ground or is it pulled up? On the other hand, what is the position of the foot when the outside is used?

To be recognised
When passing the ball with the inside of the foot, pull up the tip of the foot; when passing with the outside, turn the foot inwards – the tip of the foot points to the ground.

Extension
1. As many touches of the ball as desired.
2. Who is able to succeed touching the ball only twice.
3. Who is able to play directly?
4. We increase the tempo.

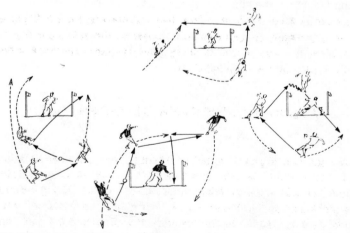

Figure 27 *The same procedure and extension as under Figure 26 but in groups of three and four*

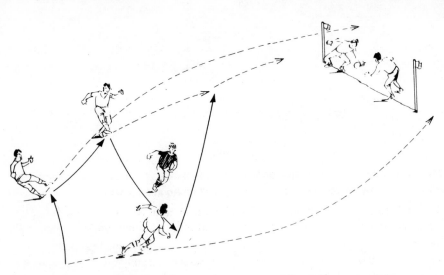

Figure 28 *Three against one round the goal*

Three link up against one fielder and two in goal. When the ball passes the goal, the defender goes into goal and one of the goalkeepers defends. After some time (5 minutes) the fielders and the defenders switch round.

Note
Within the framework of these forms of practice, all passing directions can be worked on as well as the back-heeler, including the back-heeler played across the standing leg, when the situation allows it (see diagram).

Extension
As under Figure 26.

Figure 29 *The two possibilities of the back-heeler*

Figure 30 *Two against one against or around one goal*

Two link up against one fielder and one player in goal. Who can score the most goals in the determined time (switch around after five minutes)?

Note

Adjust the technical and tactical requirement to fit the given standard of performance.

Extension

Increased tempo; play one-two movements or feint the square pass in the one-two movement with the help of a partner and then break through on your own. Conclude the one-two with a direct shot at goal. Only goals scored with the head count when two link up against one.

What should be taken into account?

Hold the ball and dribble with it; wait until your partner is ready to accept the ball before you pass it. Shield the ball in a possible tackle (your body between the opponent and the ball). Run clear when making the pass. When carrying out the one-two movement, dribble up to your opponent and select the gap to your opponent in such a way that he can be outpaced with the square pass (compare Chapter on One-Two Movement).

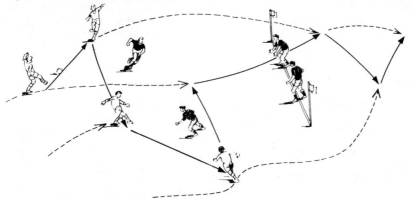

Figure 31 *Four against two*

Four attackers move around freely in the area and can change their positions as much as they wish to. The two defenders cover the area and attempt to prevent the square pass or a "solo effort". Initially, as many touches of the ball as desired and without "offside". When the ball is parried, it is played back to the attack. Change the attack and defence around either 1. after a set time, 2. when the ball has been parried three times by the defence, 3. when the ball has been shot past goal three times.

Extension
1. Increased tempo
2. Only two touches of the ball
3. Play as directly as possible

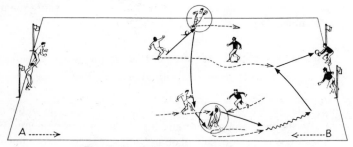

Figure 32 *Two against two plus two*

Play using two goals. A plays against B plus two players, who always switch over to the team in possession. Each team has one or two players in goal, who can switch with the field players as often as they like.

Extension
As under Figure 31

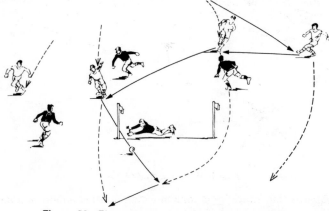

Figure 33 *Three against two (four against three)*

Three (four) play against two (three) fielders and one in goal. Proceed as under Figures 31 and 32 (one player switches to reinforce the side in possession). Extension and aims of exercise, compare under Figure 30.

NP

NP

NP = Neutral Point

Figure 34 *Three against three plus one*

Three play against three back and forth between two neutral points with a fourth player switching to the team in possession. When the defending side gain possession, the attacking and defending roles are reversed.

Note
All possible link-ups can be played by means of this form of organisation. Instead of playing towards two neutral points, two goals with neutral goalkeepers can equally well be chosen. The team which scores a goal, remains in possession. Which team can score the most goals in the set period?

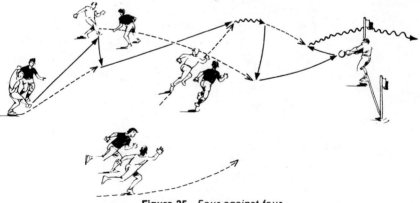

Figure 35 *Four against four*

Four play against four round one goal, in which there is a neutral goalkeeper. The team which scores a goal, remains in possession. When the defence gains

possession, it moves away and only then launches an attack when the other side
has organised its defence.

Please observe!
Cover the man! Each player has a defender opposing him
Which team can score the most goals in a set time?

Figure 36 *Three against four (or four against five)*

Interpassing with the inner and outer side against a reinforced defence. The procedure is as under Figure 35. When the defence gains possession of the ball,
they switch to attack as under Figure 35, however, one player always remains
behind to strengthen the defence.

Figure 37 *Linking up in twos or threes*

A random number of groups of two or three in a restricted area selected according to the number of groups involved. In the group of three, one plays to two, two
plays to three and back to one.

What should be observed?

Be vigilant! Wait until your team-mate is in position before you pass.

Extension

Increased tempo in enlarged playing area:

1. "Passing and moving" i. e. combine a short spurt with the pass,
2. call for the pass by spurting into the free space (running clear), otherwise as in 1,
3. carry out one-two movements

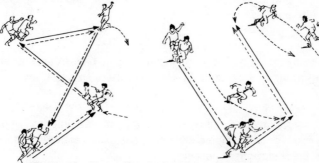

Figure 38   *"Interchanging" in the group of five*

Constant movement in changing the positions. After passing, each player runs into the position occupied by the team-mate he passed the ball to. Change at speed with the pass.

Extension

1. With two touches of the ball,
2. direct pass, always changing the type of pass (low, half-volley).

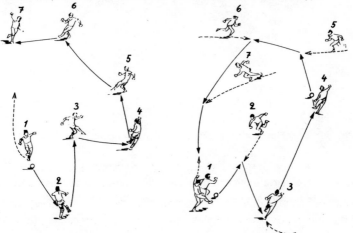

Figure 39   *Two balls are passed among a group of seven*

The ball is passed in certain sequence, from one to two, etc, and from seven back to one player one begins passing to two, four to five. Slow running tempo at first, but rapid passing.

Extension
1. Call for the ball by running clear.
2. As 1, but the player passing the ball also spurts into the open space when making his pass.
3. Fast tempo, played with two touches of the ball.
4. Fast tempo, playing direct.

Observe
Always be ready for the ball! Watch the path of both balls intensely. Where is the ball coming from, where should I pass it to, where should I run to?

Note
These exercises, played at high speed provide for great intensity of movement. Ensure there are breaks which should be made use of actively (e. g. keeping up the ball or direct stationery passing)!

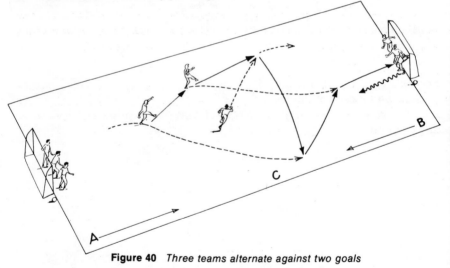

Figure 40 *Three teams alternate against two goals*

Three teams each with three players. A and B defend the goals. C attacks and attempts to score using the inner or outer side. Then B attacks A's goal and A C's, etc. Which team has scored the most goals after ten attacks?

Note
Each side has its ball. The rhythm is not disturbed by retrieving the ball.

Extension
1. Change of position, making use of square, diagonal and through passes.
2. Two touches of the ball
3. Direct passing
4. Change of tempo through running clear and "playing and moving", i. e. calling for the pass through a spurt and switching to top speed with the pass.

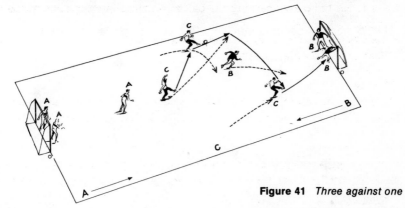

Figure 41 *Three against one*

Takes place as under Figure 40. There are now two players in goal and a further player attempts to disturb the interpassing of the attacking team, as far from his own goal as possible.

To be observed
Switch positions when linking up with one another, keeping your two partners in front of you in the process. Never isolate the man in possession, i. e. provide support and offer your support with the pass! The defender does not actually intercept but slowly backs away in the direction of his own goal along with the opposition.

Extension
As under Figure 40/1 and 2.
Play as direct as possible.

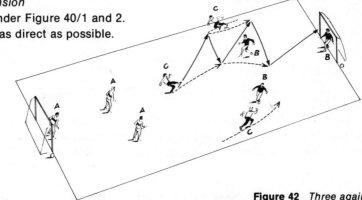

Figure 42 *Three against two*

Procedure as before. Only one player is in goal. Two attempt to break up the interpassing of the attacking side on the field.

Note

1. A successfully saved ball is returned again to the attacking side.
2. When possession of the ball is lost, the switch from attack to defence takes place; hold the ball until the third player has come out goal.

To be observed

Hold the ball and dribble with it until a pass is possible. Attempt to score goals!

Extension

1. Increased tempo   2. Aim for one-two movements.

Figure 43 *Four against two*

Procedure as before. A midfield player, who links up with two strikers, who offer their support, and a third who "stays away".

Extension

1. Increased tempo   4. Aim at one-two movements
2. Two touches of the ball
3. Play as direct as possible

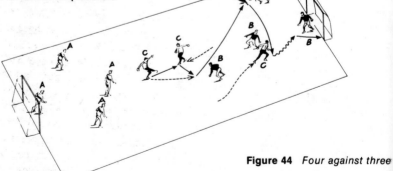

Figure 44 *Four against three*

Takes place as under Figure 42 with the same aims and extension.

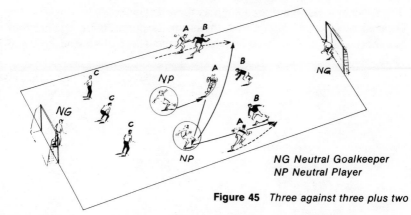

NG Neutral Goalkeeper
NP Neutral Player

Figure 45 *Three against three plus two*

Three teams each with three players are supported and strengthened in attack by two neutral players. Neutral goalkeepers are in the goals. A attacks B. If A is warded off then he takes over in defence in front of goal and B attacks C, then C attacks A, etc. Which team can score the most goals after ten attacks?

Extension

1. Two touches of the ball,
2. play as direct as possible and
3. aim at one-two movements.

Note

As there are always breaks, action can proceed at full speed. The two neutral players are replaced by two others.

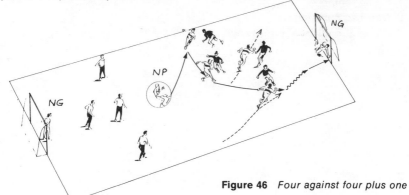

Figure 46 *Four against four plus one*

Procedure as before. Only one player strengthens the attacking team.

Note

Games involving teams of equal numbers (three against three; five against five; six against six) can take place along the same lines. In addition, all games involving sides in a restricted area such as three against one, four against two, two against one, three against two, three against three, three against four, four against six, etc., can be included, taking passing the ball with the inner and outer side into account.

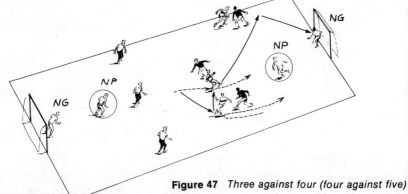

Figure 47 *Three against four (four against five)*

Procedure as before. However, now the defence in front of each goal is strengthened by a further player. When the defence has successfully warded off an attack this player moves up into attack and another remains behind in his place.

To be observed
Rapid switching from defence into attack.

Extension
1. Rapid tempo
2. One-two movements
3. Shots at goal from long-range

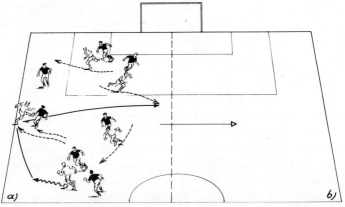

Figure 48 *An inferior number combines against a superior number*

Five against seven, six against eight or other numerical relationships play 1. in a restricted area (1/4 of the pitch), then 2. in an enlarged area covering half of the pitch, 3. between two given points, whereby the numerically superior team must observe the offside rule (procedure as I, 15).

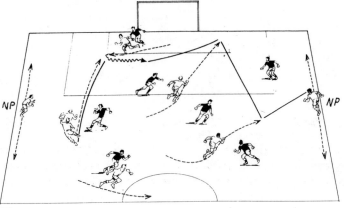

NP = Neutral Point

Figure 49

Note
The purpose of the exercise is to be found in the challenge of a minority managing to assert itself and win through against the resistance of a numerically superior team. In doing so, all technical and tactical aspects should be taken into account and made use of.
Tasks for the numerically superior side: 1. with two touches of the ball, 2. direct passing, 3. one-two movements, 4. meeting and moving with volleys, 5. passing on volleys with the head.

The main aspects of the exercise for the numerically inferior team
1. Make extreme use of the area of play; 2. attempt to pass and link up as quickly as possible; 3. aim at making a pass after dribbling past one or more opponents (do not forget to run clear); attempting to break through during the movement of all players without the ball; 5. Play one-two movements, whereby two team-mates attempt to offer their support as the "wall", whilst the others stay away and run clear (see Figure 49).

Figure 50

To be observed

When working out such technical and tactical aspects under competitive conditions, the player must always be able to decide freely about how to solve a situation! Whether a one-two movement can be completed or not, always depends e. g. on the behaviour of the opponent. Thus the ball played against the "wall" can equally well be played direct to another player (see Figure 51) or it is played on "delayed", or even perhaps, the ball must be held and dribbled with.

Figure 51

5.3. DROP-KICK

The drop-kick is employed to pass volleys on direct. The ball is not first of all brought under control and carried but instead it is passed on at the same instant as it hits the ground using the inner or the outer side of the foot, the full, inner or outer instep or even the sole (sole kick). In addition, many goalkeepers make use of the drop-kick with the instep when making clearances.

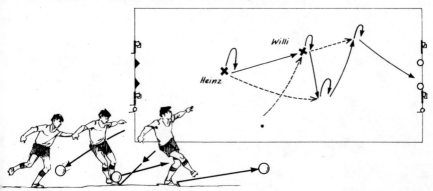

Figure 52 *Passing the ball low and high employing the drop-kick with either the inside or outside of the foot*

Three teams each with either two or three players alternate against two goals. A attacks B: Heinz throws the ball into the air and plays the ball on to Willi with a drop-kick using either the inside or the outside of the foot. Willi controls and moves with the ball, dribbles with it for a short spell and then returns it to Heinz in the same manner. The shot at goal also takes the form of a drop-kick. Then B attacks C and C again attacks A.

To be observed
The drop-kick with the inside: What is the stance on the ball and the position of the upper part of the body 1. in the case of the low drop-kick and 2. in the case of the drop-kick played high?

To be recognised
When executing the low drop-kick we stand sideways in front of the ball (Compare with meeting and moving with volleys with the inside), but behind the ball in the case of the high drop-kick, i. e. the ball bounces in front of the body so that it can be "spooned".

To be observed
When executing the drop-kick with the outside of the foot: what is the position of the foot used to play the shot?

To be recognised
The playing foot is turned inwards.

Note

Particularly in the case of the drop-kick with the outside of the foot, match-oriented forms of exercise and challenges are important in order to experience the various fine differences in the execution of the movement (See Figure 53).

Figure 53

The *"sole kick"*, allowing the ball to rebound against the sole, can be described as a further variation of the drop-kick (see Illustration 54).

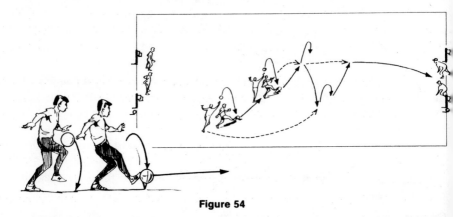

Figure 54

This form of the short pass is employed most effectively in the case of volleys passed a short distance and as a possibility to pass on falling balls which are taken on the chest, the head or the thigh, rapidly whilst keeping them low. In this way, the ball can either be played forward or diagonally to the side.

102

Figure 55 *Passing on of volleys played "short" using the drop-kick*

Organisation and procedure as under Figure 52. Heinz throws or lobs the ball with his foot to Willi and runs into position along *with* his pass. Willi plays the ball back to Heinz using the drop-kick (according to the situation either with the inside or the outside of the foot or with the sole). Heinz meets and moves with the ball before he lobs it back high to Willi.

Figure 56 *Drop-kick two against one*

Organisation and procedure as before. But only one player is in goal whereas the second begins to disturb the attacking movement as far up the pitch from goal as possible, and works himself back slowly.

1. Throw the ball up yourself
2. Execute the drop-kick following a throw or lob with the foot

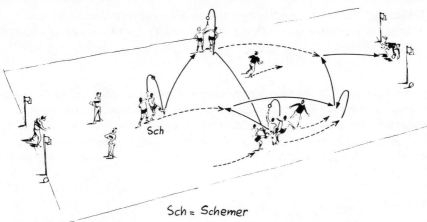

Sch = Schemer

Figure 57 *Drop-kick three against two*

Three teams each with three players. One is in goal, two defend. Otherwise, procedure as before.

Throw the ball up yourself, one player is the "schemer" who provides his two team-mates with high passes (either by throwing the ball up or lobbing the ball high with his foot). The player runs into position along with his pass and meets and moves with the balls played back to him.

Figure 58 *Four against three round one goal*

Four players form one team. The defending side have one player in goal, three field players attempts to ward off the attacks of the four attacking players. The attack and defence switch around after a certain time or if possession of the ball is lost.

1. Throw the ball up and then pass it on by means of a drop-kick, or
2. one player takes over the role of "schemer" and lobs the balls with his foot to his team-mates who run clear.

Note

In the case of such match-oriented forms of exercise, the "drop-kick" task should be regarded as the main aspect within the framework of interpassing. Should the drop-kick not be possible, then of course, every other possibility of executing a pass can be made use of with the player having free decision.

When playing with a "schemer", the pass either goes on to a team-mate who has run free or is passed back direct to the schemer.

Initially, the defence can play "at half throttle" before they increase the extent of their load by giving all they have got.

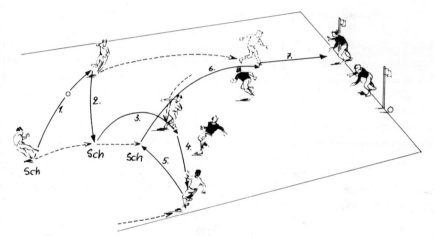

Figure 59 *"Schemer" plus three against two fielders and two in goal*

Only one goal. Each ball goes back direct to the schemer or by means of a pass to a team-mate who has run clear. Execute the shot at goal as a drop-kick.

Note

A second ball is lying ready next to the goal. Thus play can continue at once using the second ball in order to avoid any long delay if one of the players standing in goal has to retrieve a ball which has gone past.

Extension

Schemer plus three against three and a goalkeeper

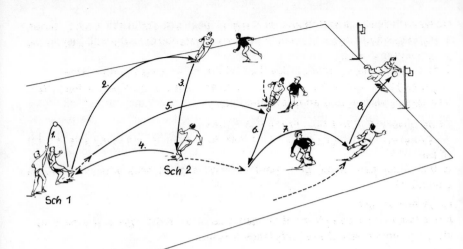

Figure 60 *Passing "long" and "short" volleys with a drop-kick*

Two schemers, one plays "long" volleys, the other takes the drop-kicks of the "strikers" and provides them again with "short" volleys, or he plays back to schemer 1, who again plays the ball "long". Following the pass, shoot at goal employing the drop-kick.
Alternate between attack and defence,
1. according to time, 2. each time the forwards lose possession or 3. if the defenders ward off an attack with a drop-kick to schemer 2 or schemer 1.

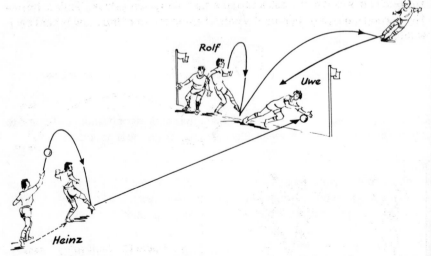

Figure 61 *The drop-kick with the instep as a shot at goal*

Heinz and Willi against Rolf and Uwe in goal. Both sides take it in turns to shoot.
1. Heinz and Willi throw the ball in the air and attempt to shoot low and on the half volley at goal.
2. The goalkeepers throw or play the ball out high using the drop-kick.
Heinz and Willi "crack the ball home" by means of the drop-kick with the instep. The sides switch round after ten shots each.

To be observed in the case of the low drop-kick
Just what is the position on the ball: 1. next to, 2. behind, or 3 to the side in front of the ball?
Is the upper part of the body bent a) forward or b) back when the shot is executed?

To be recognised
A position to *the side* in front of the ball is adopted in the case of the low drop-kick. The upper part of the body *leans forward*.

To be observed with regard to the playing leg
Does the shank swing in the direction of the shot until the leg is stretched, or does it adopt an almost vertical position when the shot is executed, and what is the position of the thigh?

To be recognised
The shank does not swing after the ball but adopts an almost vertical position when the shot is executed; in the process, the thigh is drawn up by the knee. We *compare* the features of the low drop-kick with those of the half-volley and high drop-kick (clearance from goal).

To be recognised
The position is next to the ball and in the case of high drop-kicks behind the ball. The playing leg swings behind the ball. The upper part of the body is bent backwards.

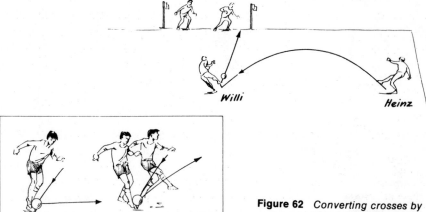

Figure 62 *Converting crosses by means of the drop-kick*

Heinz crosses from the right (A throw, a lob or "chipped" crosses which fall at the feet of the partner). Willi shoots with his right foot at goal which Rolf and Uwe are guarding. Each player has ten shots, then the players in goal switch with those on the field.

Extension
The cross is played "short" so that Willi has to run towards the ball and then shoots at goal on the turn.

Figure 63 *Using the drop-kick to attempt convert volleys*

Heinz uses the drop-kick to play the ball high over Willi, who turns towards goal and shoots at goal using the drop-kick. Procedure as before.

Figure 64 *Bringing the cross under control and shooting at goal by means of the drop-kick*

Willi uses his chest to bring Heinz's cross under control and as the ball falls from his chest he employs the drop-kick to shoot at goal. Procedure as before.

Extension
The tasks under Figures 62, 63 and 64 are carried out with opponents: Uwe covers, puts the pressure on Willi but initially does not intercept.

When you are under pressure from an opponent and in actual match situations only make use of the drop-kick when it is feasible and represents the optimal solution.

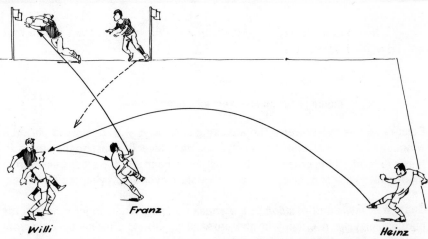

Figure 65 *Shooting at goal by means of the drop-kick following a headed pass*

Each team has three players. Heinz crosses, Willi allows the ball to "roll off" his head and Franz shoots at goal using the drop-kick. The defending side places two players either in goal or in the field. After five shots at goal, the attack and defence switch round.

Note
The defence initially adopts a passive attitude. When the defence adopts an active role, Franz also attempts to shoot balls which have been warded off direct at goal, or he plays the ball back to Heinz.

Figure 66 *Shooting balls which have been flicked on with the head at goal*

Heinz volleys the ball and Willi flicks it on with his head. Franz runs on to the ball and shoots at goal with a drop-kick. Procedure as before.

Figure 67 *Drop-kick from a "hidden" position*

Each team has five players. The attacking side plays with a midfield player, a winger and three strikers. The defence has one player in goal and the others attempt to fend off the crosses. Balls which have been warded off or passes from the forwards are shot at goal by the midfield player employing the drop-kick.

Change of tasks and position in the attacking team: The winger runs into the midfield player's position with the cross, the midfield player moves up front when he has shot at goal, a forward moves out to the wing, etc. Attack and defence switch round when each forward has shot at goal once.

5.4. VOLLEY KICK

There are many situations both in attack and defence when the "volley kick" finds its application. In the case of the defender when he wants to remove volleys from the danger zone and in the case of the attacking player to shoot crosses and other volleys at goal. When interpassing there are also situations in which a high volley can be passed on direct out of the air by means of this type of shot.
Heinz stands at the one, Willi at the other side of the goal in which Rolf and Uwe have taken up position. Heinz and Willi throw the ball up themselves, allow it to bounce and shoot the ball as it rises at goal by means of the volley kick. Then they take the ball direct out of the air as it falls. Each player shoots ten times, then they switch with the players in goal. Who can score the most goals?

Another method of organisation
One player in goal, the other in front. Switch round after ten shots. *Or:* Each player has his own goal and is goalkeeper and markman at the same time.

To be observed
What is the stance before the shot and after it?
Is the upper part of the body leaning towards or away from the ball when executing the shot?

Figure 68 *Shooting at goal with the volley kick*

To be recognised
The player takes the ball frontally, in the direction of the goal. (The swinging movement is carried out rather like a blow with a scythe.) The body turns and swings in the direction of the shot as a result of this movement.

To be observed further
Is the foot of the playing leg stretched out or pulled back? Is the shot executed under or by making full impact with the ball?

To be recognised
The foot of the playing leg is stretched out. The shot is executed hip-high making full impact with the ball.

Note ·
"Jumping into" the direction of the shot (rising slightly from the ground) is better than turning on the sole. By this means more impetus can be achieved and the danger of injuring the knee joint as a result of studs sticking in the ground is avoided.

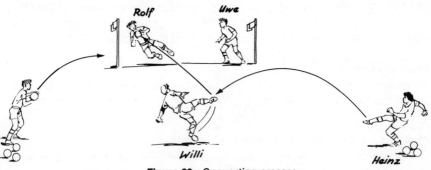

Figure 69 *Converting crosses*

Heinz throws or lifts the ball with his foot as a cross to Willi, who uses the volley kick to shoot at goal, which Rolf and Uwe are guarding. After ten shots Heinz and Willi switch, then the players in goal switch with those on the field. Which side can score the most goals?

Extension
"Collect" the ball shoulder-high.

Observe
Allow the upper part of the body to "fall away" from the ball.

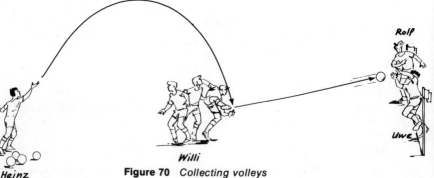

Figure 70 *Collecting volleys*

Procedure as before. Heinz throws or lifts the ball above Willi's head so that it falls as sharply as possible. Willi stands facing Heinz. He swings round and turns his body in the direction of the shot (jump round – do *not* turn on the sole) and picks up the volley, shooting at Rolf and Uwe's goal by means of a volley kick.

Observe
"Collect" the ball shoulder-high. Allow the upper part of the body to fall away from the ball! Ensure that you keep far enough away to the side of the ball to allow the playing leg enough space to make contact with the ball.

Figure 71 *Converting crosses when pressed by an opponent*

112

Procedure is as under Figure 69. Uwe now covers Willi, who attempts to hit home the crosses which are provided by Heinz in spite of Uwe's pressure.

Note
The crosses have to be played "short" so that Willi can run towards the ball.

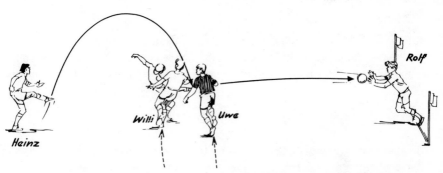

Figure 72 *Picking up volleys when pressed by an opponent*

Procedure as under Figure 70. Heinz throws or lifts the ball with his foot in such a way that they drop sharply to the side of Willi. Willi runs away from his opponent to the ball and shoots it towards Rolf's goal.

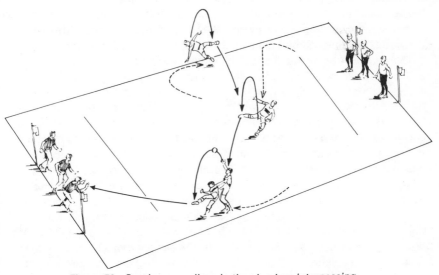

Figure 73 *Passing on volleys in the air when interpassing*

Three teams each with three players alternate with two goals. Two teams occupy the goals, the third attacks. Each player throws the ball up in the air himself, "collects" it at shoulder-height and plays it out of the air by means of the volley kick to the second player, who passes it on to the third, who in turn passes it back to the first one, etc. There is a marking line from which shots at goal are made. Then the second teams attacks the third, then the third the first, etc.

Extension
1. Following the throw, pass the ball on in a fixed sequence.
2. One player plays as schemer behind the two strikers and provides them alternately with high volleys. Pass on the ball or play it back direct to the schmer.

5.5. BALL CONTROL (MEETING AND MOVING WITH THE BALL)

Bringing the ball under control calls on the player to reveal speedy initiative in deciding upon the method of his behaviour. His behaviour when he takes over the ball and consequently, the match initiative always depends on the competitive environment (how the ball has been passed on to him) and on the behaviour of team-mates and opponents. It is essential to school this behaviour, which secures possession of the ball when interpassing in order ultimately to facilitate the scoring of goals. Meeting and moving with the ball with the inner and outer side of the foot, the instep, the chest, etc., are adapted forms of execution of the challenge as presented by the situation.
Where can the ball come from and just how will it come?
1. The pass can be low, soft and graduated, but alternatively it can be hard so that with the running speed towards the ball and under the pressure of the opponent, meeting the ball reaches its ultimate degree of difficulty.
2. The pass can be on the half volley, either "soft" or hard.
3. The pass can come as a high, short or long volley.
4. The ball can drop sharply.
All these possibilities should be worked on under the stress of match conditions. In doing so, the degree of difficulty must correspond to the player's standard of performance. The player has to learn not only to turn his attention and concentration towards the ball unconcernedly but that it is important at the same time to observe the movements and reactions of team-mates and opponents and to estimate their effects in order to orientate one's own behaviour accordingly.
Be quick in getting to the ball in order to be able to act confidently once in possession thanks to the added time at your disposal! A quick look over your shoulder helps and assures you about the behaviour and possiblities of the opposition: whether he is following so closely that he can prevent you meeting the ball or whether your running clear, the surprise move to get away from your opponent was so successful that the ball can safely be brought under control. If the

opponent is pursuing rapidly and closely than it may be possible to shake him off by dummying (e. g. left/right or right/left). Frequently, such a situation, in which the opponent is hard on your heels in going for the ball, is just right for a successful one-two movement (see one-two movement). You allow the ball being played to you "to rebound" and spurt past the opponent, whose running speed and activity are still fully orientated towards winning the ball.

The possibilities and decisions for your behaviour on the ball result from the given match situations.

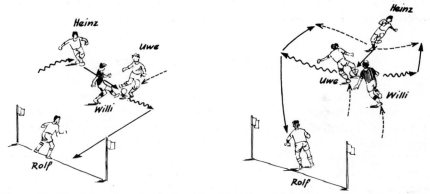

Figure 74 *Meeting and moving to the side with balls which have been played low, using the inside and outside of the foot*

Two against two
Rolf is in goal and Willi covers Uwe. Heinz plays the ball low to Uwe. Uwe runs to meet the ball and moves with it to the side using the inside of the foot. Then he plays it back to Heinz. After repeating this several times, Heinz comes into the game in that he runs into position. Heinz and Uwe attempt to score goals by linking up against Willi (2:1). After five such attacking moves, Heinz and Uwe switch positions. At the end of ten attacks, the defending and attacking sides switch round. Which side has been able to score the most goals after their ten attacks?

Note
Meeting and moving with the ball remains the main aspect of the exercise in the game 2:1 as well.
Willi as the defender watches to see that Uwe runs towards the ball, otherwise he intercepts the pass intended for Uwe. When the ball is met he should initially only put pressure on Uwe but not actively intercept.

To be observed
Is the standing leg a step ahead when meeting and moving with the ball or does it come down behind the ball?

To be recognised
Be a step ahead of the ball in the new direction you are running in!

To be observed further
Is the tip of the foot of the playing leg raised aloft or is the foot pointing to the ground?

To be recognised
The tip of the foot of the playing leg is raised aloft!

Extension
Harder passing. Run towards the ball spurting fast and then very fast. The defending player makes a match-type interception. Dummying: left/right or right/left.

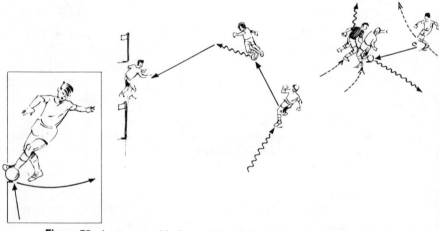

Figure 75 *Low pass with the outside of the foot carried to the side*

To be observed
Is the foot of the playing leg stretched downwards or is the tip of the foot raised?

To be observed further
If the ball is being carried with the right outer side of the foot to the right, do you adopt a stance right or left of the ball?

To be recognised
The tip of the foot of the playing leg is raised. You take up position to the right of the ball. The playing leg crosses over the supporting leg and carries the ball to the other side (the opposite is the case if the ball is being met and moved with using the left outer side of the foot).

As under Figure 74. Feint: Pretend to meet and move with the ball using the inside of the foot but then move with the ball to the other side using the outside of the foot.

Note
Practise both possibilities with the inside and outside of the foot under match conditions. The player should make his free choice according to the situation whether he allows the ball to rebound in order to start a one-two movement.

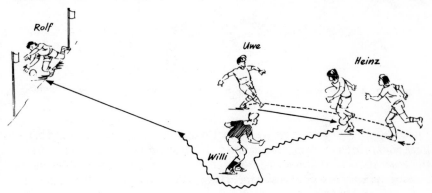

Figure 76 *Meeting and moving with balls played low in the direction of running*

Uwe plays the ball to Heinz who runs towards the ball and moves with it in the direction of running. He attempts to outplay Willi and to get in a shot at Rolf's goal. Uwe has moved into the position originally occupied by Heinz upon passing the ball. Heinz and Uwe can switch a number of times if Willi is successfully preventing them getting in a shot at goal. Each side attacks for five minutes. Which side can score the most goals in this time?

Note
If Heinz shoots at goal then he gets the ball again from Rolf and then plays it back to Uwe.

Please observe
Meeting and moving with the ball in the direction of running is most safely executed with the inside of the foot; however, some players are able to attain the same degree of safety with the outer side. Here though, the foot is turned well to the inside (see diagram).

Extension
Hard and low pass at very high speed, however, meet and move on with it "softly".

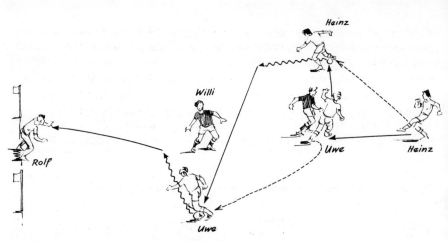

Figure 77 *Meeting and moving on with square passes in the direction of running*

Procedure as before. Heinz plays the ball to Uwe who runs towards it and plays it back square to Heinz who has run into position along with his pass. Heinz meets the square pass and carries it in the direction of running. He dribbles with the ball and shoots at goal or plays it square to Uwe, who then finishes off the move (two against one). After ten attacks or after a given period of time, the attack and defence switch round. Which side can score the most goals?

Note
Here too, the ball is met and moved on with the inner or outer side of the foot (with the outside of the foot turned towards the pass).

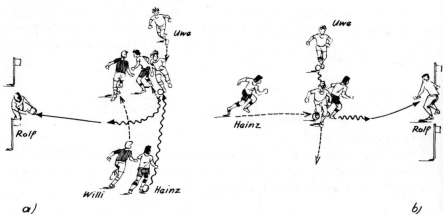

a) b)

Figure 78 *Meeting and carrying and "taking over" the ball*

Procedure as before. Heinz and Uwe play against Willi. Apart from practising meeting and moving with the ball they should also practise "taking over" the ball from a partner who is dribbling with it.

a) Heinz and Uwe approach one another face to face: Uwe dribbles with the ball and shields it from his opponent Willi who is in close attendance. Heinz runs towards Uwe and takes over the ball which Uwe has left behind him.

b) Heinz crosses the path of Uwe who is dribbling with the ball. Uwe while running stops the ball with the sole of his boot so that Heinz can take over the ball.

Please observe
The inside of the foot provides the greatest amount of security.

Figure 79 *Meeting and moving with the ball while facing the opponent*

Procedure as before. Heinz plays the ball to Uwe, who runs towards the ball, meets it with the inside of the foot and makes a turn moving with it towards his opponent (with the inside of the right foot turning right, with the inside of the left foot turning left).

To be observed
Do you take up position close to the ball or some distance to the side?

To be recognised
Ensure when meeting the ball and turning with it that the standing leg is far enough to the side of the ball. In this way, the ball can be moved out of its original direction and moved away from an opponent trying to intercept.

Extension
Hard passes and retrieving the ball at a fast running speed.

Figure 80
*Meeting and moving
with and "taking
over" the ball in
a game with one goal
and three against two*

You play around one goal with a neutral goalkeeper. A "neutral" player takes on the role of schemer for the side in possession. Which side can score the most goals in a given period of time?

Note
Within the scope of this game, all possibilities of playing behaviour with regard to meeting and moving with the ball and "taking over" the ball should be concentrated on.

Meeting and moving with hard, knee-high passes
Procedure as under Figures 74–80.

Note
Before a scoring shot is made by means of "two against one" or by dribbling, the practising player repeats meeting and moving with hard and knee-high passes a number of times.

Please observe
The inside of the foot provides the greatest security when "killing" balls played hard.

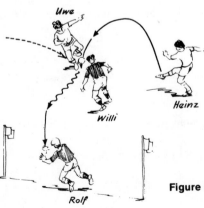

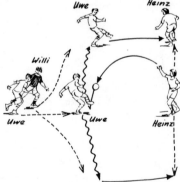

Figure 81 *Meeting and moving with carrying volleys
to the side using the inside of the foot*

Procedure as under Figures 74–79. Heinz throws or lobs the ball and passes it in such a way that Uwe can run towards the high pass. He moves with the ball using the inside of the right foot to the left or using the inside of the left foot to the right. Uwe plays back to Heinz. After several passing movements and meeting and carrying the ball, Heinz and Uwe then face up to Willi, the fielder and Rolf in goal. Then Uwe takes on the schemer's role and Heinz practises meeting and moving with the ball.

To be observed
Do you take up position a) behind, b) next to or c) to the side of the ball?

To be recognised
The stance should be to the *side of the ball* in the new direction of running.

To be observed further
Is the tip of the foot of the playing leg a) stretched downwards or b) drawn up?

To be observed
The tip of the foot should be drawn up!

To be observed further
Does the shank hang a) vertically downwards, or b) is it inclined over the ball like a "roof"?

To be recognised
The shank is inclined over the ball like a "roof".

Note
If it turns out to be difficult for some boys to meet and move with the ball from the pass then the exercise can be reduced by employing the following variations: Heinz and Willi throw the ball aloft, meet it and then play it to one another. By combining in this way they approach the goal in which Willi and Rolf are positioned, and play around it. Switch sides after a given number of attacks or according to time (see Figure 82).

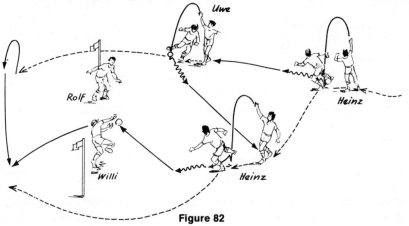

Figure 82

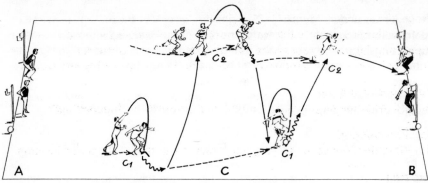

Figure 83 *Three teams alternating*

A and B are in the goals. C attacks B in that each player throws the ball aloft, meets and moves with the ball and then passes to his partner. After C has finished off the attack with a shot at goal, B attacks A's goal, etc. Each team has a ball. Which side can score the most goals in ten attacks?

Extension

The player passing the ball does so in such a way that his partner can only reach it running at full speed. The defender for his part attempts to reach the ball and puts pressure on the practising player. By dummying (left/right·or right/left) attempt to shake of the pursuing defender!

Figure 84 *Meeting and moving with volleys to the side with the outside of the foot*

Procedure as under Figure 81.

To be observed

Do you take up position a) to the right or b) to the left of the ball if the ball has to be met and moved with using the outside of the right foot?

To be recognised
The position should be to the right of the ball. The playing leg "crosses" over the
supporting leg and guides the ball round to the other side (the reverse is the case
if the ball is to be met and moved with using the outside of the left foot).

To be observed further
Is the foot of the playing leg a) stretched downwards or b) pulled up?

To be recognised
The tip of the foot of the playing leg is raised and the foot inclined inwards.

Extension
As under Figure 81. Feinting: Pretend to meet and move with the inside of the
foot and use the outside to move with the ball to the other side.

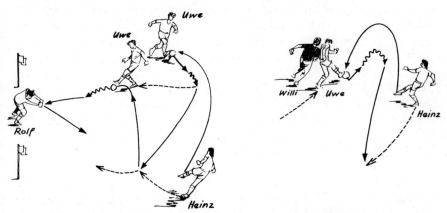

Figure 85 *Bringing volleys under control with the sole in the direction of running*

Procedure as before. Heinz uses his hand or foot to pass the ball high to Uwe
who runs towards it and uses the sole of his foot to bring the ball under control in
the direction he is running in. After repeating this several times, attempt to score.

To be observed
Do you take up position a) next to or b) behind the ball?

To be recognised
You take up position behind the ball which thus drops in front of the body.

Please observe with regard to the foot of the playing leg:
Should the tip of the foot be a) pulled up or b) stretched downwards?

To be recognised
The tip of the foot is pulled up. The foot forms a "roof" over the ball.

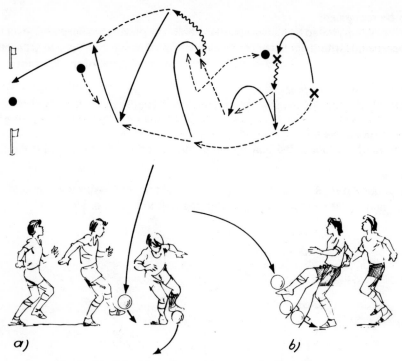

Figure 86 *Bringing volleys under control with the instep*

Note
Bringing the ball under control with the instep can be applied in two situations:
a) in the case of balls which drop sharply, b) in the case of high-angled balls.
Organisation and procedure as before. Heinz throws or lifts the ball with his foot
in such a way that it a) drops sharply and b) arches down. Uwe runs towards the
ball and brings it under control with his instep. Then he carries it with the sole,
the inside or outside of the foot, according to the situation.

To be observed
When bringing sharply dropping balls under control with the instep what should
the distance from the ground be and what is the position of the foot of the playing
leg?

To be recognised
The sharply dropping ball falls on to the foot held in a horizontal position just
above the ground. The ankle is "relaxed". "Kill" the falling ball!

To be observed
What is the distance from the ground for the playing leg when bringing arching
balls under control and what should the position of the foot be here?

In the case of arched balls, the playing leg should make contact with the ball at knee-height with outstretched instep.

Note
A skilful player is able to direct the ball with the instep in any given direction or in the one required by the situation. The final, safe controlling of the ball is executed, according to the situation, with the sole (in the direction of running) or with the inside or outside of the foot in any other direction.

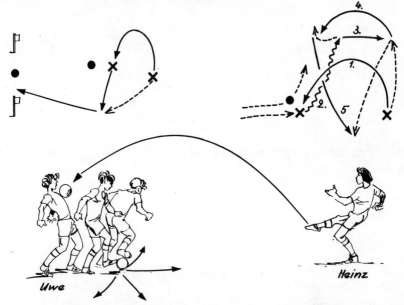

Figure 87   *Bringing volleys under control with the chest*

Procedure as before. Heinz throws or passes the ball high in the air. Uwe brings it under control with his chest and moves with the ball falling from his chest employing his sole (in the direction of running), or the inside or outside of the foot in any other direction.

To be observed
Should the pelvis be a) thrust forward or b) thrust backward?

To be recognised
The pelvis is thrust forward. As a result, the back is hollowed and this is essential in order to "catch the ball on your the chest".

To be observed further
a) Does the chest give way upon contact with the ball and should it be pulled in or
b) does it remain concave?

To be recognised
The chest remains concave! As a *result the ball remains against the body.*

Variations of Figure 87.
a) Uwe moves with the ball to the side using his chest and then proceeds to bring the ball falling from his chest under control as above (see diagram).

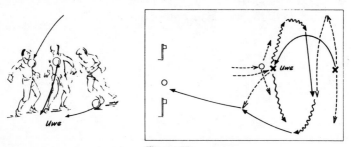

Figure 88

b) Uwe jumps, stops the ball in the air with his chest and then moves with the fal-ling ball.

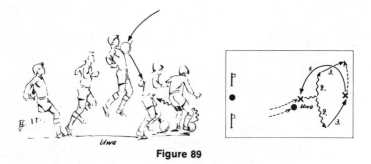

Figure 89

c) Uwe jumps, turns to the side in the air with the ball against his chest and moves with the falling ball.

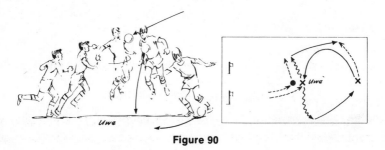

Figure 90

126

d) Uwe meets the ball with his chest and plays the falling ball in the air or as a drop-kick to Heinz who has run clear.

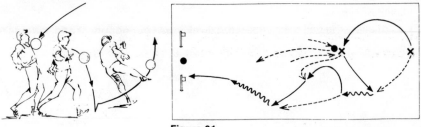

Figure 91

e) Uwe brings balls which are shot hard against his chest under control.

To be recognised

Allow your chest to give way, pull it in in order to "deaden" the impact of the ball. Bring the ball dropping from your chest under control – do not allow it to bounce out of control.

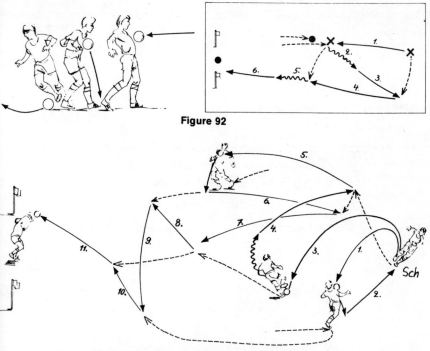

Figure 92

Figure 93 *Three against three with "schemer"*

Three forwards run clear against three defenders. The "schemer" throws the ball to them or plays it to them high in the air. Bring the ball under control according to the situation, then play it brack to the schemer. When each player has been on the ball once, shoot at goal.

Please observe
Do not allow the ball to bounce! Run away from your opponent and towards the ball! Accurate throwing or passing of the ball is essential.

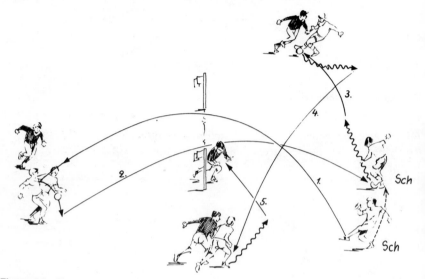

Figure 94 *Three against three with a neutral schemer on the side of the team in possession*

Keep far apart from one another and play around one goal. The schemer distributes the ball using high passes. Shoot at goal only after each player has been on the ball at least once. Every pass goes back to the schemer until the shot at goal is undertaken.

Figure 95 *Three against three with the two goals a fair distance apart*

Each team has a midfield player, who passes high to the three strikers. Each pass is returned to the midfield player until a shot at goal is feasible.

Note
In order to ensure that an optimal training effect is attained, it is essential that the midfield player plays all possible forms of volleys from half-volleys to sharply dropping balls.

5.6. HEADING THE BALL

The significance of playing the ball with the head is to be found in passing on balls in the air direct when interpassing or in rounding off an attacking move with a header at goal. Solid heading ability can often be decisive in a game for the defence as well.

Playing against a reinforced opposing defence – a quantity which is continuing to develop even further – necessitates forceful attacking moves over the wings. But what use is this tactical requirement if it cannot be rounded off in front of the opposing goal by forwards who are sufficiently athletic, with the necessary jumping ability and above all, sufficiently resolute to assert themselves by means of a purposive and powerful header. On the other hand, the attacking game played by the opposition over the wings means that defenders who are strong in the air are needed, who can match up to the opposing strikers.

It is becoming increasingly evident that crosses are not just simply "soft" nowadays when they arrive in the penalty area, frequently they are fired in hard and relatively low. The forwards move towards the ball explosively and surprisingly and flick it – according to the height of the cross – either with the head or foot or by some other means towards goal. In Mexico, the English practised this way of rounding off their attacks over the wings, particularly when it came to corners (balls fired in towards the near post) with great success (two goals against Germany). Such tactics were based on the consideration that balls lobbed softly into the penalty area are easily gobbled up by the goalkeeper and the tall lads in defence.

Being able to come to terms with the competitive environment and the challenge linked to it, of judging the strength and height of the ball in the air and adopting the proper behaviour to meet the situation are of particular significance for effectively practising heading. It is also essential to eliminate the reluctance revealed by many players to play the ball with their heads, as soon as possible. As a result of its great tactical importance "heading the ball" is a subject which should be included in training at all stages whether lads in the "groundwork" stage are concerned or the "finished" player who has reached top performance level. Man against man duels are not simply settled on the ground but also to a high and often decisive degree in the air!

It appears to me that here in particular there is still a lot of ground to be made up in order to at least counter-balance the advantage that others seem to have in heading the ball.

Figure 96 *Scoring with the head (one against one)*

Heinz up against Rolf in goal. Heinz throws the ball up and heads it towards Rolf's goal. After ten headers, they switch. Who can score the most goals?

To be observed
Which part of the head is used to head the ball?
When executing the header should the head be drawn back or should the chin be pulled in to the chest? Should your eyes be open or closed?

To be recognised
The ball should make contact with the forehead. The chin is pulled in to the chest. The neck should be stiff. The eyes open.

To be observed further
Is only the head used to strike the ball or should the whole body be arched?

To be recognised
The whole body is arched.

Note
The header can be executed by means of a twisting turning movement of the upper part of the body or by means of a straight draw back and follow through movement. The header has more force when carried out by means of a twisting movement, which we also apply when leaping to attempt force home crosses. It can be observed that when attempting to score with the head, those engaged in the practice session attempt to make the goalkeeper go the wrong way by carrying out deceptive movements of their own accord. Recognise and develop special features of movement taking the essential characteristics into account!

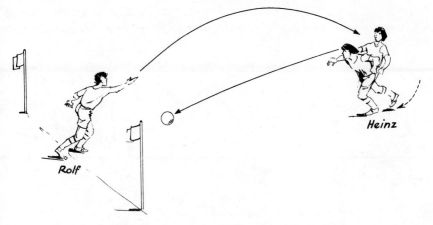

Figure 97 *Heading home balls coming straight towards you*

Rolf in goal throws the ball to Heinz who head the ball back towards goal. Procedure as under Figure 96.

Extension
Head the ball towards goal when running towards it.

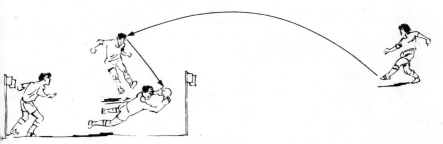

Figure 98 *Converting crosses*

Two in goal against two field players, one of whom crosses the ball whilst the other tries to nod it home with the head (either throw the ball in or use your foot to cross). The two field players change round after ten attempts then the two sides switch places. Which team can score the most goals?

Extension
Run into the crosses, whereby the crosses are thrown or hit harder.

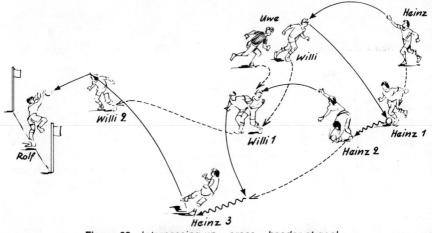

Figure 99 *Interpassing up – cross – header at goal*

Rolf is in goal, Uwe covers Willi, Heinz throws the ball to Willi and runs into position. Willi plays the ball to Heinz with his head. Heinz meets and moves with the ball before he returns it to Willi. The move is set up in such a way that Heinz finally crosses from the wing and Willi heads the cross towards goal (see Figure 99). After five headers at goal, the two field players change over, then the defence and attack switch round.

Extension
Heinz throws or plays the ball harder and from a greater distance. Willi runs onto the pass.

Figure 100 *Jumping to head the ball at goal*

Rolf and Uwe are in goal. Heinz stands next to the goal and throws the ball in an arch in such a way that it falls in front of Willi. Willi jumps up and heads the ball goalwards. Procedure as before.

To be observed
When must you jump? Are the legs a) together or b) spread out the width of your body when leaping?

o be recognised
The leap towards the ball must be effected in such a way to facilitate a high-angled movement towards it. Only in this way can the ball be headed properly with the forehead. Do not leap towards the ball from underneath it and make contact with the top of the skull! When leaping, the legs should be spread out the width of the body!

How to learn the process of "bracing yourself"
a) The boys jump in the air and again land on the point of take-off. Next, they attempt to knock the ball out of their partner's hand with their stomach while leaping, but be careful to land on the point of take-off again!
b) The partner holds the ball aloft at an angle. The player who is practising jumps up, bends his body and makes contact with his forehead against the ball.

Other Possibility
Procedure as Fig. 96. Throw the ball up yourself, jump to reach it, brace yourself and head the ball downwards towards the goal-line.

Note
The practising player is called upon to head the ball powerfully by means of this exercise.

Figure 101 *Leaping to the ball and heading it home when running*

Procedure as before. Heinz throws the ball so that is drops in front of Willi. Willi runs towards the ball, leaps using one leg and heads the ball at goal.

To be recognised
Time your leap properly and use only one leg!

Extension
Uwe covers Willi and jumps together with him but initially does not intercept.

133

Figure 102 *Heading home crosses in the air*

Rolf and Uwe are in goal. Heinz throws or crosses the ball which Willi head at goal, leaping into the air and twisting his body. Otherwise procedure as before.

To be observed
When and how does your leap to the ball take place? How is the movement to connect with the ball take place carried out?

To be recognised
Leap soon enough to be able to execute the connection properly! When heading the ball from the side then twist the upper part of your body round to connect with the ball.

Extension
Willi attempts to reach the cross by running two or three steps towards it; Heinz puts in the crosses harder.

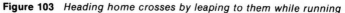

Figure 103 *Heading home crosses by leaping to them while running*

134

Rolf is in goal and Uwe now covers Willi. Willi runs towards the crosses, jumps using one leg (cross from the right – use left leg to jump), turns and twists the upper part of the body and heads the ball at goal using his forehead. Uwe jumps at the same instant and puts pressure on Willi but initially does not intercept. Further procedure as before.

Note

The twisting turning movement in the case of the header when leaping sideways is something which should be constantly practised outside the exercise sequence, for instance during the warming-up programme.

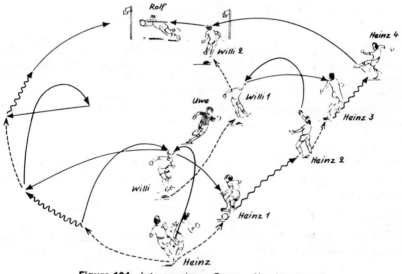

Figure 104   *Interpassing – Cross – Header at goal*

Rolf is in goal and Uwe covers Willi. Heinz, the "schemer" throws the ball up for Willi or lifts the ball with his foot and runs into position. Willi leaps and heads the ball back to Heinz, who first meets it and moves with it and then plays in back high to Willi. Heinz takes up position in a semi-circle in front of goal so that he can cross from the sides and Willi heads the crosses at goal. Further procedure as before.

Extension

Uwe attempts to intercept against Willi by heading the ball away. His clearance should also reach Heinz.

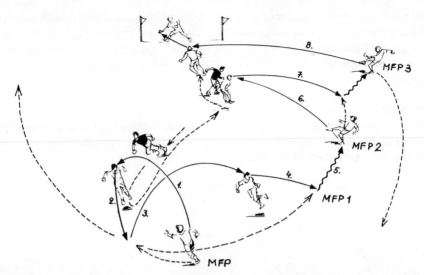

Figure 105 *Midfield player – two spearheads – two defenders (midfield player and three against two)*

Procedure and extension as under Figure 104

Note
The midfield player alternates between hard hit and soft crosses.

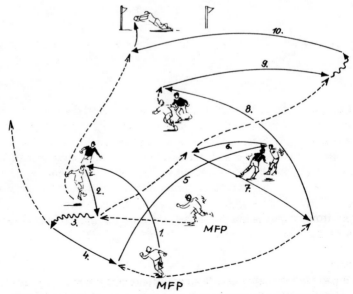

Figure 106 *Passing long volleys and attempting to convert crosses*

Midfield player 1 provides three strikers with long volleys. Midfield player 2 runs clear, meets the passes from the strikers and plays the ball back to midfield player 1. Midfield player 2 runs clear orientating himself towards the wing from where he crosses. The three strikers attempt to score from the crosses. The goalkeeper returns the ball to midfield player 1.

Extension
The defence attempt to intercept the ball. If the ball is successfully cleared to midfield player 2 then the three strikers switch with the three defenders. The two midfield player retain their positions.

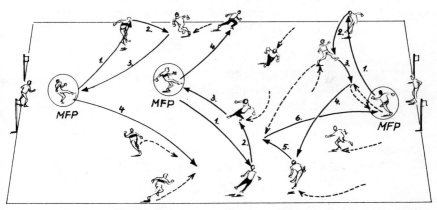

Figure 107   *Three groups of four with a midfield player executing volleys and headers between two goals*

A midfield player feeds four strikers with long volleys from goal to goal in which there is a neutral goalkeeper. Each volley from the midfield player is played on with the head and then passed back to the midfield player. Every attack is rounded off with a cross and header at goal. Which team can score the most goals following ten attacks?

Note
Volleys which cannot be played with the head are passed back immediately to the midfield player.

Extension
A and B organise the defence in front of the goals. C attacks in the direction of A as under Figure 107, A attacks B, B attacks C, etc.

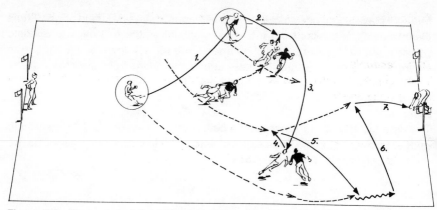

Figure 108   *Three against three plus two players teaming up with the side in possession with two goals*

Five play against three from goal to goal concentrating on volleying and heading the ball (two players always strengthen the side in possession). Each side remains on the ball for as long as it takes the three players to win it. Which team can score the most goals in a given period of time?

Extension
a) Only one player more, b) same number of players

Note
All other team games using either one or two goals can also concentrate upon volleying and heading the ball with a final header at goal.

Figure 109   *"Diving" headers*

Procedure as under Figures 97 and 98. Observe how the body is supported when falling.

To be recognised
When falling, the body is supported with the arms which are bent to ensure a soft and springy effect!

6. EXCURSUS: TRAINING WITH THE BALL PENDULUM (SUSPENDED BALL)

The Apparatus
There should be at least four suspended ball in every hall. *The cord* should not be too thick or too heavy and it must run through stainless, smooth guiding rings. The last ring on the ceiling should be flexible to ensure that no undue strain is imposed on the cord. Do not employ grooved wheels to guide the cord (they frequently stick!). The height of the ball must be easily adjustable for every practising player. *The ball* should be obtained from a qualified source.

Ball pendulum on the training ground
Height 5 to 6 metres, rigid construction in order to ensure a smooth pendulum effect. Set up vertical mast between U-beam by means of two screws. In this way you can remove the pendulum by slackening one screw in order to replace a frayed cord easily.

Range of applications
The ball attached to the cord facilitates manifold training possibilities on one's own and supports the attainment of technical accomplishments. If the intensity of movement is correspondingly increased a greater training effect can be achieved. *Important:* Ensure that the exercises and work on the suspended ball provide match-orientated impressions.

Exercise and Training Examples

Figure 109 A *Footwork*

1. Keep your movements constant and relaxed. Play the swinging ball according to the appropriate match situation with the inside, outside or the instep. Meet and move with the ball in between. The ball should also be played outside the "zero point".

2. We hit home crosses and make contact with high dipping balls direct in the air by means of the volley kick, knee-high – hip-high – shoulder-high. Please observe: bend your body away from the ball, stretch your instep!

Figure 109 B *Training with the head*

1. We jump up to play the ball with the head accurately into the path of a team-mate or head home crosses with a flick to the side turning from the hip, first without any opponents, then with one and finally with several. Do the same while running; then: jump using *one* leg!

2. Hip-high balls should be headed goalwards by "diving" at them. Please observe: leap towards the ball – make contact with the full forehead – brace yourself as you fall with your arms, ensuring a soft landing through bending them elastically – get up immediately and follow the pendulum swing, prepare yourself once more and "dive" into the ball as it swings towards you.

Figure 109 C *Special training for goalkeepers*

1. Leap and fist the ball straight, first of all without any opponents challenging, then with one and finally with several. Please observe: jump at the right moment and high enough – make full contact with the ball from the chest with clenched fists. Do not hit the ball from above!

2. Fisting crosses away to the side with both fists, then with one fist, without any opponent and then with one. Please observe: Keep your eye on the ball – jump at the proper moment and in such a way that you make contact with the ball in front of the body.

7. TACTICAL TRAINING

7.1. DRIBBLING AND TACKLES

Dribbling with the ball, the skill of the individual player to move with the ball in the competitive environment and to take on and assert himself against the opposition is an important tactical prerequisite for successful playing behaviour in the modern, progressive game.

Strong sides are characterised in that their game is to a large extent shaped by players who know how to dribble with great skill, revealing cleverness both technically and tactically and who above all, can come out on top man-to-man. The object of the exercise is the tactical application of dribbling as adjusted behaviour in certain match situations (see Chapter "Attacking Play").

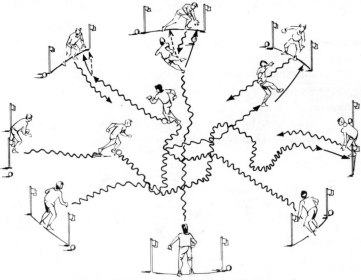

Figure 109 D   *Dribbling and shooting at goal*

Goals are set up around the edge of a circle. Three players form a training group and alternate in dribbling towards two goals lying opposite one another. A and B are in the goals. C begins and dribbles changing direction as frequently as possible (to the left, to the right, turning in a circle, straight ahead) and a) shoots at B's goal from a given line or b) attempts to outplay B in goal. Then B dribbles towards A, A towards C etc. Who has scored the most goals following ten attacks?

Note

The players engaged in dribbling meet in the centre of the circle and must make way for one another.

To be observed

When dribbling with the inside should the tip of the foot of the playing leg be a) pulled up or b) flexed downwards?

To be recognised

When dribbling with the inside of the foot, the tip of the foot of the playing leg should be pulled up.

To be observed when dribbling with the outside

What is the position of the foot and the tip of the foot if we are dribbling straight ahead? On the other hand, where should the tip of the foot be pointing when dribbling to the side or in a circle?

To be recognised

When dribbling straight ahead with the outside, the foot should be turned inwards and flexed downwards. When dribbling with the outside to the side or in a circle, the tip of the foot should be pulled up!

Extension

Increased pace in general. Change, reduce and suddenly increase the pace with ever-changing steps and changes of direction. The players dribbling towards goal dribble in the middle of the circle in a bunch until the coach gives a sign for them to make for goal.

Please observe

Keep the ball close to your body when dribbling. Engage in "mock battles". Take the special features of the players into account!

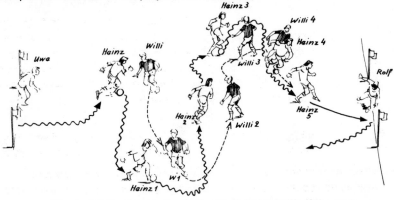

Figure 109 E *One against one with defence at "half throttle"*

Two pairs play against one another. Heinz and Uwe against Willi and Rolf. Heinz begins and dribbles against Willi, who slowly retreats always remaining in Heinz's way. As a result, Willi compels Heinz to change direction constantly. Shortly before the marking line is reached, Heinz suddenly bursts past Willi and shoots at goal. Willi takes over in goal and Rolf now dribbles against Heinz towards Uwe's goal, then Uwe dribbles against Rolf, etc.

Note

The player dribbling with the ball drives his opponent in front of him constantly varying, surprise changes of direction whilst the defender acts in such a way that he is constantly challenging him.

Please observe

Control the ball close to your body with short, ever-changing steps! When bursting past an opponent make sure you place your body between your opponent and the ball! The ball must thus be controlled by the leg which is turned away from your opponent so that as a consequence it can be shielded from the opponent with the body!

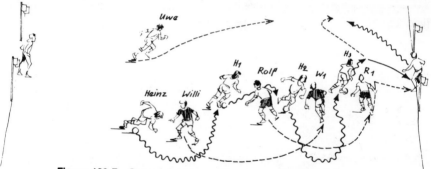

Figure 109 F   *One against two with defence at "half throttle"*

Procedure as Figure 109 E. There are three player on each side. One player dribbles with the ball against two members of the opposite side, who, lined up one behind the other, pull back as under Figure 109 E. If he dribbles round one opponent, the second bars his path to goal and the first opponent who was "outplayed" immediately runs into position behind his team-mate. In this way, the player practising always has two opponents in front of him.

Note

The presence of the second opponent means that the practising player is forced to keep *the ball under control close to his body* when spurting past the first one.

When attacking, the second attacking player moves up behind the player dribbling with the ball so that the organisation of the defence is ensured should the other side gain possession and attack.

145

Figure 109 G *One against one*

A contest to get the ball and goals! Two sides each with three players, with two of them in goal and one against one on the field. Which side can score the most goals within a given period of time?

Please observe the behaviour during a tackle: Shield the ball with your body. Keep your body between your opponent and the ball! If the ball is lost, *go after* your opponent (!) and show the *will* to win back the ball!

Note
As "one against one" calls for great intensity of movement, the players on the field and in goal should switch frequently!

Figure 109 H *One against two*

Organisation as under Figure 109 F. The player in possession must take on two opponents and assert himself against them. A second player moves up along with him and can take over and continue dribbling with the ball. Which team can score the most goals in a given period of time?

Note
The defence should make "genuine" efforts to intercept the ball.

Please observe
Should possession be lost, then immediately switch to defence: the second player adopts "delaying tactics" and the player who lost the ball runs into position behind his team-mates

146

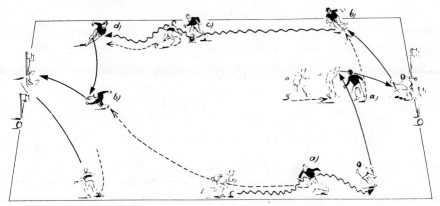

Figure 110 *Dribbling up the wing – cross – shot at goal*

Three teams each with two player alternate against two goals, with two neutral goalkeepers. Team A starts and one player dribbles up the wing with the ball. The second player moves inside to in front of team B's goal and connects with the cross. Then team B attacks team A's goal in the same manner. Which team has scored the most goals after ten attacks?

Please observe
Rapidly switch to attack! Whoever gains possession, dribbles with the ball and attacks. If the goalkeeper has the ball, the attack should start with a player bursting up the wing!

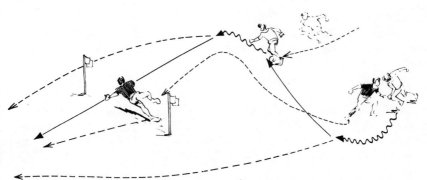

Figure 111 *Dribbling during interpassing (two against one with one goal)*

Play round one goal. Two sides each with two players. One side attacks whilst the other defends with one player on the field and a second in goal. After a certain time, the attacking and defending teams switch round. Which team can score the most goals?

Please observe
When dribbling be vigilant and keep your eyes open! Do not pass the ball until you can interpass properly with your partner as a result of dribbling and running clear! In a tackle, get between your opponent and the ball!

Figure 112 *Three against two with one goal*

Procedure as Figure 111. Two teams with three players. The side defending has two fielders and one player in goal.

Please observe
Get away from your opponent and run clear by dribbling, create opportunities to pass the ball. Dribble up to your opponent and initiate a "one-two movement".

Please observe further
Recognise and exploit chances to move through and break through on your own (prerequisite: change of pace, the attacking player runs clear rapidly without the ball).

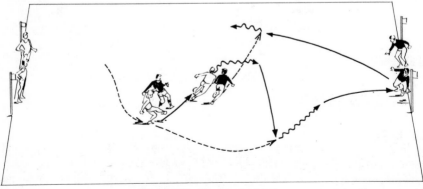

Figure 113 *Two against two*

Two team each with four players, two of whom are in goal and the others who play two against two on the field. The field and goal players switch around whenever it is suitable.

Please observe
Dribble and run clear in order to move some distance apart and create openings. *Or:* Dribble with the ball towards one another and take it over. Demonstrate the will to assert oneself on the ball. *Thus:* Keep between your opponent and the ball in a tackle! *Or:* Attempt to break through on your own!

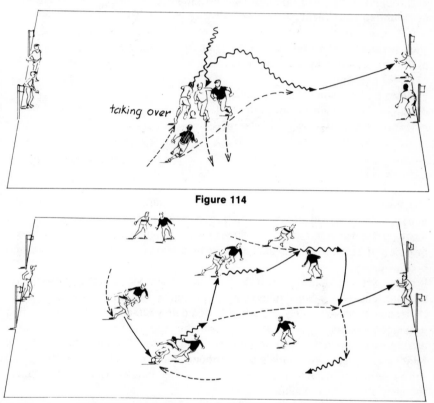

Figure 114

Figure 115 *An inferior number against superior odds*

Three against four (five); four against five (six); five against seven (eight).

Organisation
a) In a limited area, b) between two goals with neutral goalkeepers. The side which scores a goal stays in possession and attacks the other goal in the opposite direction. If the team with the superior number of players is on the ball, the

149

offside rule must be observed! Each goal scored by the team in the minority counts double.

The main aspects of the exercise for the side in the minority:
a) Dribbling in order to create openings together with team-mates who run clear.
b) Dribbling and "outplaying" two or more opponents, and then first passing.
c) Dribbling, taking advantage of team-mates rapidly running clear and then attempting the break-through on your own.
d) Dribbling and setting up "one-two movements".
e) Dribbling and "taking over" the ball.

Main features of the exercise for the team in the majority
a) Playing with two touches of the ball.
b) Direct passing.
c) Bringing long volleys under control.
d) Playing volleys and heading the ball.
e) Dribbling and "taking over" the ball.

7.2. FEINTING

The surprise feinting manoeuvre can often be an important and decisive means of asserting oneself in a tussle. Your opponent is forced into making the wrong move so that you can realise your intentions. The ability to "dummy" is the expression of a high degree of skill of movement and adapted, thoughtful playing behaviour.

It is quite self-explanatory and certainly no world-shattering tactical observation that the success of a side depends greatly on the number of tackles it can win. In this respect, it is extremely important to dedicate yourself to practising feinting as a tactical means. This should be done at the "groundwork" stage in order to ensure that it becomes part of the player's make-up. Cunning and successful feinting also strengthens one's self-confidence and it goes without saying that the performance of the team as a whole is improved thanks to the increased playing strength of the individual.

The more surprising a match situation turns out to be, the more intuitively feints are executed. They are always a component of overall behaviour just like every other technical act of movement.

Frequently, however, it is possible to consciously set up a feint or even to provoke your opponent into adopting certain behaviour in order to be able to successfully assert yourself by means of a trick, as e. g. when Wolfgang Overath applies his "trick with the sole". In the case of Franz Beckenbauer and also of other good dribblers, overall dribbling close to the opponent represents a constant deceptive manoeuvre: he keeps the ball close to his body so that he can control it all the time; surprise change of pace, change of direction and fast turns on the spot to move away from the direction his opponent is moving in are all characteristics of his behaviour in tackles.

When practising tricks, the situation must be set up in such a way that the practising player learns about the possibility of application and consequently the purpose behind it. His opponent initially acts passively and provides help in simulating the situation as genuinely as possible. As the opponent is aware what the player who is practising the feint intends to do he should not ambitiously go out of his way to destroy the execution and effect of the feint. In any case, it is essential that a feinting move should be practised and experimented with against an opponent. The range of possibilities should be as diverse and variable as possible and the successful adoption and application of feints should help enhance the characteristics in playing skill which are already present.

Figure 116 *"Trick with the sole"*

Two or three players form a practice group. The one player practises the move, the other opposes him.

To be observed
What position should you adopt with regard to your opponent and the planned direction of attack – a) facing him, or b) should we "show him the cold shoulder"?

To be recognised
We should dribble parallel to the goal line and "cold shoulder" him. The ball is there as bait on the "presentation plate" and is moved with the leg nearest your opponent in order to invite him to intercept.

151

If your opponent tries to intercept then the ball is pulled back with the sole light-ning-fast and then carried forward with the inside of the same foot in the direction of attack (90°) by means of a simultaneous turn of the body. Your opponent is left kicking at air and the forward exploits this successful deception by dribbling as fast as possible.

Figure 117   *Sole – inside of the foot*

To be observed
How should the deceptive movement be executed and just what is the deceptive effect?

To be recognised
The ball is briefly pulled back with the sole and then carried in the same direction by means of the inside at the highest possible speed. The *deceptive effect* is based on the fact that the opponent assumes the "trick with the sole" is about to be executed and reacts correspondingly.

Figure 118   *Simple feint*

Dribble towards your opponent, feint as if to go past your opponent to the left and then sprint past him on the right (and vice versa).

To be observed
How should the weight of the body be balanced and how should the shoulders "turn"?

To be recognised
If I want to pass my opponent to the right then I must pretend to break-through *on the left,* whereby the weight of the body is completely supported by the left leg and the shoulders turn in the direction of the feint. If I want to pass my opponent to the *left* then I have to reverse my behaviour.

Figure 119   *Double feint*

Shift your weight and turn your shoulders as in the case of the simple feint. If I want to pass my opponent to the left then: pretend to go left – feint towards the right – then move left and pass your opponent (the opposite procedure of course, if I want to pass my opponent to the right).

Note
This feint can also be applied if the opponent is in pursuit and is breathing down my neck.

Figure 120 *Left-right, right-left*

Application

a) The opponent is squaring up to you. b) The opponent comes from the back.

To be observed

How should the ball be moved when executing the feint?

To be recognised

If I want to pass my opponent to the left then the ball must be played rapidly with the inside of the left foot against the inside of the right one. In the process, *the ball runs straight under* the body and *not* towards the opponent (the reverse procedure in the case of the other side).

If your opponent suddenly moves up behind you than the ball should be played *in front* of your body with the same fast rhythm. In the process, the shoulders should turn in the direction of the feint.

Figure 121 *The "locomotive" or the "Leo" feint*

Application

Shaking off an opponent who is running side by side with the player dribbling with the ball in order to overtake and intercept.

154

Sequence ot the feint
The ball is moved with the outer leg, i. e. the one turned away from your opponent. The player dribbling with the ball keeps his body between it and his opponent. The playing leg swings back and then forward again to carry the ball on again like the back and forward movement of the connecting rod of a locomotive. When the leg is swung back, your running speed is reduced for a brief instant; your other leg then executes a short, compensatory hop in order to facilitate a burst of speed again upon landing and to exploit the deception.

To be observed
What stance do you adopt on the ball – a) close to the ball or b) to the side of it?

To be recognised
You adopt a stance to the side of the ball in order to ensure that the swinging playing leg can freely move past it to the side.

To be observed further
When you begin to execute the swinging feint should the heel of the playing leg be behind or in front of the ball?

To be recognised
The heel of the playing leg should be in front of the ball. In this way, the back-heeler ("Leo") is feinted.

Note
This deceptive manoeuvre is particularly effective if there is a team-mate behind the dribbling player in position and who calls for the back-heeler by shouting "Leo".

Variations of the feinted "Leo"
In the situation, two against one, the defensive player who is squaring up and covering can be outplayed in that you pretend to pass the ball to the side with the outside of the foot: the player who is dribbling swings the playing leg as if he were kicking it to the side over the ball and then carries it with the inside in the opposite direction to the one he has just feinted in. When swinging the playing leg, the "compensatory hop" (see above) is important in this case too!

Figure 122 *"Shearing" over the ball*

Application
The player dribbling with the ball finds his opponent approaching from the side. He shears over the ball with the leg nearest his opponent and then carries it on with the inside of the other foot.

To be observed
Should the leg shearing over the ball be put down again a) in the same instant as the ball is moved on or b) should there be an interval in between?

To be recognised
The ball is moved on with the inside of the other foot at the same time as the "shearing" leg is put down again and speed picked up.

Note
The leg shearing across must land at a sufficient distance from the ball to ensure that the ball can be moved on freely and easily!

Figure 123 *Feinting a shot*

Application
A player on the attack, who is approaching the penalty box, can put himself in a better shooting position if he deceives the defender squaring up to him by pretending to shoot at goal and dribbles past him by means of the deceptive effect. Or: the winger pretends to cross the ball. The defender reacts by jumping to reach the presumed cross. The winger, however, carries the ball past the defender and has a better chance to finish off the move by doing so.

To be recognised
When shaping up for the shot or pretending to cross make sure you do so clearly and convincingly!

156

Figure 124 *The Mathews trick*

Application

This feint is used above all, by wingers. Stan Mathews could execute it in exemplary fashion and indeed the outstanding English winger could bring even world-class defenders to the verge of desperation with it. "Stan" Libuda is able to use this same trick almost as effectively.

Procedure of the feint

The winger approaches the defender dribbling in a restrained manner. He dribbles with the ball, cutting inside sharply, controlling the ball with the inside of the right foot. In this way, the defender is enticed away from the line. Suddenly and surprisingly, he then takes a lunging step to the left (in the process the ball can easily be barried with the inside of the foot), and in the same moment, he breaks past his opponent on the outside using the outside of his right foot to carry the ball.

Note

Such feints should be practised and consolidated as main aspects of training by teams playing against one goal or between two goals and in the scope of games involving a majority against a minority.

7.3. SO-MANY-A-SIDE IN A RESTRICTED AREA

Games involving teams in a restricted area are only then worthwhile in the tactical learning process providing that the interpassing called for in such games has a direction and purpose and also that defensive behaviour also corresponds to match conditions. The aim of the exercise when 3:1, 4:2, 2:1 or 3:2 are involved is to make use of the determined area by means of running clear. The defensive players attempt to ward off the attacking move of a superior number of forwards and cover the area in the direction of the target of the attack.

In order to create a playing concept which is both concrete and apparent for those practising, the match situation must be ascertained along with the positions involved and related to the "game itself".

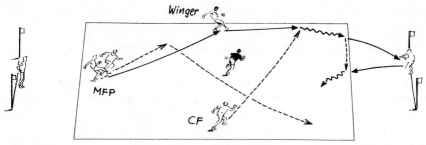

Figure 125 *3:1 on the wing*

Playing concept
Midfield player, winger and centre-forward against one defender in the direction
of the attack with the move to be rounded off (shot at goal).

Procedure
One team has three players in attack, the other one player on the field and two in
goal. The attack moves back and forward between the two goals. After five attacks in each direction, the attack and defence switch round. Whoever rounds
off the move with a shot at goal then takes over the role of the midfield player in
the opposite direction.

We observe the playing behaviour and recognise
a) Both team-mates off the ball are in position to the side of the opponent on the
perimeter of the playing area, offering themselves "short" (triangle). b) *With the
pass,* move towards the man on the ball!

Note
"Moving towards the man on the ball" (running clear and taking up a free position ready to meet the ball) should be carried out purposively in order to arrive at
the final shot at goal quickly. *Please avoid stereotyped behaviour!* As a result, it
is most reasonable and purposeful with regard to running clear if the midfield
player runs through diagonally in the direction of the touchline together with his
pass. The through pass he has called for and receives, he then shoots at goal. In

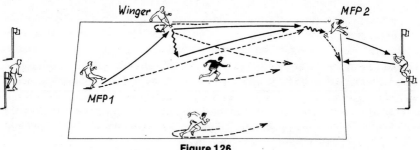

Figure 126

158

the process, the second striker moves up with him and the winger takes over the "cover-up" position in the attacking triangle (see Figure) together with his pass.

c) The midfield player moves up diagonally as in the Figure, but he does not play the through pass but instead dribbles inside and sends the midfield striker away or then plays the ball to the midfield player on the wing. d) The winger or centre-forward "takes over" from the midfield player. e) Taking over, feinting (possibly making use of the back-heeler ("Leo") f.) Switch among one another at high speed varying the technique (low, half-volley, high) and take all possible special aspects into account.
The defender covers the space against the superior number of attackers!

Note
When practising interpassing with the inside and the outside of the foot, the behaviour was experienced in the case of 3:1.

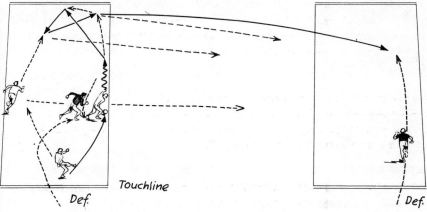

Figure 127   *3:1 On the wing with a switch to the other wing*

Playing concept
A midfield player plays together with two strikers against a defender from marking line to marking line. When interpassing ensure that you move wide on the wing and swing the ball over to the defender who is running clear on the other wing.

Procedure
Thoughtful running clear during the 3:1 game on the wing. A defender runs up the line in a second, relatively distant area. When he runs clear, far away from the ball, the ball is swung over to the other wing. Together with the long pass, three players run into the other area and again link-up 3:1. Whoever reaches the area last plays as the defender. The other defender stays behind in the other area and brings the game back into his area again by running clear.

Figure 128 *4:2 on the wing*

Playing concept
A midfield player with winger – a spearhead and a deep-lying striker. The winger and deep-lying striker "move in", the spearhead stays away.

Defensive behaviour
One defender marks the man in possession, the other covers the area behind him.

Procedure
The ball should reach the centre-forward from the midfield player *as quickly as possible*. The centre-forward shoots at goal. Then he starts up the attack in the opposite direction taking over the role of midfield player. The ball should run, according to the way the defence reacts, sharply through the "gap", diagonally or even back again to the midfield player, who moves up again with the back-pass. After five sorties ending with a shot at goal in each direction the defenders and attacking players switch round. Who can score the most goals?

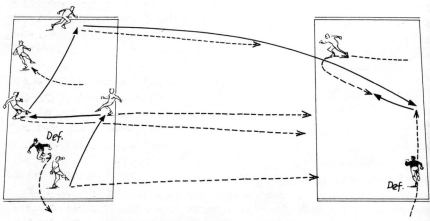

Figure 129 *4:2 with switching of the wings*

Playing concept and procedure

Play 4:2 on the wing as before. In the distant area, a winger and defender are on the wing. While the 4:2 are practising (the winger and defender on the other wing should also participate), the winger moves off the wing and comes in short. The defender sprints up the wing in the second area and calls for the change of wing. Together with the long pass, the four attacking players switch to the other wing. The last to reach there then take over the defensive role. The defenders who have remained behind then function as winger and defender and bring the game back to their wing. Whoever loses the ball, switches with the defender who has won the ball.

Note

As part of the tactical learning process, the "direct game" can only be strived at when playing 3:1 or 4:2. Even although the attack is numerically superior, the man in possession must frequently first have to assert himself against an opponent who is pressing him hard, in order to pass the ball and be able to secure possession of the ball for his team!

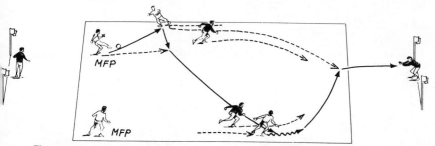

Figure 130 *Two midfield players plus two strikers against two defenders*

Playing concept

Make use of the playing area! The two strikers run clear. They interchange among themselves as well as with the midfield players. Make for the marking line as swiftly as possible and round off the move with a shot at goal. The defence should cover the zone.

Procedure

Free but directed interpassing among the attacking players against two defenders covering the zone, back and forward from goal to goal. After five attacks in each direction, the attack and defence switch round.

Main features of the exercise

a) Thoughtful running clear, hold the ball and dribble with it, fast and safe passing, facilitate the diagonal pass. b) The attack plays with two touches of the ball. c) The attack plays as direct as possible. d) Change positions. e) Take over the ball and feint taking it over. f) In direct play, switch from one form of passing to another as often and surprisingly as possible (low, half-volley, high).

Note

In the case of games played in a restricted area the area itself should be rectangular with the goal on the short side in order to facilitate diagonal running and passing. The defenders should begin their delaying and intervening tactics far enough in front of goal. Further a-side games in a restricted area:

a) Superior number in attack: 2:1, 3:2, 4:3, etc.
b) Same number in attack and defence: 2:2, 3:3, 4:4, 5:5, etc.
c) Superior number in defence: 1:2, 1:3, 2:3, 2:4, 3:4, 3:5 . . . 5:7, 5:8.

Please observe

When playing such types of games, it is essential for an optimal training effect that clear targets and playing concepts (at the most two) should be passed on by means of introducing new aspects from the field of technique and tactics. As a result the player practising finds himself constantly motivated and interested even although the form of organisation remains the same. Such aspects should not be understood as being of a stereotyped pattern but as worthwhile exercise targets. In this connection it is equally important to recognise and carry out other forms of solving a match situation.

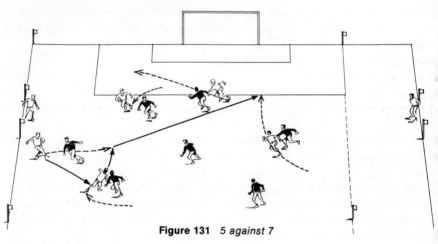

Figure 131 *5 against 7*

Playing concept and procedure

Five attacking players should assert themselves whilst interpassing under pressure from five opponents covering the man and two covering the zone. The groups should be set up according to team-tactical considerations (a midfield player, two strikers, two defenders or a midfield player and four forwards). First of all, the game is played in a relatively large area with marking lines, then from goal to goal (the narrower the area, the more difficult the interpassing). If a team manages to round off an attack properly then it remains in possession in the opposite direction. Should goals be in use, then the numerically superior side must observe the offside rule (fast switching from the one cover zone to the other).

162

The exercise starts in that a number of minutes are played without any particular target (To get used to the competitive environment with the high demands it poses). Make sure that the two sides make use of the playing area (two players move towards the man in possession, the others stay at a relative distance or far away).

Main aspects of the exercise for the minority

a) Dribbling and holding the ball, seeking the quickest possible possibility for passing the ball by running clear.

b) Attempting to break through by dribbling combined with switching positions and running free.

c) Dribbling and asserting oneself in tackles (practise behaviour in tackles with feints).

d) Taking over the ball and pretending to take it over.

e) "Playing and moving" (creates more possibilities of behaviour on the ball).

f) Seeing the one-two movement and other possibilities of behaviour (situative adjustment). From a deep-lying position play forward short to the marked man.

g) Striving towards interpassing to gain territory rapidly. By means of an initial short pass, look for the long pass. Look beyond the immediate restricted situation.

Main aspects of the exercise for the majority

a) Two touches of the ball.

b) Direct passing.

c) Passing to the player furthest away – meeting and moving with volleys in the process.

d) Using the head to pass on crosses.

e) When playing from goal to goal, change wings and only attempt to score with your head.

f) Dribbling and outplaying at least one opponent. The ensuing pass should then be played to the team-mate who is furthest away. Make sure that you concentrate both on what is occurring in your immediate vicinity and overall.

g) Executing one-two movements.

Please observe

There can be no form of training without a clear end target! Work on the main aspects of technique and tactics in match situations. Learn to recognise alternative possibilities in the process!

7.4. GROUP TRAINING

A group of players whose number remains constant is formed according to team-tactical considerations. As a result of ever new exercise forms and targets taken from the technical and tactical field of competition, interest, responsiveness and vitality are mobilised by means of each alteration. Such forms of training are extremely intensive with regard to movement and as a consequence belong to the specific training programme to improve speed and stamina in football.

Training examples for a group of five (a midfield player + two strikers + two defenders)

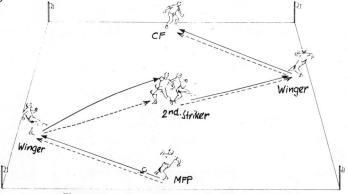

Figure 132 *Warming up – using the area of play*

Procedure

Change positions at warming-up pace. Each player follows his own pass and runs to take up the position of the man he has played it to.

a) The ball is met and carried.

b) Direct passing.

c) Direct and varied passing (low, half-volley, high).

d) The ball is passed on direct in the air.

e) The ball is passed on in the air with two touches of the ball (e. g. meet the ball with the chest and play it on with the foot).

Note

It is left to the imagination of the trainer to supplement the warming-up programme within the given framework.

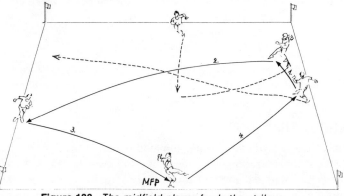

Figure 133 *The midfield player feeds the strikers*

Procedure

The strikers change positions as under Figure 132. Change positions at a slow pace; in the process the ball is passed from one player to another. Together with the third (second) pass, which is played to the midfield player, positions are changed at a fast pace. The midfield player passes the ball direct.

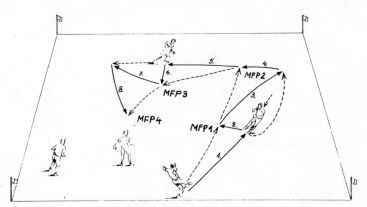

Figure 134 *The midfield player sets up one-two movements*

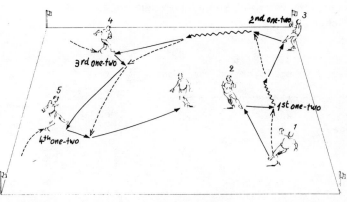

Figure 135 *Each player links up with the others acting as the "wall" to execute a one-two*

Procedure

Numerical sequence. 1 plays the one-two with 2 as the "wall", then with 3, etc. 2 takes over the ball from 1 and executes the one-two as 1 did previously. All the players keep switching positions in the process.

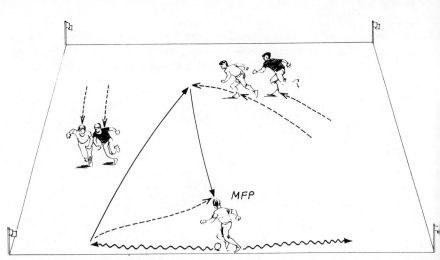

Figure 136 *Running clear, one plus two against two*

Procedure

The midfield player dribbles and holds the ball until at least one forward has been successful in shaking off his opponent (determine the moment for passing the ball). The strikers should make use of the area in that the one should "come" and the other "move away". Should the defenders gain possession, attack and defence change round.

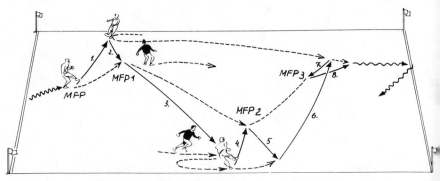

Figure 137 *The midfield player forces the strikers*

Procedure

The midfield player forces the strikers on to the marking lines. He sets up the one-two movement and offers himself as the wall with every pass. Each pass is returned to him until the line is reached.

166

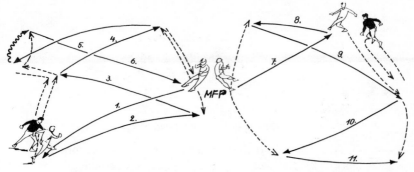

Figure 138 *The midfield player between two groups of two*

Procedure

The midfield player plays a number of passes alternately to the strikers who are running clear. With each turn (pick up and carry the ball facing your opponent) the forward begins to run clear. If he loses the ball, the defender switches to attack. The midfield player switches with one of the forwards.

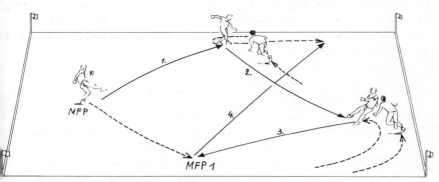

Figure 139 *Midfield player plus two against two*

Procedure

The midfield player is on the side in possession. Link up freely. Hold the ball and dribble with it, take over the ball, one-two movement and other important aspects.

Note

All these games are extremely intensive regarding movement so that following a certain imposition of strain, there should be an active break (keeping the ball up for a minute).

Figure 140 *One against two with two end positions*

Procedure

Whoever is on the ball should attempt to assert himself for as long as possible against two players in defence. "Flying" changes between the man on the ball and one of the end positions.

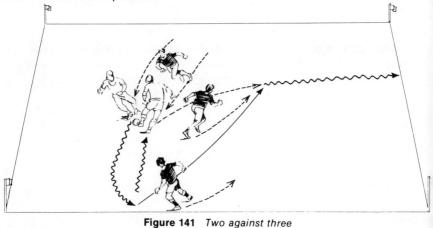

Figure 141 *Two against three*

Procedure

Two link up against two opponents marking the man and one marking the space.

Main aspects of the exercise for the two . . .

a) Hold the ball and dribble with it, seeking a chance to pass the ball as quickly as possible.
b) Take advantage of your partner's presence during tackles. Pretend to pass the ball and go it alone.
c) Take over the ball and feint as if to take it over.

Main aspects of the exercise for the three players

a) Two touches of the ball.
b) One-two movements (see the alternatives!)
c) Dribble with the ball, engage in tackles and attempt the break-through.
d) Run clear taking advantage of the space: one player moves in close, the other stays away.

168

7.5. RUNNING CLEAR AND COVERING

The exercise targets in the following playing forms are *running clear*, something which is so essential for interpassing, and *covering*, something which of course provokes running clear, as an important means of defensive behaviour.

The opponent who is marking the man ensures that the player practising is clearly aware of "being marked" thus forcing him to attempt free himself of this restriction to his play by running clear.

When goals are used in the exercise, playing at the goals helps to encourage thoughtful running clear when interpassing.

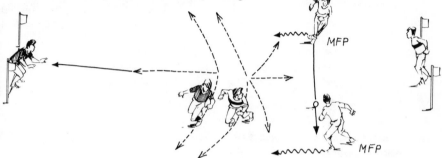

Figure 142 *One against one with two neutral schemers*

Playing concept

Two sides each with one player in goal and a player on the field. Two neutral midfield players feed the side which is attacking from behind.

Procedure

Only the striker can score goals. He concentrates upon turning on a burst of speed and spurting away from his opponent in an attempt to shake him off. Run clear moving towards *the man in possession* in order to create chances for passing and to ultimately get into a scoring position. When the midfield players pass the ball to one another, the defender switches the side he is covering and always covers on *the side nearest the ball*. Following a shot at goal, the player in goal then attacks together with the two midfield players. Which team has scored the most goals following a given number of attacks?

With regard to *behaviour when running clear* the following has to be observed: a) Watch your opponent and partners, orientate yourself regarding the overall picture, b) surprise initial burst of speed, c) make use of surprise effect and increase intitial pace, d) prepare for behaviour on the ball (see Chapter on Running clear).

Note

The tactically correct behaviour when running clear should be actively built up by the player solving "integrally" set partial tasks (e. g. "try and shake off your opponent!"). The coach watches the player's behaviour and points out possible mistakes, e. g. that there is no surprise initial burst of speed. He now sets the task that the defender should catch the forward who is practising (tag!). It is observed here that the player who is practising now orientates himself towards his opponent and through feinting ("doubling back") and an explosive burst of speed, gets away from the would-be catcher. The practising player executes a type of behaviour which corresponds to the aim of the exercise, i. e. running clear. This experience of movement and behaviour from another sphere normally leads to the target.

Covering

The defender positions himself in such a way that he combats his opponent from the *"inner line"* (stand nearer to the goal than your opponent!) and the side "nearer the ball". He attempts to

a) Intercept the pass before his opponent,

b) to disturb him when he is trying to control the ball or

c) let him come, bar the direct path to goal and then to tackle his opponent when he tries to break through (see Chapter on Defensive Play).

Note

Even given correct defensive behaviour (covering, pursuing, marking and attacking the opponent in possession) initially only the proper way to pursue and mark the opponent should be worked on together with the player who is practising. He should learn first of all how to adapt himself to the situation by means of systematically and purposively ensuring that he is ready for action so that he can react quickly (observe the opponent who is to be covered and the player with the ball!): "Position yourself in such a way that you can intercept the pass!". As the two midfield players pass the ball back and forth, the forward stands still and initially acts passively. The defender who is practising soon realises that he has the best possibility to act from a position to the side and behind his opponent, on the side nearest the ball. At the same time he now must learn how to deal with the "actively" attacking player and to differentiate between having to move in and intercept and staying away, or how he must react towards an opponent dribbling

Figure 143 *Two against two with two neutral midfield players*

up to him or against a superior number of opponents (see Chapter on Defensive Play).

Playing Concept
Two forwards run clear and shoot at goal with two midfield players setting up the chances behind them.

Procedure
a) The team on the attack remains in possession until a scoring shot is attempted. If the defence should intercept the ball in the course of the attack, it is returned to the midfield players.
b) If the ball is intercepted, then attack and defence switch round. The ball is passed to the midfield players who launch an attack in the opposite direction.
After every attack a player on the field switches with the one in goal.

Extension
Increased tempo.

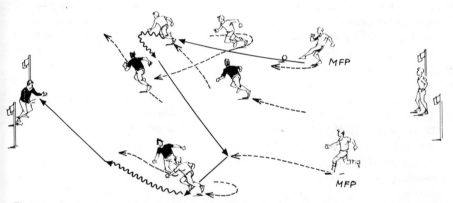

Figure 144 *Three against three with two midfield players playing for the side in possession*

Playing concept as under Figure 143. The midfield player who is playing behind the strikers passes the ball in the same moment as a forward runs clear. The forward who picks up the pass then plays it back to the midfield players. This passing sequence is continued until a shot at goal is possible. Which side can score the most goals in a given period of time?

What must be observed?
The forwards run clear along with each return pass to the midfield players; two move in ready to accept the ball (they run towards the man in possession) whilst the third stays away. Make use of the available space properly! The midfield

players run into position to accept the ball again along with their pass. The defenders cover the forwards on the "inner line" and bar the direct route to goal. Observe defensive behaviour as under Figure 142!

Figure 145 *Running clear – pass or go it alone*

Playing concept
The midfield player plays as before, exploits the possibility of running clear as an alternative to breaking through and shoots at goal.

Procedure
Each team has five players. The side on the attack plays with one man in goal, a midfield player and three strikers. The team defending is composed of three players covering the man and two in goal, one of whom takes over the role of midfield player when they switch to attack.
The midfield player feeds the strikers who are running clear and has the ball returned to him each time. Suddenly, he runs clear in order to break through on his own and shoots at goal. The strikers also continue to work towards goal and attempt to score.

Figure 146 *One plus three against three plus one*

172

Playing concept and procedure as before

Three strikers run clear, the midfield player directs the passing sequence. We should attempt to concentrate upon interpassing with one another (where is the ball coming from, whom should I pass it to?), with the midfield player remaining the free point to pass the ball; he feeds and directs the forwards. In defence, three players covering the man and behind them a "libero" covering the space. *Observe running clear in such a way as to utilize space!*

Other aspects

Change of tempo and rhythm, reduced and subdued running pace alternating all of a sudden with top speed. The midfield player holds the ball and strives towards setting up the most advantageous pass.

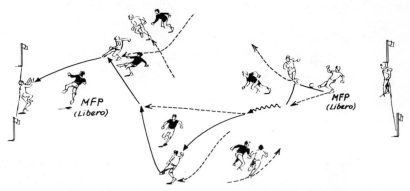

Figure 147   *Five against five between two midfield players*

Playing concept

Extend the playing environment. Switch pace and rhythm. Switch wings (run clear when at a distance from the ball not just when close to it). The midfield players set up one-two movements.

Procedure

The midfield player directs the interpassing. The pass follows to the player making a surprise movement to run clear. Or: Pass the ball in such a way to draw your team-mate and an opponent towards the ball in order to set up one-two movements. The ball is returned each time to the midfield player until a shot at goal is feasible. In defence, the midfield player takes over the role of "libero".

Note

Size of goal: 5 metres or normal size.

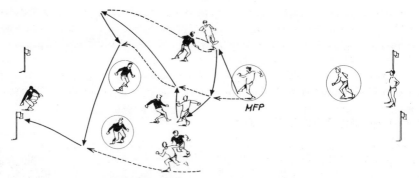

Figure 148 *One plus three against five*

Playing concept

Run clear against a reinforced defence. The strikers are covered man-to-man. Two defenders covering the zone are behind them; one of whom operates in attack as midfield player whilst the other stays in defence.

Figure 149 *Two plus four against six*

Playing concept

Four strikers run clear against four defenders who are covering the man and two the zone. The two midfield players play some distance away from one another, each behind a winger.

Procedure

Three teams alternate in attack and defence. A attacks B, then B attacks C, C then A, etc. Counter-attacking, swiftly reverting from defence to attack should take *place under the aspect of running clear.* Should A lose the ball to B, then A responds to B's counter-attack by *pursuing* B (until the midfield line). If A manages to win the ball again then it launches an attack in the direction of C.

The midfield players direct operations and initially have the ball returned to them each time; then free play under consideration of all the main aspects of the exercise practised up till now: the timing of when you should run clear – running

174

clear to gain ground – the timing of the pass – passing during a one-two movement – running clear and breaking through on your own – running clear and securing possession of the ball (where does the ball come from and in which manner? Get ready to decide on how to act when in possession) – change of pace and rhythm – counter-attacking. The throw-in is also something which should also be practised time and time again under the aspect of seeking the space!

7.6. THE ONE-TWO MOVEMENT

The one-two movement is a completed sequence of two passes, of which at least one must be played direct. The players responsible for its execution link-up a little distance apart, with one player serving as the "wall" – he passes back the ball played to him, as if it had bounced off a wall, straight into the path of the other player who has run into the open space along *with* his original pass.

The one-two movement has a surprise effect, it confuses the opponent and is thus dangerous – on account of the combination of a rapid series of passes and explosive running clear with the aim of finding a way through the defence as quickly as possible.

As the one-two movement, if it is to be played properly, also presupposes that the opposition will react accordingly thus the players engaged in executing the one-two must also have alternative possibilities worked out. Thus on no account must they commit themselves to simply playing the one-two movement, instead they should make use of the effect of instigating the movement in order to seek success just as surprisingly by other means of attack. Thus an effective alternative instead of passing the ball to the "wall" that is to the other player involved in the sequence who is going "through", is to pass it to another player altogether, especially if the player directing operations recognises that a defender has anticipated the through pass. In this case, the one-two movement initiated on the one wing can be an extremely effective alternative in attack when there is a surprise switch to the other wing.

The one-two movement calls for composed and perspicuous conduct on the part of the players involved, above all, from the player directing it.

The ability to learn how to read alternative and indeed better behaviour and to carry it out surprisingly should be included in the training process.

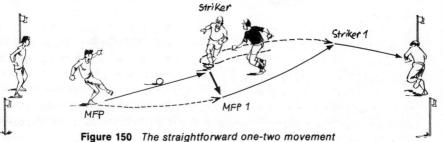

Figure 150 *The straightforward one-two movement*

Playing concept and procedure
Midfield player and striker, with a defender opposing them. The midfield player passes the ball short to the "striker" and moves up to offer himself as the "wall" laterally. His partner runs towards the ball, draws the defender with him and allows the ball to rebound direct *onto the foot* of the midfield player. He moves up at an angle along *with the square pass.* The "wall" plays the ball direct into the path of the onrushing forward.

The positions and tasks should now be switched round and the one-two movement runs in the opposite direction.

To be observed
The "wall" should on no account run into position too far to the side! If he does so then the square pass is too long and the defender finds time to rush back to position himself in such a way that the one-two movement cannot be played. Here, two passes played direct in rapid succession are linked together to form a one-two movement.

Note
The exercise can be carried out between two goals in which case, the one-two is rounded off with a shot at goal. Who is able to score the most goals?

Figure 151 *Dribbling and the one-two movement*

The playing concept is the same as under Figure 150.

Procedure
The defender does not allow himself to be drawn towards the ball. He remains in the area he is defending, awaiting the attack. The striker executes a short turn in order to face the defender and dribbles at speed towards his opponent. The "wall" moves up laterally (as a result, there are alternative possibilities). Once the distance between himself and his opponent is short enough, the striker plays the ball up against the "wall" and spurts past his opponent in order to receive the return pass.

176

To be observed

The distance between the player on the ball and his opponent should be such that he can spurt past him along with the square pass, but it should not be too short otherwise the defender can use a sliding tackle to deprive the forward of the ball. Be prepared to deal with this move by the defender! Fractions of a second can decide on success or failure, whether the situation can be successfully rounded off by playing the ball against the "wall" or whether you should attempt to break through on your own.

Note

When linking up in this way with the timing such an essential factor, it can often happen that the through pass cannot be executed because the player acting as the "wall" must first of all wait to see whether his partner can successfully spurt past the defender who is chasing him.
The following possibilities result here:
a) The midfield player executes the one-two with a slight delay.
b) He plays the ball direct to another player.
c) He changes the attacking area immediately or after holding the ball for a short time by means of a long pass.
d) He dribbles with the ball and attempts to link up with another player or decides to go through on his own.

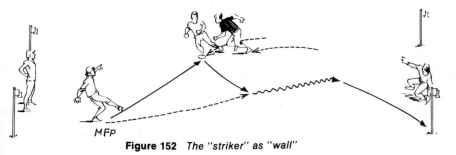

MFP

Figure 152 *The "striker" as "wall"*

Playing concept as before.

Procedure

The midfield players passes the ball short to his partner and by doing so draws the defender out of the defensive zone. The midfield player once again spurts laterally into position, moves with the square pass which has been played direct to him in the direction of attack and goes through on his own without faltering in his step.

To be observed

The pass to the onrushing midfield player can be executed as follows a) it is concealed, i. e. allow the ball to rebound from the inside of the foot across the standing leg, or b) use the outside of the foot to "cut the ball into" the path of the midfield player. When passing the ball do not turn your body in the intended direction of the pass!

Note
The behaviour of the defender should be restrained while the basic possibilities of the one-two movement are acquired until alternative possibilities have been worked out.

Figure 153 *Breaking through on your own instead of playing "against the wall"*

Playing concept and procedure as under Figures 150 and 152. The midfield player sets up the one-two movement with a pass to the forward and simultaneously moves up laterally to offer himself as the "wall". The defender anticipates the square pass and adopts an appropriate position. The forward moves with the ball and heads for goal after turning quickly, going through on his own.

To be observed
En route to the ball, make sure you observe your opponent and his behaviour closely (compare with Meeting and Moving with the Ball when Facing your Opponent).

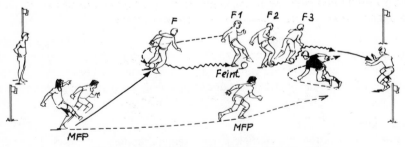

Figure 154 *Feinting "playing against the wall"*

Playing concept and procedure as under Figure 151. The striker dribbles towards the defender, the midfield player is at his side to act as "wall". The striker pretends to play the square pass against the "wall" but instead breaks through on his own after a successful feint.

We observe how the deception is carried out and recognise: that instead of hitting the ball with the outside of the foot when executing the pass, the forward swings his playing leg over the ball. He then executes a "compensating hop" with his standing leg, moves the ball to the side with the inside of the playing leg and then dribbles past his opponent in the direction of attack (compare with Chapter on Dribbling and Tackles).

Note

Meeting and moving with the ball in the direction of attack as well as feinting the square pass are alternative possibilities of behaviour in a given situation. They are effective as a result of the setting up of the one-two movement and the presence of a team-mate as the "wall".

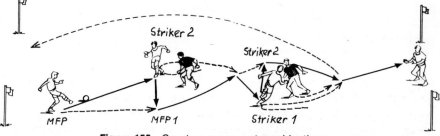

Figure 155 *One-two movement combinations*

Playing concept

One midfield player plus striker number two and striker number one. The two strikers are covered man-to-man. The third player on the other side goes into goal. The midfield player starts and executes a one-two with striker 2. Then striker 2 plays the same one-two with player 1, who rounds it off with a shot at goal (one-two movement is executed as under Figure 150). Player 1 spurts back to take up position in goal; the midfield player covers the forward striker, player 2 the deeper striker of the other team (switch over roles).

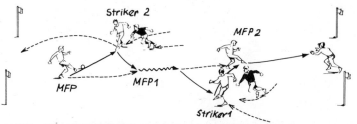

Figure 156 *The midfield player moves up along with two one-two movements*

The one-two is executed as under Figure 153. The midfield player carries out the one-two movement together with the second striker and then with the forward striker as "wall" and shoots at goal. When it is the other team's turn to attack, the midfield player covers the second striker, player 1 the forward striker and player 2 goes in goal. (The other team also switches roles in the same fashion).

Note
During the initial learning process, the team defending should allow the one-two movement to be carried out only then to provoke other attacking possibilities through their active involvement. The one-two movement should remain the object of the exercise but it is up to the individual to decide freely on what other move would best suit the situation.

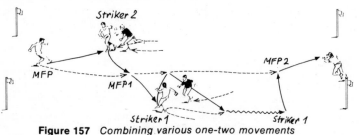

Figure 157 *Combining various one-two movements*

Playing concept and procedure as under Fig. 156. The midfield player moves up with player 2 as "wall" and then passes to player 1 whilst he himself acts as the "wall". Together with his through pass he runs into position and shoots player 1's cross at goal. The attack in the other direction takes place when the defence of the side switching to defence has set itself up as under Figure 156.

Note
In this case too, ensure that the planned one-two movements can initially be executed through setting up the defence accordingly. Genuine match behaviour with all its possibilities and variations.

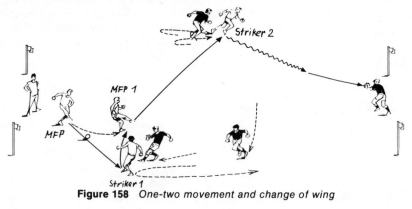

Figure 158 *One-two movement and change of wing*

Playing concept
Two sides each with a midfield player and two other players. In defence two players covering the man and one covering the zone.

Procedure
The midfield player sets up the one-two movement on one side. The players spurt quickly upfield, facilitating the through pass, drawing the defender covering the zone in the process. Player 2 on the other wing feints as if to accept the ball "short" and the spurts past his opponent in the direction of attack. The "game with the wall" switches to the other side.

Note
The effectiveness of this one-two combination depends on rapid running of the players on the one wing and skilful and well-timed running clear on the other.

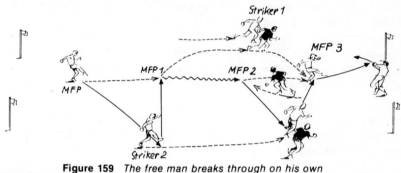

Figure 159 *The free man breaks through on his own*

Playing concept as under Figure 158

Procedure
The midfield player attempts to break through on his own. The last player of the opposing team moves up to intercept him before he is within shooting distance. Both strikers move up with him laterally. Once the gap between the midfield player and his opponent is short enough, he makes use of one striker as the "wall" and spurts past his opponent together with his pass. He picks up the rebound from his partner and shoots at goal.

Note
Within the framework of all other games involving sides – either with the same number of players, a minority or a majority in attack or in defence, the one-two movement, with all its possibilities and variations, represents an essential main aspect of training. Forming groups of two or even three is an important prerequisite for setting up and successfully playing one-two movements. One-two movements also create moments of surprise.

181

8. SPECIAL TRAINING FOR THE TEAM POSITIONS

The harmony and proficiency of a team depend upon just how the individual players perform in the interests of the team. Each player has caertain basic tasks to perform within the basic order of the playing system, tasks which result from the position he is playing in. Quite apart from these basic duties, each player fulfils other functions within the bounds of his possibilities. Thus a defender surprisingly moves up into attack and strikers take over defensive duties. Each player is only then able to fulfil his role optimally if he possesses the necessary gifts and continues to develop these qualities by means of purposive special training. Such inherent abilities also enable the player to take over the role of a certain team position. He feels secure in this role; he enjoys fulfilling his duties and is able to provide evidence of his capabilities best of all here. The proficiency of a player finds its expression in his technical-tactical behaviour and in the effectiveness for the overall performance of the team.

The target of special training is to improve the player in his technical-tactical basic behaviour and in addition, to extend the possibilities of his game. We must concentrate on strengthening consciousness governing performance and the aplomb of the individual player.

Direct contact between the coach and each individual player is of fundamental significance for the success of training, particularly with regard to team sports. The player must on no account have the feeling that the coach merely has a general, superficial interest in him. He must at all times feel that the coach is concerned with him personally and with his individual improvement of performance. Thanks to such direct work revolving around the individual player, the coach helps to increase his willingness to train. The coach sets the tasks which the player actively has to come to terms with; he avoids offering patent solutions. The player should be the one who trains and not the one who is trained! The coach for his part keeps a close watch on his charge and knows exactly how to motivate him by setting intermediate tasks or reducing or increasing targets and to guide him towards experiencing success.

During special training, the coach can devote himself to the individual player with all his individual characteristics. Above all, in the psychological respect, the coach finds he has the best chance here to get close to the player and exert his influence on certain behavioural characteristics of the player governed by the psychical sphere.

The player trains in his radius of action and within his competitive surroundings, i. e. so that opponents and team-mates stimulate his attention and concentration. Against this competitive background, adjustment reactions are fostered through continually new situations and as a result, the technical-tactical behaviour is schooled. The coach controls the play of the player's opponent so that initially it is reduced to more or less passive behaviour, only then to instruct him to increase his resistance in order to achieve a stress situation as near to real match conditions as possible. The player should attempt to find the solutions on his own and be stimulated into acting creatively.

Special training calls for great intensity of movement and in conjunction with technical-tactical instruction, it represents the best means of circulatory training which will ensure peak fitness.

8.1. THE GOALKEEPER

The goalkeeper is the last line of defence. The skill and reliability he displays in preventing goals stimulate and consolidate the playing strength of the whole team. He sets up an attack by means of a well-directed kick or throw. When kicking or throwing the ball the object should be to ensure that the attack is initiated as quickly as possible before the opposing forwards have been reprogrammed from attacking to defensive behaviour. The prior condition here is that each player immediately switches to attack as soon as the ball has been successfully brought under control by the defence. The restrictive "hedgehog" position is opened up and the playing area made use of by running into open positions. The effectiveness of attacking play is decisively influenced by means of this surprise, rapid running clear and the cooperation between the goalkeeper and the field players when initiating an attack. Such rapid switching from defence to a well-directed attacking move must be practised incisively during training in all playing forms in which the goalkeeper is involved.

The goalkeeper plays in that highly precarious field of tension in front of goal, where the will to attack and the will to defend clash with the utmost intensity. The challenge made on the intellectual-mental components of the performance capacity of the players, experiences a climax in front of goal, something which presupposes that the goalkeeper in particular should be equipped with especially well-accentuated capabilities in order to be able to assert himself properly.

His performance profile is marked in particular by the following features: The goalkeeper should be athletically built. Greater-than-average height provides him with playing advantages (command of the area).

With regard to his fitness, excellent all-round mobility and acrobatic manoeuvrability should stand out. Similarly, his elasticity should be outstandingly developed in order to ensure optimal performance when spurting or leaping for the ball or when fisting it.

The main technical aspects to be concentrated on should be catching and holding the ball in every position, getting hold of balls which have been hit low and fisting the ball away. He is able to master the instep kick when taking a goal-kick or clearing it out of his hands as well as throwing out the ball overarm or roundarm. In addition, he is capable of diverting balls past the posts or over the bar.

He reveals his tactical ability

a) in his positioning,
b) by the way he commands the penalty area, comes out of goal, whether he fists or catches the ball,
c) how he organises the defence and directs it and
d) in his attacking behaviour.

8.1.1. Positioning

The goalkeeper takes up position in front of the goal-line. In the process he narrows the angle for a shot at goal in order to ensure that he has the optimal possibilities for defending to either side of him and also to be able to reach high balls which dip over his head.

As an aid to orientation, the goalkeeper marks the middle of the goal between the posts before the game gets underway. How far he can move away from the goal-line and move towards the ball depends on his stature, his spurting speed and his jumping ability. In the case of crosses near the touchline or when corners are being taken, the goalkeeper should stand near the far post, in the rear third of the goal. From here, he is in a position to reach crosses which are passing over his head and falling beyond the far post. At the same time, he must be able to rush out from his position in the rear third of his goal to reach crosses shot hard towards the near post. A physically large defender with quick reactions and strength in the air should be positioned at the near post to support him. When a corner is being taken, another player should also be positioned in the rear third to secure the goal in order to provide cover for the goalkeeper if he must leave his goal in order to attempt clear the ball. The goalkeeper's positioning is of extreme importance for his further tactical playing behaviour. Special training strengthens the goalkeeper's confidence with regard to his positioning in that he has to ward off shots and crosses from various positions in rapid succession during match-oriented situations.

8.1.2. Commanding the Penalty Area

The goalkeeper must be able to read the attacking şituation as rapidly as possible in order to decide whether he should leave his goal or stay in it. If he does leave his goal, he must be certain that he is going to reach the ball. If he has freedom to act, he should clutch the ball, for this is always the safest defensive move on the part of the goalkeeper. If he is aware that when leaping to reach the ball he is under pressure than he should fist the ball as far away from the danger zone as possible. This can be done safest of all – providing that the situation and his position with regard to the ball allow it – with both fists or failing which, with one fist. The ball pendulum is an important piece of training equipment for the goalkeeper in order to be able to train such skills. The optimal training effect can only of course, be reached through match-oriented situations, which call for speed of decision and the ability to adapt to the situation. Crosses from both sides, which are curved towards or away from the goalkeeper, which are hit either hard or soft, as well as balls which are punted into the penalty area from midfield, should be saved by the goalkeeper while up against five opposing forwards moving around in the area.

The tempo and the sequence of shots must be directed by the coach so that the goalkeeper can decide upon his move from his starting position.

8.1.3. *Organiser and Director of the Defence*

Experience reveals that good goalkeepers are also good field players. This helps them a great deal when they must direct moves. A good goalkeeper follows everything happening during the opposing attack and observes the defensive behaviour of the men in front of him at the same time.

The goalkeeper sees the game in front of him and as a result can also best recognise possible mistakes in the organisation of the defence which he then should correct by shouting instructions clearly. However, any such possible correction or direction should take place early enough to ensure that the goalkeeper is concentrating entirely on his own role during the final phase of the opposition's attack. The libero in actual fact is mainly responsible for directing proceedings. In this respect, the goalkeeper exercises a final control function.

8.1.4. *Behaviour in Attack*

When he is in possession of the ball, the goalkeeper is his team's first attacking player. Whether he throws out the ball, or kicks it from out of his hands or launches the attack by kicking the dead ball – what is always at stake is to retain possession in order to be able to carry out an effective attacking move. Of course, when the ball has been parried successfully all the players must quickly revert from defence into attack and make themselves available in order to ensure that the goalkeeper can make use of the ball constructively. All the field players should spread out the length and breadth of the playing area in order to make it possible for the goalkeeper to play the ball to the player who is best placed. First and foremost, he directs his attention to the midfield player directing operations, as he possesses the best prerequisites for developing the attack further. Once the goalkeeper has caught the ball, he often has the possibility of playing the ball to a defender who had moved into a free position on the wing as he saved the ball. If the goalkeeper's team has been subject to strong pressure by the other side, it is often very dangerous for him to make a short pass. For this reason he should clear the ball downfield, trying to find the spearhead. In such a case, the ball should not be played direct to the centre-forward because the defender marking him has always the advantage following such a clearance from goal; instead, the ball should drop to the side of the centre-forward so that he must run towards the ball and so that he can make use of his superiority in running to reach it. In this case too, the goalkeeper must always decide on the best way to start an attack, depending on the given situation. Experience has shown, however, that such linking-up between the goalkeeper and the field players which is of cardinal important when launching an attack is far too often neglected during training. For this reason, it is important to ensure that the throw-out, the goal-kick and other clearances should be practised under match conditions during all training sessions involving the goalkeeper.

8.1.5. *Special Traits*
The goalkeeper's playing behaviour and his possibilities are governed by intellectual-mental features related to temperament and aptitude.

A strong, inner driving force, the impulsive desire and the will towards self-assertion provide him with the readiness to resist the attacking strength of the opposition at the very centre of the complex situation in front of goal. His speed of decision requires him to be able to read situative match associations as rapidly as possible and to recognise the attacking intentions of the other side. However, it is also essential when he is in a position to read given situations that he does not determine his course of action too prematurely for he must keep the door open to other possible reactions which might become necessary.

His powers of concentration and attentiveness enable him to grasp situations which have changed rapidly and to adjust himself to them. He is in a position to concentrate on that which is the most essential – in spite of the range of impressions obtained from the action taking place in front of him.

An able goalkeeper has a stimulating effect on the whole team by the very self-confidence he displays. He is also characterised by emotional stability and he is not particularly prone to fluctuations of temperament. On no account must he allow himself to be influenced by experiences of lack of success during the course of the game or by negative reactions on the part of the spectators. Resignation or capitulation are foreign words to him.

8.1.6. *The Goalkeeper and his Training*
All performance characteristics should be developed and consolidated by means of diligent, collected and thoughtful training work. Only through displaying great zeal in training can the goalkeeper apply his technical and tactical qualities with self-confidence and concentrated imperturbability in order to provide his side with the support so necessary to ensure inspired performance.

With regard to training for the goalkeeper in particular, it should be observed that the training effect is provided by means of the frequency of repetitions. Thus shots at goal should also provide the goalkeeper with some sort of chance of saving them. If the goalkeeper is put under pressure with two balls then the sequence of shots should not be too rapid otherwise the technical execution is bound to be bad. The final round of shots, above all, must act as a challenge to the goalkeeper and make him reveal all his skill in order to wind up the training session with a number of great saves which serve to build up the goalkeeper's confidence. Goalkeeper training must on no account be a presentation of shooting power on the part of the coach but instead it should build up and consolidate the goalkeeper's awareness regarding his own ability and his self-confidence.

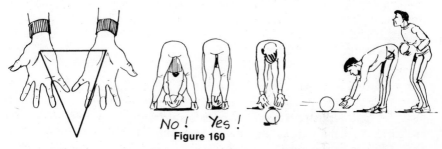

Figure 160

1. The goalkeeper clutches the rolling ball in that he scoops under the ball with his hands well-spread out and then pulls it towards his body. He stands behind the ball, when bending down he flexes his knees and the legs are spread apart in such a way that no ball can pass between them.

Figure 161

2. The goalkeeper catches waist to chest-high balls with his hand spread well apart with the backs of his hands facing downwards. For safety's sake he again pulls the ball against his body. Always make sure your body is behind the ball!

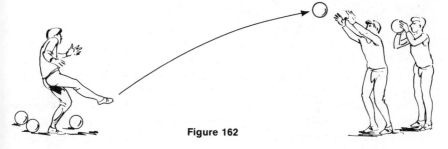

Figure 162

3. Thrust your hands out to clutch chest-high or high balls and pull them towards your body. The backs of the hands should face upwards. If the goalkeeper catches the ball after running out and jumping up for it, he should leap in the air using one leg only.

Figure 163

4. If opposing forwards jump for the ball together with the goalkeeper, he should use both fists if at all possible to clear any possible danger. Starting from the chest, quickly push out the clenched fists which should cover as wide an area as possible to make contract with the ball and punch it well-clear of the danger zone with a powerful blow.

Figure 164

5. In the case of a shot in the air to the side of the goalkeeper, he must throw himself at it and if he intends to clutch it, the palms of his hands must be behind the ball. Once he has caught the ball safely he then pulls it to his body and clutches it to him. When falling avoid landing on the stomach on the elbows (danger of injuring the mucous membrane)!

Overarm-Throw   Roundarm-Throw   Ground Clearance   Drop-Kick

Figure 165

6. The precision of a clearance, whether as a drop-kick or kicked from the hands, goal-kicks or throwing the ball out, determines whether an attack can be launched successfully. The goalkeeper obtains the necessary feeling of security through repeating exercises under simulated match conditions, time and time again.

Figure 166

7. Crosses which drop beyond the far post are pushed away by the goalkeeper before the forwards and defenders jumping to head the ball can get to them. Thanks to the frequency of the situative challenge, the goalkeeper is able to learn how to judge the flight of the ball and the proper moment to leap for it. A correctly-timed, high leap to the ball ensures that his technical execution is precise. Here, pushing away crosses under pressure.

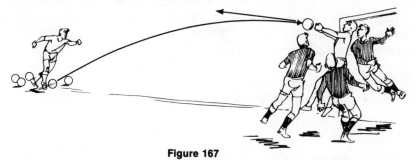

Figure 167

8. The goalkeeper should school his match behaviour in match-oriented forms of training under pressure. He must keep his eye on the ball and work on clean, technical execution. A high leap towards the ball is an important prerequisite in preventing an opponent getting his head to the ball by fisting it away.

As the last man in defence, where he also has to act as an attentive director of operations, and as the first man in attack, the goalkeeper has responsible tasks to fulfil. By dint of his ability, his confidence, his resolute engagement in the heat of the battle or in fending off difficult shots which extend him to the full, he strengthens the backbone of his side. Self-confidence and determination emanate from him and considerably influence the fighting morale of his team-mates. The goalkeeper is only then able to improve and consolidate his tactical ability if he is confronted during training with a whole range of typical competitive situations and in this way learns how to apply his means and possibilities consciously and successfully. He must learn – against the background of a whole host of momentary impressions provided by his environment – to concentrate on the ball and the possible kicker. Clever *positioning* provides the goalkeeper with the best possible chance of saving the ball in every situation. It is expedient to mark the centre of the goal. The goalkeeper does not stand on the line itself but instead moves a few paces in the direction of the shot in order to narrow the angle and to close the gap for shots coming from the side at a very acute angle. He takes up his position in such a way that he is also able to reach balls lobbed over his head and to divert them over the bar.

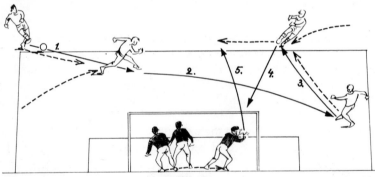

Figure 168

1. In this exercise, four forwards link up freely over the breadth of the pitch in front of goal. Each one follows his pass. Shots at goal should only be taken from outside the penalty box. The goalkeeper is required to continually change his position on account of the ball being moved about so frequently.

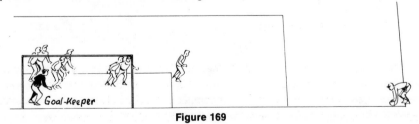

Figure 169

2. The goalkeeper stands in the rear third of his goal in order to save long crosses put over from close to the goal-line. He also stands there when a corner is being taken.

Figure 170

3. If the attacking forward is dribbling along the goal-line and approaching the goal, then the goalkeeper must take up position at the near post in order to prevent the possibility of a direct shot at goal.

Figure 171

4. If an opposing forward breaks through on his own and is moving towards goal, the goalkeeper approaches him in a crouching position. In this way he narrows the angle and forces the forward to attempt play the ball past him. When the forward attempts this, the goalkeeper throws himself at the ball.

Figure 172

5. The forwards combine freely and set up attacks from the wings. The goalkeeper catches the crosses and by throwing the ball out he at once changes the direction of attack. The goalkeeper has to learn how to command the penalty area.

Figure 173

6. Once again, attacks are launched up both wings. The crosses should drop on or about the penalty spot. The strikers attempt to convert the crosses. The goalkeeper fists the ball well clear of the danger zone. Extend the exercise in that the forwards engage themselves under real competitive conditions after initially being passive.

Figure 174

7. Throwing and kicking the ball clear. After successfully saving the ball the goalkeeper initiates an attack by quickly throwing or kicking the ball to a team-mate in a free position. If his own side has been under pressure, then it is advisable for him to clear the ball as far upfield as possible where the centre-forward is lurking. The rule dictates that the goalkeeper is only permitted to take four steps with the ball before releasing it.

Exercise: An inside forward who hits high crosses time and time again into the penalty area; three strikers attempt to convert the ball under pressure from three defenders. When the goalkeeper saves the ball, the forwards hinder him from throwing or kicking the ball clear, while the players who had been in defence up till that point switch to attack and quickly run clear. Perpetual switching between attack and defence when the goalkeeper is in possession. Throw the ball out to the wing or kick it out to the inside forward who is running through.

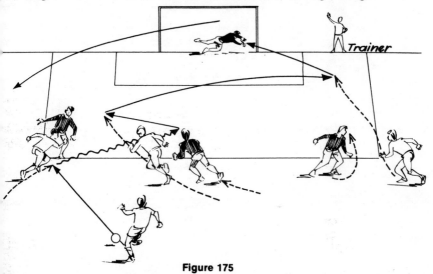

Figure 175

8. Four play against three with one goal. In this game, the coach directs and corrects the action. The overall tactical behaviour of the goalkeeper should be practised as the main object of the exercise. He should control his positioning, direct the defence, be on the alert for concealed shots fired at him unexpectedly, catch high crosses in the area when free to act, fist the ball away when under pressure or, if he recognises that he cannot get to the ball, stay in goal. Rapidly switch to attack.

More than any other team position, a good performance in goal depends on talent. The ability to sense and consciously anticipate dangerous situations as well as reacting quickly to unexpected and unpredictable balls are special qualities of the goalkeeper, which can only be improved and consolidated by means of match-oriented training.

Intensive, thoughtful realisation of the conditional basis as well as competition-oriented coming to terms with technical and tactical training tasks form confidence in one's own ability and as a result, the goalkeeper's self-confidence which is so essential for the solid foundation of a side. While the coach works with other team groups, the goalkeepers should keep themselves occupied with self-training outside the goal.

Duration of each exercise: 1 minute, then 1 minute gymnastics with the ball as active recreation.

Figure 176

1. Throw the ball in the air whilst running smoothly, jump up to reach it, collect it as high in the air as possible and clutch it to your body safely.

Figure 177

2. Two balls, one lying within jumping range to the left, the other to the right of where the goalkeeper has positioned himself. The goalkeeper dives alternately to the left and right and uses both hands to grip the ball. *To be observed:* When diving for the ball, land on the side of your body, not on the stomach and elbows!

194

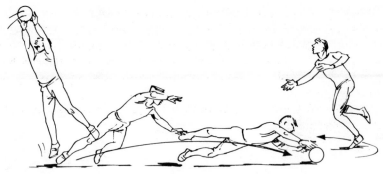

Figure 178

3. The goalkeeper throws one ball up in the air *vertically* and then dives for a second ball, which is lying within jumping range to his side (see Exercise 2). He rises as quickly as possible from the ground in order to collect and catch the falling ball if possible by leaping towards it. The ball is allowed to bounce once to begin with.

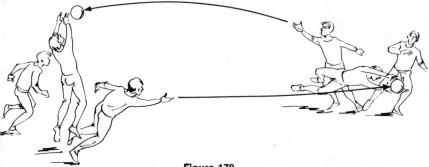

Figure 179

4. Two goalkeepers stand facing one another some 10 to 15 metres apart. They throw the ball to one another alternating between low, half-volley, high or sidewards. In the process, the goalkeepers spurt quickly to change positions with one another.

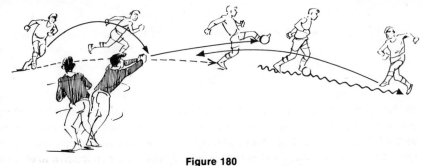

Figure 180

5. Two goalkeepers, the one throws or crosses the ball high in the air to his partner and spurts sidewards into position. The goalkeeper leaps up and fists the ball back sidewards to the new position taken up by his partner.

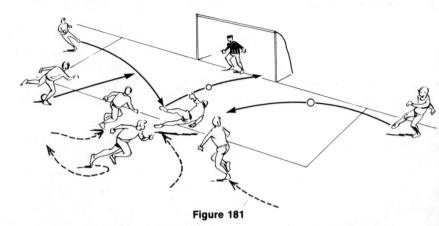

Figure 181

6. *"Pressure training"*. One goalkeeper in goal. Crosses are alternately sent over from the left and the right and shot at goal from outside the penalty area. Four or five forwards are distributed in front of goal, ready to convert the crosses. The forwards should rapidly interchange with one another when shooting from outside the area.

8.2. THE BACK DEFENDER

The two defenders have to ward off the opponent's attacks up the wings. Their direct opponents are nifty, fast, can turn on the spot and are full of tricks. Their prime task in terms of tactics is to roll up the defence out on the wings. Previously, we have mentioned the significance of man-to-man marking which is to be preferred to marking the zone. The defender and his playing behaviour is now analysed from this basic position.

The defender also possesses certain characteristic traits which suit him for the role, a role in which he feels at home and can reach his optimal performance capacity. Thus each defender must possess the talent to fulfil basic tasks. However, practice reveals that defenders can be split up into two basic types, whose range of functions differ from each other. First of all, there is the defender who faces up to and adapts himself to his direct opponent furnished with unlimited concentration and attentiveness, who effectively combats him and achieves his optimal top performance. The type of defender, who feels at home and is full of confidence and who appears to be bursting at the seams regarding his enthusiasm to defend, providing that is, he has a definite task to fulfil, but who possesses only limited possibilities when it comes to attack. The other type is the defender who

196

not only masters the basic task of marking his man but who can rapidly and flexibly adjust himself to the characteristics of other defenders and who also masters all the possibilities of attacking play.

Once again we are faced with the fact that both types can effectively fulfil their basic tasks but as a result of individual traits and extended qualities with regard to their talent, their means of functioning can be different.

The development of the game is of course tending towards the type of defender who is just as skilfully able to take part in attacking play over and beyond his defensive qualities and who produces a surprise moment of danger in front of the opposing goal by dint of his verve and penetrating skill. The tactical basic tasks of the defender are

a) Positioning
b) Defensive engagement
c) Attacking play

8.2.1. *Positioning*

As the winger's direct opponent he takes up a position in such a way that he
a) is nearer to his own goal than his opponent, on the "inner line",
b) covers from the side nearest the ball, i. e., from the side from where a pass can be expected,
c) ensures he keeps a sufficient distance from his opponent so that his speed suffices to intercept his opponent's pass, or in the case of a through pass, he takes advantage of the shorter distance which he has to cover and arrives on the ball before his opponent,
d) manoeuvres an opponent who is dribbling with the ball out to the touch-line thus narrowing the space he can move in,
e) follows the movement of the interchanging winger along the "inner line" and
f) covers the area, i. e., he increases the distance between himself and his opponent (in the direction of the near goalpost) if the action on the ball is remote from him and his direct opponent is not in a position to accept the ball.

Together with the libero, who orientates himself more towards the ball, he takes up position behind him to provide for additional cover in the area. When doing so, he selects the distance between himself and his opponent in such a way that should there be a sudden switch from one wing to the other he can get back in position again fast enough in order to cover his opponent.

8.2.2. *Defensive Involvement*

Good positioning, the ability to interpret the opponent's attacking intentions rapidly as well as powerful, but at the same time collected behaviour in combating the opponent in possession govern the defender's defensive involvement. Concentrated observation and surveillance of the opposing side's attacking play at all times as well as the ability to recognise the playing traits of his direct opponent are essential prerequisites for fast and controlled defensive behaviour.

197

The good defender knows how to adjust himself to the type of opponent as rapidly as possible. As a rule, he knows his opponent from previous games and can then programme himself in advance correspondingly and concentrate on his opponent's special traits in special training.

The technically gifted player who can dribble strongly and who is full of tricks should on no account be allowed to start revealing his special qualities. Consequently, the defender must attempt to prevent his opponent getting to the ball. He should intercept him at the very latest when he is collecting the ball, powerfully but fairly. When tackling him, the defender must concentrate on trying to blunt the edge of his technically brilliant opponent, who frequently is a sensitive player; to try and reduce his attacking enthusiasm and enjoyment of the game. Should the strong-dribbling and tricky winger be in possession and approaching the defender, the defender must prevent him from cutting inside and should force him out to the touch-line. In this way he narrows the space the winger has to move in, and is able to combat him more effectively in this position (sliding-tackle). If the winger dribbles up towards him and has a team-mate in position nearby then there is a strong possibility of a one-two movement. In this case, the running speed with which the winger approaches the defender is greater than when dribbling towards him bent on making use of a deceptive manoeuvre. In the latter case, the winger tends to approach the defender stealthily in order to deceive the defender with a sudden change of speed and surprise alterations of movement and attempt the break-through.

Feints are intended to cause the defender to commit a false movement. E. g. short, restrained dribbling inside followed by a sudden burst of speed to get past the defender on the inside is intended to cause him to follow this movement. This feint, which indicates that the winger is about to break through via the dangerous inside route to goal requires the defender to cut off this dangerous route. The winger takes advantage of this in order to suddenly spurt past the defender on the outside. Then the winger attempts to shake off the defender by means of the "locomotive" or by "shearing over the ball" or other possible deceptions (see Chapter on Feinting).

Some wingers are able to feint the break-through inside and then on the outside, only then to cut inside again. This example reveals that it is essential for the defender to come to terms with strong-dribbling opponents in special training in order to learn how to apply his speed of reaction properly and in a controlled fashion.

Frequently, defenders become the victims of their own unbridled defensive drive in that they follow up every feint. It can often be observed that such defenders allow themselves to be outmanoeuvred in that the winger draws the defender with him by dribbling for a short distance in the direction opposite the one of attack only then to turn suddenly in the direction of attack and leave the defender behind him. Thus the conclusion which should be drawn here is that the defender should on no account follow up deceptive movements which are designed to draw him away from the "inner line". It is far better to allow the winger to "come" in order to intercept him when he is attempting the decisive break-through.

Strong-running, athletic wingers make the attempt to outrun the defender by dint of their speed. Usually, they do not possess the variable playing skill of the tricky dribbler but instead they are far more straightforward in their plaxing behaviour and as a consequence, easier for the defender to read. This type of winger should basically be covered from a distance by the defender. In such cases, he must be on the watch for one-two movements and other forms of the through pass. Frequently, they dribble towards the defender at full pelt and play the square pass to the "wall" from a distance of some 5 metres; at the same time, they move forward in top gear in order to reach the through pass before the defender.

This underlines once again the importance of marking at a distance in order to counter-act sprinting speed as a tactical means.

It is impossible to determine and describe all the variations of the winger's game. In the end effect, a player's behaviour is not calculable. It results from the type of challenge posed by a playing situation, the player's genius and his intuition. Thus the defender has to learn through special training how to adapt himself to this multitude of possibilities in the winger's behaviour. Above all, he has to learn to differentiate between when to attack and intercept his opponent or whether he should stay at a distance and allow him to come towards him.

8.2.3. Attacking Play

Once the defender has regained possession of the ball, he immediately switches to attack. His defensive action is not over and finalised until he has got an attack going safely and purposively.

He launches an attack by

a) passing the ball safely. In this connection, the midfield schemer, who is best able to continue the attack thanks to his special qualities, should have priority here, providing of course, the ball can be passed to him without risk. Long square passes in front of your own goal are dangerous and should be avoided if possible.

b) The defender counter-attacks by "driving" the ball forward. He should dribble without taking any risk and rounds off his move with a shot at goal or a cross.

Once the attacking move has been concluded, he moves back to his defensive position as quickly as possible. While he is up in attack, the libero takes over the organisation of "covering his back".

Counter-attacking by the defender is particularly effective if it takes place in the right moment. That is to say, if the opponent has just been robbed of the ball after putting all he had into the attacking move and the defender has managed to leave his opponent behind him as a result of his interception, e. g. if he has managed to intercept his pass, or his opponent has fallen to the ground as a result of a sliding-tackle, or the goalkeeper has caught the ball and the defender leaves his defensive position and runs clear as rapidly as possible towards the touch-line.

The defender's task of actively participating in attack and consequently in the efforts of his team to score goal stands in contrast to his defensive behaviour with regard to his inherent qualities and the specific nature of the challenge. As a defender, he reacts to the ideas and actions of his direct opponent. As an attacking player, he is transformed into an active and creative player in that he now must reveal initiative and must attempt, employing the means of good attacking play, to assert himself on the ball and retain possession of it until he has concluded the move constructively.

This in fact should be the point of application in special training – designed to expand the limitations of his game in attack and his individual possibilities.

Here, there is also the chance for the coach – given the still persisting tendency towards reinforced "defensive might" – to improve the offensive strength of teams by improving the attacking qualities of the defenders and thus bring about a balance between attacking and defensive strength. Coaches can make a considerable contribution here with regard to maintaining and increasing the attractiveness and popularity of football.

The defender's attacking game takes place on the wing and from the wing and thus resembles the winger's game. The defender must move upfield with the ball, play one-two movements, be able to cross the ball and score goals. As far as possible, he should not get involved in senseless tackles whilst moving upfield. Notwithstanding, skilful behaviour in tackles is an important learning objective during special training. It appears important to me to realise that the defender should only participate in attack within the bounds of his own individual capabilities and that the possibility of improving his attacking game by means of directed training is only provided for within these bounds. Every attempt to copy highly talented defenders who are capable of exhausting and commanding all the possibilities both in defence and attack is doomed to failure. In fact, it leads frequently to the wrong behaviour in attacking play and can easily bring on uncertainty and frustration which affects his overall performance.

Thus, first and foremost, the defender is a defensive player and surprisingly becomes, in the tactically correct moment, a dangerous attacking player, within the bounds of his individual capabilities.

8.2.4. *Special Traits*

The defender is usually a thickset, athletic player type of medium build. He possesses the explosiveness to make him quick off the mark and strong in jumping. This explosive speed is allied to speed of reaction, acrobatic manoeuvrability and dexterity. The stamina he is equipped with, enables him to fulfil his tactical duties, duties such as executing rapid, reactive movements in defence, lightning-fast counter-attacking and taking part in attack and falling back immediately to take up his position in defence following the conclusion of his attacking

Sharp concentration, constant and directed attentiveness and the utmost vitality are the prerequisites for adjusting and reacting to the surprise actions of the opposing side as quickly as possible.

Furthermore, resolution and steadfastness mark his powerful engagement. His drive and strength of purpose provide him with the necessary basis of performance for effective attacking play as well.

8.2.5. *Special Training*

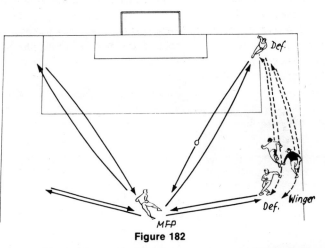

MFP

Figure 182

1. A midfield player passes the ball "short" or "through" into the area. The defender sprints after the ball, reaches it before the winger and plays it back to the midfield player. The winger puts the defender under pressure but initially makes no move to disturb the technical execution.

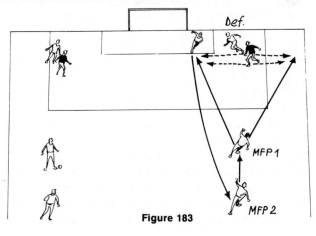

Figure 183

2. Midfield player 1 plays the ball to the left and right of the defender into the area.
a) The defender dribbles clear and then passes a "long" ball to midfield player 2,
b) plays the ball direct to midfield player 2.
The defender's pass to midfield player 2 is passed on direct to midfield player 1 (without holding up the ball).

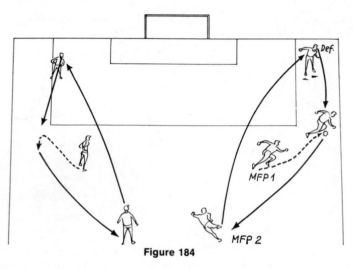

Figure 184

3. Midfield player 2 puts over crosses to the defender, who heads them accurately to midfield player 1 who has moved up in support. Midfield player 1 then passes the ball back to midfield player 2.

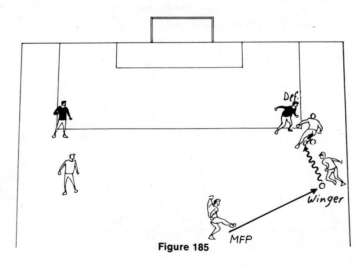

Figure 185

4. The defender observes that he cannot prevent the winger from collecting the ball. He does not attack him but lets him "come" instead. The winger tries to pass him, he feints and provokes him into making a move. The defender stops him from cutting inside. He leaves the gap on the outside free; in this way, he can react if the winger tries to pass him (possibly by means of a "sliding-tackle").

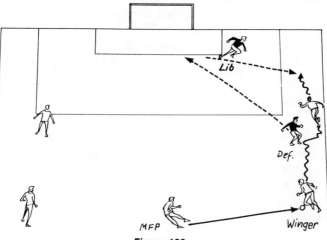

Figure 186

5. The winger has outplayed the defender. Pursuit is senseless. The "libero" challenges the winger and the defender races to take up the "libero's" position. If the libero is able to deprive the winger of the ball, he passes to the midfield player and the defender and the goalkeeper attempt to gain possession of the ball before the centre-forward.

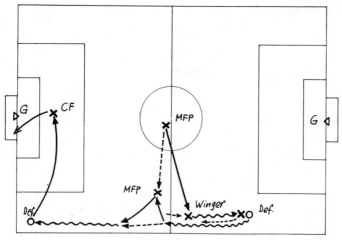

Figure 187

203

6. The midfield player passes the ball to the winger, who dribbles towards the defender. He loses the ball in his attempt to beat the defender. The defender counter-attacks, spurts up the wing, sets up a one-two movement with the midfield player, dribbles on and rounds off his action with a cross to the centre-forward who is lurking there ready to hit it home. Now, develop the same set-up starting from this goal in the opposite direction.

Note: These tasks require great intensity of movement, thus it is advisable to work with both full-backs alternately. The player opposing the defender should initially only put him under pressure but not disturb the execution of the move. Then, he increases his activity to real competitive behaviour.

8.3. THE CENTRE-BACK (STOPPER)

The centre-back, who is also known as the "stopper", plays in the centre of the defence against the centre-forward or the opposing side's spearhead. The task of combatting this striker who is usually strong both in shooting and in the air, requires athletic basic qualities. Jumping ability and speed of the mark, rapid and unperturbed reaction, strength in the air as well as thoughtful play using the instep are among the main characteristics of his playing behaviour. By means of rapid, space-bridging dribbling, rounded off with a shot at goal, he surprisingly moves up to take part in attack.

His tactical basic duties are the same as those which the full-backs have to fulfil (see Special Training for Defenders). His positioning is also based on the "inner line" and he covers his direct opponent from the side nearest the ball. Similarly, he attempts to cut off passes intended for the centre-forward before they reach him or to be quicker to the ball when a through pass is made.

If the spearhead moves out to the wing, he should pursue and combat him using the same means as we described in connection with full-backs. He carries out his defensive commitment powerfully but also perspicuously and thoughtfully. He analyses and recognises the essential traits and strengths of his opponent and knows how to adjust himself to his play in such a way that he is able to dominate him and consequently restrict his attacking effectiveness to as large a degree as possible.

With regard to attempting to intercept the ball before the pass reaches his opponent, he must be certain when spurting towards it that he will be able to get to the ball before his opponent does. If he should not reach it in time, there is the danger that he will be outmanoeuvred by the spearhead by means of a one-two or skilful turning and moving off with the ball.

It can often be observed that when the centre-back is attempting to cut off the short pass to the centre-forward that his opponent places himself so cleverly in the way of the centre-back on the ball that the defender finds he has been thrust out on to the "outer line" when the spearhead turns in the direction of attack.

Thus the centre-back must when spurting towards the ball at all costs avoid running too closely up against the spearhead. He must maintain his position on the inner line and select the distance to his opponent in such a way that he can separate the centre-forward from the ball while he is turning in the direction of attack. If the centre-back should be stranded on the outer line then it is up to the libero to pursue and combat the centre-forward as he breaks through. The centre-back immediately drops back to occupy the libero's position in order to establish the double-cover set-up once more.

He initiates his attacking play with a pass up the wing, to the spearhead or he gains territory with a long pass up to the foremost striker. He also counter-attacks and takes part in attack in the tactically appropriate moment and should attempt to round off his contribution to the attack with a shot at goal.

Should he take part in attack as an additional striker then it is essential that he is also brought into play and that an attempt is made to round off the attacking move using his services. Only then is it possible to take advantage of the centre-back moving up as an extra striker without the risk of weakening your own defence. The attack must be concluded in such a way that the centre-back has sufficient time to drop back to his defensive position.

8.3.1. Special Traits

The centre-back is big, strong and athletic. A physically strong and robust type of player is particularly essential in the centre of defence where the opposing attack is concentrating on scoring with all the means at its disposal. His playing behaviour is marked by strong fighting qualities but he must also be thoughtful. The centre-back is strong of will, uncompromising, purposive and consciencious. Even under extreme pressure he is able to remain cool an unperturbed thanks to his psychical stability. You can depend on him. He emanates coolness and is thus a pillar in the centre of the defence.

8.3.2. Special Training

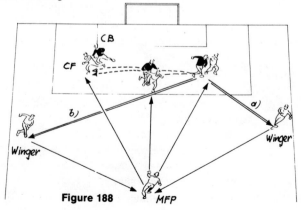

Figure 188

1. *The centre-back should intercept the pass intended for the centre-forward.* The centre-forward runs clear and the midfield player provides him with a pass either to the side, or a short or a through pass. Once the centre-back has successfully won the ball, it is passed back a) to the winger nearer the ball or b) to the winger further away on the other wing. *Note:* The centre-forward initially does not intervene, then genuine match behaviour.

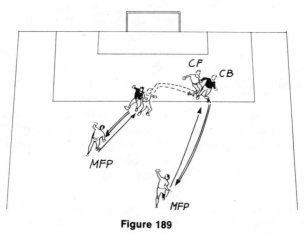

Figure 189

2. *Watch your positioning!* Always take up position at the side of your opponent from where the pass can be expected. Two midfield players, each with a ball. The centre-back should alternately react first to a short and then a long pass (passes, low and half-volley). A constructive pass is returned to the midfield player.

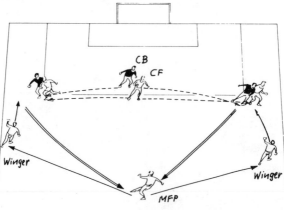

Figure 190

3. *The centre-back combats the centre-forward on the wing.* The midfield player alternately feeds the wingers. The centre-forward then breaks out to the wing and receives a through pass from the winger, which the centre-back should intercept. A constructive pass is returned to the midfield player. *Note:* The midfield player waits with his pass to the winger until the centre-forward and centre-back are back in the centre again.

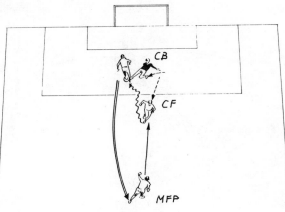

Figure 191

4. *The centre-back challenges and combats the dribbling centre-forward.* The centre-back is unable to prevent the centre-forward meeting the ball. The centre-forward dribbles slowly and provokingly up to the centre-back. *Note:* Do not allow yourself to be provoked so that you "make your thrust" prematurely; react and "make your thrust" when the centre-forward is trying to spurt past you (sliding tackle).

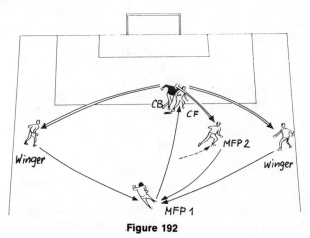

Figure 192

5. *Training with the head.* The midfield player sends in high volleys, which the centre-back either a) heads short to the midfield player 2 who is running clear or b) heads long to one of the two wingers. Midfield player 2 and the wingers pass the ball to midfield player 1. *Extension:* Place the centre-back under pressure with a number of balls and rapid passing sequences. The centre-forward increases his activity.

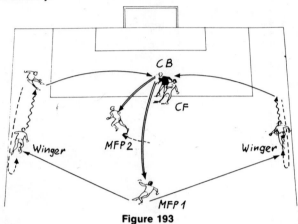

Figure 193

6. *The centre-back wards off crosses.* The midfield player alternately passes to the wingers; they dribble with the ball and cross it. The centre-back heads the crosses short to midfield player 2 or long to midfield player 1. *Extension:* Two and more opponents, who behave increasingly in a competitive manner. Use a number of balls and put the crosses over in more rapid succession.

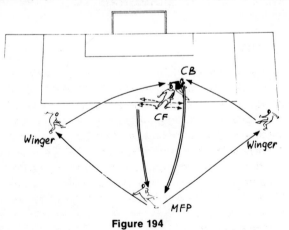

Figure 194

7. *The centre-back practises the "volley kick".* The midfield player and the two wingers put over volleys or crosses into the centre-back's defensive zone. The

centre-back uses the "volley kick" to pass the balls to the midfield player who feeds them back to the wingers. *Note:* Select other possibilities of passing the ball if the "volley kick" is not feasible. Extension: A more rapid sequence of balls.

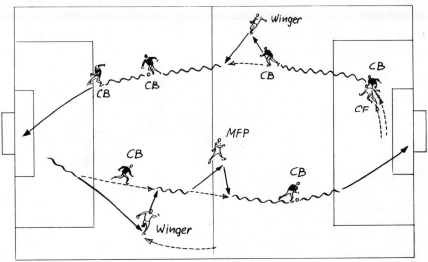

Figure 195

8. *The centre-back counter attacks* after winning the ball. a) The centre-back dribbles upfield, plays a one-two with the winger or midfield player, b) he moves up to the winger along with his pass, has the ball returned, dribbles, executes a one-two and rounds off the move with a shot at goal. *Note:* Include all technical and tactical main aspects. Build up the same situation and task from the other side.

8.4. THE "LIBERO"

The provocative trait in the development of the game of football continues to be the reinforced "might of defence". The former "double stopper" or sweeper as he is known in England, experienced his rather dubious moments of glory as far as the game was concerned during the 1962 World Cup in Chile. At the time, many were concerned about the beauty and attraction of the game of football and quite justifiably so, for here, quite in contrast to the actual basic concept of the game of adopting a positive approach to the scoring of goals, the prevention of goals occupied pride of place in the prevailing types of system. The defence was reinforced and the "sweeper" became the key figure in this reinforced defence. All over the world, a warning finger was raised pointing to a destructive development of the game. However, in Chile, the German team, managed by Sepp Herberger, actually played with what was for the time a very progressive sweeper in the person of Karl-Heinz Schnellinger, who readily moved up into attack and who introduced the functional development of the modern "libero", as is for instance, incorporated nowadays in a brilliant manner by Franz Beckenbauer.

The "free defender" has for long now been by no means identical with the stopper of earlier years. Indeed, nowadays the libero has a whole range of concrete duties to fulfil which have raised him to the level of a dominating playing personality. He covers the zone behind his fellows who are marking man-to-man and he is equally free in deciding whether to move up to take part in attacking play until it is rounded off by a shot at goal or to send one of the defenders who are marking man-to-man up front to reinforce the attack. As a consequence the libero has emerged as the central figure in the reinforced defence but also as the driving force for more powerful and penetrating attacking play which has developed from this reinforced defence.

The tasks linked to this position call for perspicuity, imperturbability, a comprehensive understanding of the game, determination and qualities of leadership They can only be fulfilled by an experienced, responsible and consciencious playing personality.

The libero must master both zone defence and man-to-man covering and in addition, be aware of exactly how to react in attack. This functional diversity calls for certain qualities which the libero must possess.

The tactical basic duties of the libero are:

a) He is the boss and director of the defence. You should also hear him during play if for instance, he has to correct mistakes made by his team-mates by shouting instructions to them or if he calls on one of his fellow defenders to move up in order to counter-attack.

b) He operates freely in the zone behind his fellow defenders covering the man and guards the "lanes". He lies in wait in this deep position, concentrating fully, ready to cut off through passes.

c) He covers the back of his team-mates in front of him, in that he challenges and combats the opponent who has outplayed one of his team-mates. The defender who has been outplayed moves back as swiftly as possible to take up the libero's position.

d) He bars the path of attack of an opponent who has moved up to reinforce the attack in that he challenges and combats him outside scoring range. He moves out of his deep position early enough in order to be able to challenge the additional opponent in attack surely and safely. He should on no account venture too far outside the funnel-shaped defensive zone in front of goal nor for instance, attack the opposing player dribbling towards him too soon or overhastily. By means of such behaviour he would be outplayed thus surrendering the advantage of the numerically superior defence. On the other hand, if he challenges his opponent too late or even remains rooted in his deep position covering the zone, he would provide the opposing player with the chance to unleash an undisturbed shot at goal.

Switching from the zone defence to covering the man is something which the libero must practise time and time again in special training in order to acquire the proper feeling for timing with regard to this functional transformation.

e) He covers up for the defenders covering in front of him when they move up to take part in attacking play.

f) Finally, the libero himself takes part in attack and strives towards scoring success. He counter-attacks and covers the territory leading to the opposing goal at maximum dribbling speed. En route, he exploits the possibility of one-two movements in that he uses the spearheads as the wall (see Chapter on One-Two Movement).

However, on no account should he allow himself to be too one-sided and stereotyped in the application of his attacking means. Above all, the one-two should not represent the only means of penetrating into the opposing penalty area. In front of the densely populated box in particular, the surprise shot at goal still represents the most effective alternative to the one-two movement. While the libero moves up into attack, a midfield player stays back for safety's sake. This safety measure is necessary in order to delay the opponent's counter-attack sufficiently in the event of the libero losing possession so that he is able to return to his defensive position as rapidly as possible in order to strengthen the defence.

8.4.1. *Special Traits*

The libero combines the qualities of the defender with those of the midfield schemer. As a defender he is the type of player who is able to rapidly adjust to new situations and other opponents. His position as the last defender with the task of covering the zone, to act flexibly as "double cover" behind his fellows in front who are covering the man, calls for comprehensive tactical playing understanding, circumspection and anticipation.

Thus his overall attentiveness and ability to concentrate is an essential special trait, which differ from the related qualities of back defenders and centre-backs which concentrate on one particular focal point. Having talked to defenders and centre-backs who have played in the libero position simply because no one else was available, I am aware how uncomfortable they felt and were bound to feel in their task of defending the zone. Here, it once again clearly emerges that special traits govern a player's suitability for a given position. A player can only then reach his optimal performance capacity when the tasks he is required to fulfil in the position he is playing in correspond to his specific inherent qualities. His ability to make contact and adapt himself enable him to fulfil both the tasks of covering the zone as well as the man. His understanding of the game qualifies him for the role of schemer. He organises the defence employing his qualities of leadership and produces impulses for thoughtful attacking play. His tactical duties, which require a large radius of action from him, in that first of all he must be on the scene when danger threatens from the opposing attack and on the other hand, he should be there to help round off his own side's attack and then drops back as rapidly as possible, mean that in terms of condition, he must be quick off the mark and possess stamina. Similarly, the libero should be an excellent technically adept player who commands the ball during rapid combinations involving both short or long passes and who is also good in the air. He is able to dribble trickily and is in a position to assert himself in tackles.

Only a strong playing personality with diverse inherent traits and talent is able to embody the role of the libero optimally.

8.4.2. *Special Training*

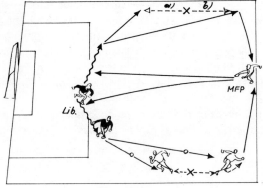

Figure 196

1. *The "libero" stands in his defensive zone ready to intercept* long, low and high passes from the midfield player. He moves to the side with the ball and plays it to the winger who a) moves in close to offer his support, b) moves up the wing. *Extension:* The libero plays direct to the winger, heading should be taken into account!

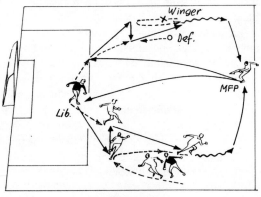

Figure 197

212

2. The libero intercepts *long passes* and sends the winger off by means of the "one-two". A defender covers the winger. If the one-two movement is not possible, he plays the square pass direct to the midfield player.
Please observe: Along with the pass to the winger spurt into position to the side of him in order to be able to play the square pass direct!

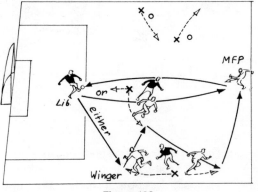

Figure 198

3. *Intercepting volleys.* The pass is made to the forwards running clear at high speed (maintain a fair distance to the libero!). Decide whether a pass is possible or not! Otherwise, pass to the midfield player. The forwards play the ball back to the midfield player. Attack and defence switch round when possession is lost.

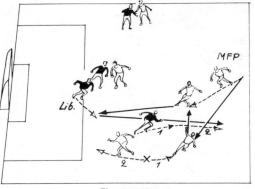

Figure 199

4. *The libero guards the "lanes".* The midfield player sets up a one-two with the winger or the centre-forward.
Please observe: The libero *should not yet* be standing in the "lane"! In this way, he provokes the one-two and is then able to intercept it. His attacking play is executed by passing to the counter-attacking defender or the midfield player.

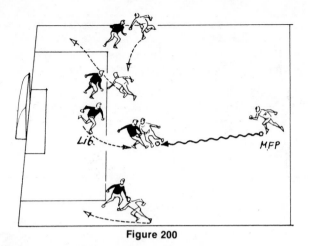

Figure 200

5. *The libero challenges and combats the free opposing attacker.* As Figure 199. The midfield player should now attack and dribbles in the direction of goal. The strikers interchange. The libero moves up and challenges his opponent outside goal-scoring range.

Please observe: Do not combat your opponent by "launching your thrust" at him until he attempts to pass you!

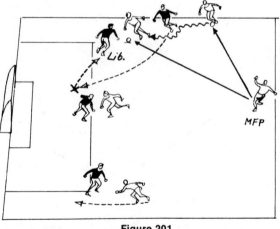

Figure 201

6. *The libero takes over the opponent of an outplayed team-mate.* As Figure 200. The opponent is outplayed a) by dribbling. The libero challenges and combats the opponent (see Figure 200). The opponent is outplayed b) by means of a through pass. By means of a *sliding tackle,* he is able to reach the through pass just before the opposing attacker.

214

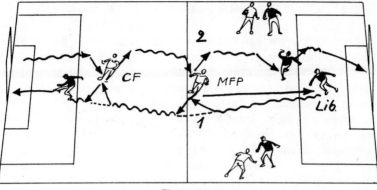

Figure 202

7. *The libero counter-attacks* himself and attempts to round off the move with a shot. Procedure as before. The libero in possession dribbles at high speed towards the opposing goal. In the process he sets up a one-two with the midfield player and the centre-forward. He then rounds off the move with a shot at goal. *Extension:* Moving in the other direction, he must penetrate the opposing defence, a) by shooting at the right moment at goal or b) by means of a one-two. *Please observe:* Attempt to counter-attack without risk!

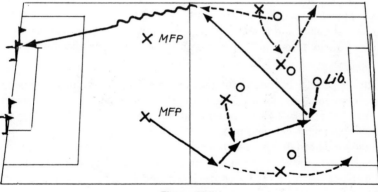

Figure 203

8. *The libero as defensive general.* Play attack against defence with two midfield players, four strikers, opposed by four man-to-man defenders and the libero. The defence counter-attacks against two goals marked by flags. a) The libero counter-attacks himself, b) he takes up the position left empty by his fellow defenders counter-attacking, c) he directs a counter-attack by the whole defence. *Please observe:* Attack in a deep-set formation so that if the ball should be lost, your defence can be formed as quickly as possible again.

8.5. THE MIDFIELD PLAYER

No matter which system the available types of players are classified and coordinated in the midfield always bears the major responsibility for forming attacking play. This is where the decision is made whether the attacking game is carried out at a more reserved pace, wait-and-see with surprise changes of tempo, if for instance, an already organised defence has to be overcome, or whether the midfield should be covered as rapidly as possible in a single move as for instance, in the case of the surprise counter-attack and moving up of a defender. No matter what the overall situation with regard to the manoeuvering of team-mates and opponents is, a corresponding adjustment is demanded from the midfield player. In midfield, three types of players are coordinated who, according to their special traits, have certain basic tasks to fulfil:

a) the creative schemer,
b) the primarily defensive midfield player and
c) the midfield player operating as "second spearhead".

The creative schemer in midfield directs and moulds attacking play. Günter Netzer and Wolfgang Overath are outstanding models in this position. The midfield schemer fulfils his tasks with intelligent, tactically clever playing understanding, alert concentration, wide-ranging attentiveness and command. He is full of temperament and dynamic, full of inner driving force, but at the same time controlled and perspicuous, responsible, consciencious and purposeful. He possesses excellent physical condition and he distinguishes himself through comprehensive technical ability and special playing skill. If the other side is in possession, he knows how to assert himself both in covering the zone and the man.

His tactical basic duties are:

a) Creatively setting up thoughtful attacking play. He determines the pace and rhythm of the game and knows exactly when to select the tactically appropriate moment to pass the ball. He is always ready to take over the ball in order to properly fulfil his match-forming role.
b) He is the motor in that he displays his temperament by driving on the spearheads with territory-bridging passes. He initiates one-twos and acts as "wall".
c) He executes the "one-two" with the spearhead as "wall" and attempts to penetrate on his own and shoot at goal.
d) He dribbles with a sudden burst of speed when he sees openings and strives – in conjunction with the strikers who are running clear and interchanging – to penetrate on his own and shoot at goal as an alternative to passing the ball.
e) He is able to assert himself and come out on top in tackles.
f) He is not only the schemer, but also lethal and with finishing ability.
g) Once possession is lost he at once switches to defence, delays the opposing attack in midfield, drops back at the same rate as the opposing attack into the defensive zone in front of goal and marks and combats an opposing attacker. After

concluding his defensive task he immediately runs clear in order to be able to take over the ball again.

8.5.1. *Special Traits*

The midfield schemer is an athletic type of player, possessing stamina and special creative ability. He possesses a strong inner driving force, an impulsive sense of urgency and strength of will, by means of which he determines his playing behaviour according to free decision. He also has the gift of intensive and steadfast concentration and wide attentiveness. These qualities make it possible for him to anticipate, comprehend and read the most complicated events of play and to operate over an extensive area. His effervescent brilliance is expressed by the surprise change in his attacking means. He is brimming with temperament, full of elan and dynamism, but at the same time, controlled, self-possessed and balanced. He is untiring in his operations and resignation is an unknown quantity as far as he is concerned. Expecially when he is being pressed by a determined opponent or the opposing side has won the initiative. His motorial talent and adaptability make it possible for him to control the ball at top pace and in the most precarious match situations. The midfield player is a playing personality of a particularly differentiated and diverse mould.

8.5.2. *Special Training*

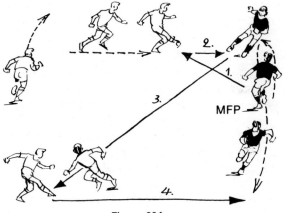

Figure 204

1. *The midfield player practises the "short" pass.* Three or more players move freely in a restricted area. Each pass to one of the players running clear is passed back to him. The midfield player plays a) with two touches of the ball, b) direct. He alternates between low, half-volley and high balls and the returns to him are carried out in similar fashion. Run clear to the side of his pass!

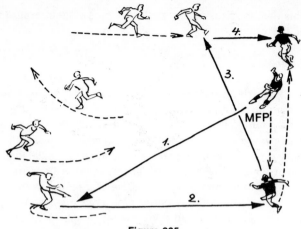

Figure 205

2. *The midfield player practises the "long" pass.* Procedure as in Figure 204. The midfield player passes the ball at a distance of some 30 metres using his instep into the path of his team-mates as they run clear. Passing variations as in Figure 204. The return passes should be brought under control. *Extension:* Make two touches suffice!

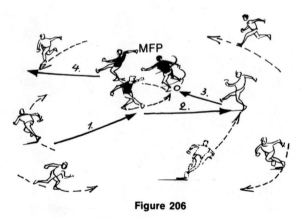

Figure 206

3. *Meeting and moving with the ball with a short turn in the direction of attack.* The midfield player operates between two groups of players and meets and moves with the balls played to him from the one group with a short turn facing the other group of players. Once the midfield player has the ball safely under control, his pass is called for by swiftly spurting clear. *Please observe:* Run towards the ball as it is passed!

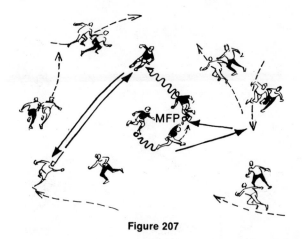

Figure 207

4. *Hold the ball and dribble with it.* Decide on the *moment for passing the ball.* Three against three in two playing areas bordering one another run clear. The midfield player operates between the groups. Each pass is returned to the midfield player. He alternately links up with both groups and passes the ball only then when the possibility has arisen as a result of running clear. Practise "long" passes by increasing the distance between the playing areas.

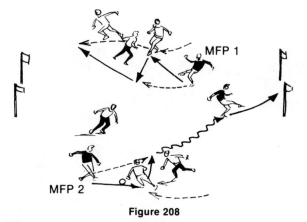

Figure 208

5. *The midfield player practises "one-two movements".* Three against three between two goals. The midfield player runs into position along with his pass and offers himself as the "wall". When he receives the square pass, he returns it as a through ball into the path of the forward as he runs clear. Following a shot at goal, he then joins forces with the other group in the direction of the second goal. This time he moves up with the square pass and adopts a striking position and shoots at goal.

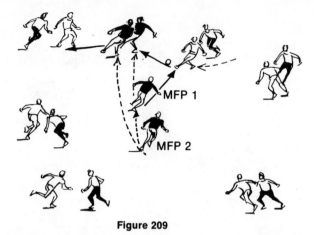

Figure 209

6. *The midfield player practises tackles.* Procedure as under Figure 207. Two midfield players, who play opposite one another and who, when in possession, alternately pass the ball to their fellow players in the two playing areas. They must now attempt to run clear, assert themselves and having come out on top, play the ball into the other area under pressure. Practise "long" passes by increasing the distance between the playing areas!

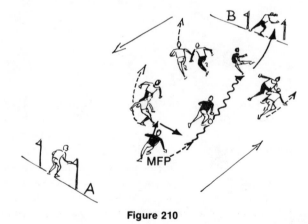

Figure 210

7. *The midfield player practises shots at goal from long range.* The midfield player plays with three strikers against three defenders between two goals. With A against B in the one direction, with B against A in the other. Interpassing, each pass is returned to the midfield player who then a) while dribbling make use of the forwards running clear and round off the break-through with a shot at goal. b) Shoot at goal following one-two with the sparhead. c) Convert return passes.

220

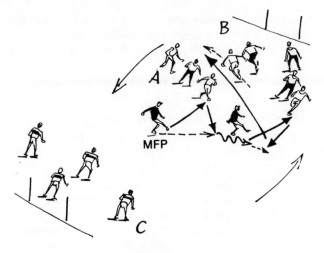

Figure 211

8. *The midfield player drives on the strikers.* Three teams alternating against two goals. Together with A he attacks B, together with B he plays against C, with C against A, etc. When attacking, each pass is returned to him until a shot at goal is possible. a) Midfield player initates "one-two movements" in that he offers himself as "wall" along *with* his pass, b) practise surprise switch of wings as a main aspect.

8.6. THE DEFENSIVE MIDFIELD PLAYER

This type of player is equipped primarily with defensive qualities. He masters both covering the man and the zone and usually faces up the second spearhead unless special tactical measures require him to cover another opponent (both in England and Mexico, Beckenbauer played against the English schemer Bobby Charlton). His actions in defence and active are characterised by a strong driving force and never-tiring involvement. His attacking actions are restricted to a relatively narrow area. His capacity to concentrate and attentiveness are more of a restricted nature and consequently orientated to the more immediate playing environment. He drives the attack on his side forward and largely links up with the winger. But he is also strong in dribbling and tackling and lethal.

Through his extremely strong involvement in attack, he is able to commit his direct opponent to defensive duties as Franz Beckenbauer demonstrated against England in Mexico. In terms of fitness, this type of player has to be quick off the

221

mark, manoeuvrable and endowed with a great deal of stamina. This midfield player with his versatile qualities is first of all an essential factor in defence but equally effective in attack by dint of his dynamic offensive drive and is a strong support for the schemer.

8.6.1. *The "Second Spearhead"* (The front midfield player)

In the basic system he plays behind the centre-forward. His range of action is by far the widest. He pops up lethally in the foremost striking position on both wings and drops back to take over defensive duties in front of his own goal.

His tactical basic duties are consequently very varied:

a) His clever play off the ball. By running to make use of space he opens up "lanes" and gives his team-mates the chance to interchange and switch around as well as providing the man on the ball with a chance to penetrate.

b) He is there to receive the ball from the other two midfield players and from the defensive player moving up in attack.

c) He attempts to break through on his own in order to score. He e. g. makes use of the lethal centre-forward moving out to the side and running clear in order to go it alone, executes the one-two with the centre-forward as "wall" and during interpassing moves to take up the spearhead position.

d) If the schemer or defensive midfield player moves up front, he ensures their back is covered in midfield.

e) His defensive operations concern the pursuit and challenging of the opponent in possession who is in his vicinity, delaying in midfield and integrating himself in the defensive block in front of goal.

8.6.2. *Special Traits*

The basis for such a range of operation is overall good physical condition. He is exemplary with regard to stamina, which he allies with steadfast preparedness "to do battle". Speed off the mark, versatility and creativity – these are qualities evident in his attacking game and he reveals the ability to react when he is in attack. He fulfils his tasks diligently, conscienciously and thoughtfully. No distance is ever too great! He is perpetually in motion – unselfishly, and as a result, the manifold attacking means of his team-mates, above all, those of the schemer are triggered off and can really become effective.

The type of player who plays as the "second spearhead" makes contact easily, is ready to integrate himself and in all cases plays in the interests of his side.

Well harmonised midfield play in which each of the midfield players fulfils his basic duties according to his special inherent traits, but which first really blends properly as a result of their integrative coordination, is the heart, the driving force of a good playing side.

8.7. THE CENTRE-FORWARD

We immediately associate two names with the position of centre-forward: Uwe Seeler and Gerd Müller. The centre-forward plays as the lethal finisher in the foremost striking position.

His tactical basic duties are:

a) To score goals either by going it alone or by finishing off a move, no matter from where he approaches goal, from midfield or when converting crosses to round off an attack up the wing.

b) As the foremost spearhead he can meet territory-bridging through passes. He serves as the "wall" during one-two movements.

c) By means of surprise changes of speed and variable running, without the ball, close to goal, he puts himself in a scoring position or ties up opponents, thus creating space for other strikers moving up to penetrate and shoot at goal.

d) The centre-forward pursues his opponent if he loses possession and fights to regain the ball.

8.7.1. *Special Traits*

A sense of purpose, a strong will and inner driving force, the determination to assert himself and steadfastness enable him to come out on top and assert himself in the explosive, all-deciding field of tension in front of goal.

Mental stability and robustness enable him to perform in a seemingly carefree and calm fashion even in the tighest situations. He aims for the fastest possible solutions to given situations – also when interpassing. He plays simply and safely.

The ability to be able to act and react at lightning speed facilitates surprise, intuitive behaviour in the tightest penalty area situations under great pressure. The centre-forward lies in wait, vigilantly, ready to get to the ball and to take advantage of a scoring chance in a split second in front of his opponent's goal. He possesses strong fighting qualities and allows no ball to go lost unchased. The centre-forward is an athletically strong and resilient type of player. He is characterised by his speed off the mark and his spurting speed as well as his outstanding jumping ability. A further characteristic is his greater-than-average manoeuvrability.

Technically speaking, he employs the simplest means to master the match situations he has to solve. He packs a strong shot and can head the ball accurately in all situations. Indeed, his will to get to the ball before his opponent is most pronounceably evident when it comes to heading the ball.

The centre-forward who has the prime responsibility of getting the ball in the back of the opposing net is a decisively important player personality. But he too, needs other players to help him, for only through their effectiveness can he really unfold his own qualities.

8.7.2. Special Training

1. *The centre-forward dribbles and forces his way towards goal.* Two defenders bar his path without moving in to intercept. Once a defender is outplayed, he immediately spurts back to take up position behind the second one. The centre-

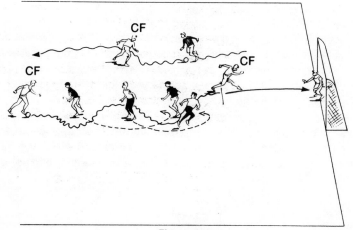

Figure 212

forward shoots at goal from a marking line. Another player moves with the ball trying to pass him in the opposite direction and the centre-forward practises defensive behaviour.

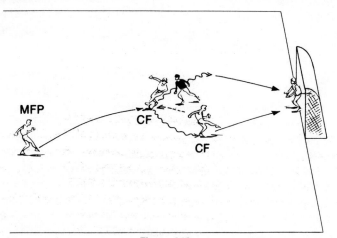

Figure 213

2. The centre-forward brings low, half-volley and high passes under control against the resistance of an opponent and then heads at goal. Meet and move with the ball employing the inner and outer side of the foot, the chest, the instep, etc.

Free yourself from your opponent at the proper moment and run towards the ball.

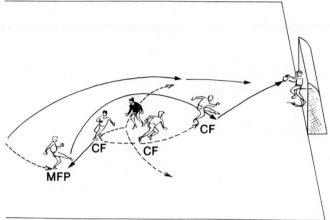

Figure 214

3. The centre-forward runs clear and converts the pass direct – if at all possible. The centre-forward also runs through the centre and meets the pass which has been lobbed over his head in the direction of running and shoots at goal. Or: the centre-forward moves up "short" and allows the ball to rebound to the midfield player, then moves through and picks up and shoots the ball played over his head at goal.

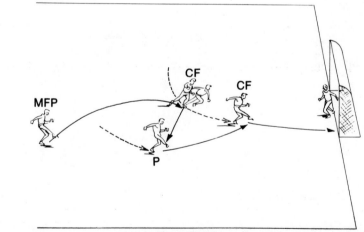

Figure 215

4. The centre-forward plays the long passes he receives from the midfield player direct to player 2 who runs clear and spurts into a free space along *with* his pass. He meets the return pass from player 2 and moves towards goal and shoots.

225

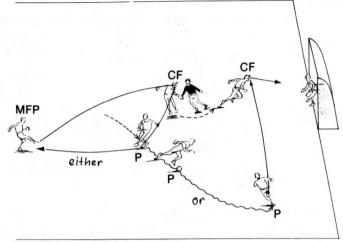

Figure 216

5. The midfield player plays long high balls which the centre-forward nods down to player 2 running clear. Player 2 either returns the ball to the midfield player or dribbles up the wing from where he crosses the ball either "soft" or "hard". The centre-forward runs to meet the crosses and heads at goal.

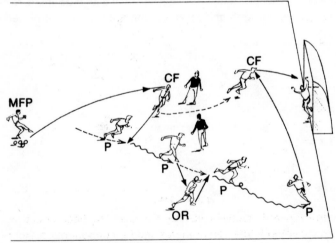

Figure 217

6. The centre-forwards uses his head or a volley (volley kick) to hit home crosses in the air. The crosses are passed in quick succession either "soft" or "hard" using the head, to player 2, who switches with the right-winger on the wing, linking up by means of a one-two movement, before crossing the ball. The two defenders maintain pressure but initially do not stop the execution.

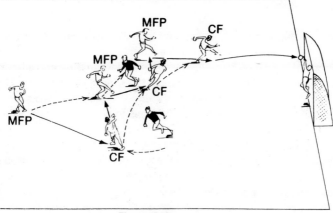

Figure 218

7. The centre-forward asserts himself against two defenders. By means of constant free running, he provides the midfield player, who should vary the manner of passing, with a chance to pass the ball. Only the centre-forward shoots at goal; he should create his own chances and make use of them.

Variations
Try to score from long range or to score only using the head.

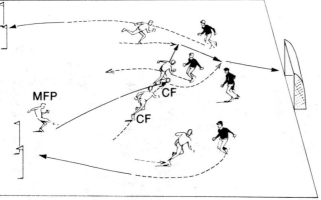

Figure 219

8. The centre-forward practises main technical and tactical aspects in a competitive environment with three team-mates and four opponents. a) Running clear, bringing himself into the game and creating openings, b) set up a one-two movement, in the process of which he acts as "wall" for the onrushing midfield player or returns his pass, runs through himself and calls for the one-two, c) the defence counter-attacks against two mini-goals marked by corner flags, the centre-forward chases after his opponents, delays them in midfield and attempts to regain possession.

8.8. THE WINGER

The winger is usually a compact, resilient type of player. He can turn on the spot, is strong in dribbling and clever in tackles, moves fast, is quick off the mark and lethal. He is distinguished by match cunning, determination and a never-say-die spirit. Apart from these traits and qualities, the winger must be able to meet and move with both low and high balls, to initiate and play one-two movements, to cross the ball at high speed and of course, has to possess an accurate and hard shot.

His tactical importance within the context of attacking play is particularly great nowadays in view of reinforced defensive formations. As a result of his play both on and from the touchline he makes openings, creates playing space for his team-mates and provides for a surprise switch of the ball and the attack from one wing to the other. By dint of his penetrating dribbling skill he is able to pierce the opposing defence. Once he has outplayed his opponent, he "cuts" the path of the opponent in pursuit and heads for goal. He rounds off his attacking move with a shot at goal or with a cross.

The winger also orientates himself to the inside and in the course of interpassing frequently switches to the other wing. In the process, he changes positions with the inner strikers or makes room on the wing for an onrushing defender. His direct task in defence is to cover the opposing defender when the opposing side initiates an attack or to thwart the defender's intentions by immediately setting

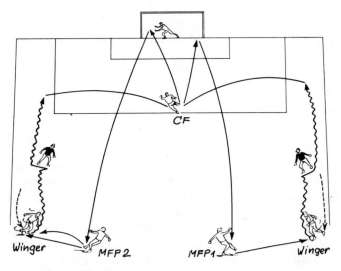

Figure 220 *The winger controls low and high passes*

off after him. Similarly, he also takes part in the midfield defensive measures (delaying) and in the organisation of the defence in front of goal. When the other side is taking a free-kick in front of his own goal, he should cover the wings alongside the defensive wall and is also in a position to cover up for a defender should his team-mate move up into attack.

All these possibilities of behaviour must be impressed in his consciousness by means of special training.

The midfield player plays low cross passes and volleys which the winger meets and moves with. The winger dribbles with the ball and outplays the defender. The centre-forward converts his crosses. The goalkeeper plays the ball to midfield player 2, who similarly serves the outside-left with low and high crosses.

Note

The defender initially acts in a passive fashion. He puts pressure on the winger, but initially does not hinder the execution of technical moves.

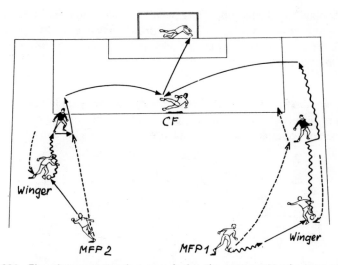

Figure 221 *The winger meets a low pass facing the opponent and moves with the ball*

Procedure as under Figure 220. The midfield player's pass to the winger is either transverse or straight through. The winger comes to meet the ball and then turns in the direction of attack. He then dribbles up to the defender, either executes a one-two movement with the midfield player as "wall" or exploits the possibility of a one-two to break through on his own. His crosses, alternately hit hard or soft, are converted by the centre-forward.

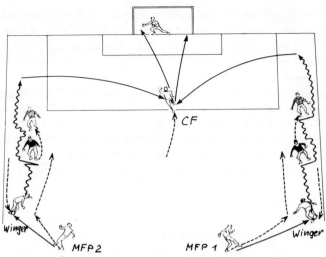

Figure 222 *Dribbling – feinting – behaviour in tackles*

The midfield player lends his support as "wall" when linking up with the winger. The winger dribbles up to the defender, who drops back in a "delaying" fashion in order to constantly bar the way for the winger who attempts to break through using simple and double feints.

Other Feints
Pretend to execute the "Leo" trick (Locomotive), "shear" your leg over the ball, left/right – right/left, "Mathews trick", pretend to burst through on the inside only to pass your opponent on the outside, pretend to cross the ball (see Chapter on Feinting).

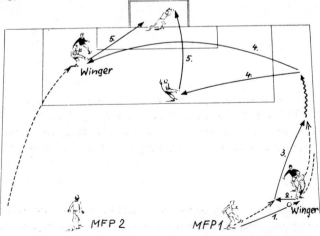

Figure 223 *One-two movements – short and long crosses*

a) The midfield player passes "short" to the winger and draws the defender to the ball. The winger allows the ball to rebound and moves through. The midfield player puts the ball through. The cross comes over hard and short to the centre-forward or long to the other winger.

b) The defender is not drawn towards the ball. The winger turns with the ball to face his opponent, dribbles at speed towards him, plays the ball against the "wall" and spurts past the defender. Meet and move with the through pass from the midfield player and then cross the ball.

c) The defender attempts to intercept the square pass from the midfield player. The winger moves through on his own and crosses the ball.

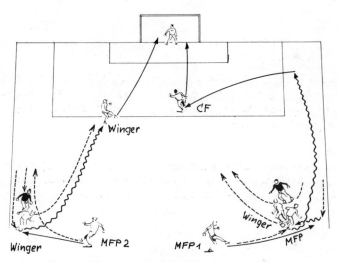

Figure 224 *Leaving and taking over the ball*

The midfield player passes the ball either square or diagonally to the winger and moves up with his pass. The winger dribbles inside with the ball; the defender moves with him along the "inner line". The midfield player takes over the ball from the winger's foot, carries it up the wing and crosses it for the centre-forward.

Variations

The midfield player pretends to take over the ball from the winger but the latter maintains possession. The centre-forward moves out to the wing and the winger shoots at goal himself.

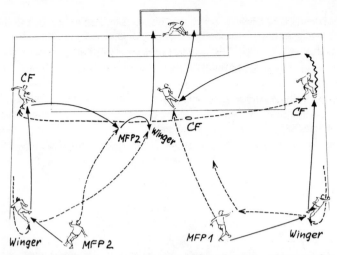

Figure 225 *The winger "sends-off" the centre-forward with the ball*

The centre-forward moves out to the wing along with the square pass from the midfield player to the winger. The winger plays the ball through to the centre-forward, while the midfield player runs to take up the centre-forward berth. The winger switches to the midfield position and covers up. The centre-forward puts the ball back to the winger, who shoots at goal.

Variations

The centre-forward crosses on to the midfield player's head, who allows the ball to fall to the winger, who then shoots at goal (drop-kick or a volley out of the air).

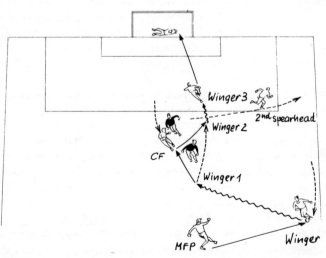

Figure 226 *Switch between the second spearhead and the winger*

Meeting the midfield player's pass, the winger dribbles inside whilst the second spearhead moves out to the wing. The winger passes the ball to the centre-forward and sprints past the defender in the direction of goal. The centre-forward moves towards the ball, draws the centre-back with him and allows the ball to rebound into the path of the winger by means of a "concealed" pass. The winger moves with the ball and shoots at goal.

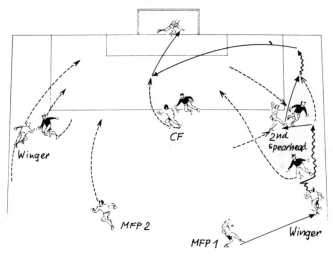

Figure 227 *Winger against defender and libero*

Attack against defence. Two midfield players with four strikers against five defenders. The winger dribbles with the midfield player's pass and outplays the defender. The libero challenges him. The winger plays the ball square to the second spearhead ("the wall"), collects the direct through ball and crosses it.

Variations
The winger loses the ball to the libero, who immediately counter attacks. The winger chases after him and combats the libero.

Note
All technical-tactical main aspects of the winger's game can be practised within the complete playing environment as provided by the "attack against defence" game.
"Attack against defence" is played in both halves of the field. The two midfield players take over the attack set up by the defence and continue into the other half of the field. Both sets of attackers play with the same wingers, who play outside-left in the one direction of attack and outside-right in the opposite direction. If the defenders move up in attack, they then take over the defender's role.

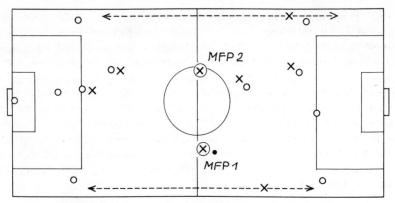

Figure 228 *The winger as outside-left and outside-right*

8.9. "ATTACK AGAINST DEFENCE" (TWO PLUS FOUR AGAINST FIVE)

An attacking formation plays against a correspondingly organised defence. This is based on the assumption that the attack functions with a forward striker and a second striker as well as two wingers. The strikers are directed by two midfield players. The defence organises itself using the centre-back, two back defenders, a defensive midfield player and the libero covering the zone.

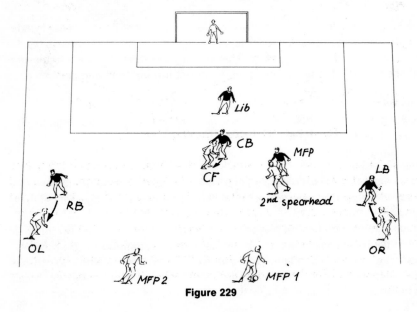

Figure 229

In the context of this exercise, all conceivable technical-tactical main aspects of both general as well as specialised nature are worked on (particularly tactical measures against a given opponent). "Main aspects" are not to be interpreted as stereotyped determination of behaviour – this would no longer be in the interests of the game –, but should be strived for freely according to the possibility offered. The prime object of the exercise must remain the player's intuitive and creative freedom, to adjust himself to each new situation and to execute his playing behaviour according to free decision. In the case of the aspect "playing one-two movements" for instance, it is up to the player to decide whether to complete a one-two movement which has been initiated or whether there is a better and more thoughtful solution of the playing situation which should be selected in preference of the one-two movement.

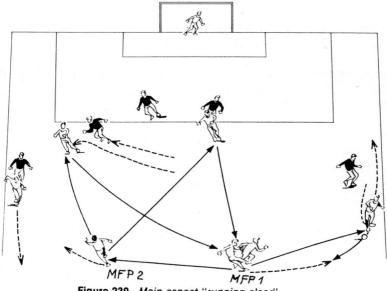

Figure 230 *Main aspect "running clear"*

Two midfield players behind the attack are delegated with passing the ball as quickly – but also as safely as possible. This calls for surprise running clear and change of pace on the part of all the attackers. Each pass to the attack is returned to one of the midfield players, which is the signal for the forwards to begin running clear all over again. Once the defence has won possession, it starts up an attack which runs until it reaches the midfield players, with the defenders dropping back into position again. When the midfield players are interpassing, the inner defender and the libero should switch the side they are covering (side near the ball).

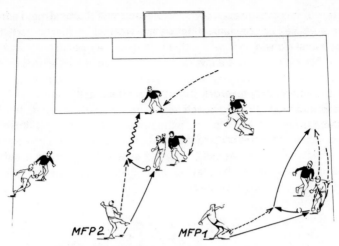

Figure 231 *Setting up one-two movements*

a) The midfield players move up with their pass and lend their support as "wall" in order to send off the strikers.
b) The midfield players use the strikers as "wall" and break through alone.

Note
The libero is called upon to challenge the forward who has run clear in the proper moment and to combat him.

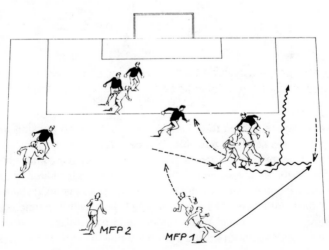

Figure 232 *Leaving and taking over the ball*

Dribble and run towards one another. The partner of the player who is dribbling takes over the ball from his playing leg. (Do not pass the ball from a short distance any longer!)

Further main aspects of training
Dribbling and attempting to break through,
meeting and moving with volleys,
heading the ball,
long-range shots (from the second row).

Figure 233 *Counter-attacking by the defenders*

"Attack against defence" is played in both halves of the playing area; the two midfield players alternately direct first the one, then the other attack.
The defender who wins the ball, counter attacks and moves up to help attack the other goal. One of the midfield players hangs back and covers up for him. The defender who is counter-attacking should round off his attacking move.

Note
This form of organisation in particular caters for all possibilities of competition-oriented attacking and defending behaviour and is extremely effective for rounding off the game "attack against defence".

9. FITNESS TRAINING

9.1. EXAMPLES WITHIN THE FRAMEWORK OF A GROUP OF TWO

It has been pointed out elsewhere at an earlier stage in this book that the game of football requires speed, stamina and strength, in a very specific form. Sprinting ability or being quick off the mark are always linked tactically to a competitive situation with or without the ball. Thus the "start" in the case of tactically running clear is a surprise burst of speed which usually is preceded by a deceptive burst of speed in the opposite direction.

Running and speed of running during a game are no linear, constant quahtities. They vary too, in their pattern of movement. The tactical efficiency of running during a match lies in the change in running direction and speed according to the situation as well as the differentiated running traits of the individual players. This situative running behaviour signifies – when compared to running straight ahead on a track – quite a different kind of neuro-muscular load as well as imposition on the circulation. Fitness has different interpretations!

The match-specific speed, stamina and strength make it possible for the player to adjust himself to the manifold challenges provided by an ever-changing competitive environment. An improvement in these match-specific fitness principles can thus best be arrived at within the context of technical and tactical training forms, that is to say match-oriented challenges. Fitness training governed by competition itself is accepted by the player as a far more sensible training load corresponding both to his nature and mentality. The technical and tactical solution of a competitive task represents a challenge to his own willingness to exert himself – not the trainer. Such a range of training possibilities is oriented towards motivating him and as a consequence, it is both attractive and effective.

Warming-up
Several pairs link up at "warming-up pace" in a restricted playing area as they mill around. The marking lines are the goal-lines at which the interpassing is aimed:
a) short passing in a narrow area,
b) in an enlarged playing area, bridge the distance with long passes (low, half-volley, high).
Technical-tactical objectives within the framework of warming-up:
a) Make use of the playing space and head for the marking lines.

b) Select the right moment to pass, when the way to your partner is clear and he is ready to accept your pass.

c) Aim to pass the ball as quickly as possible.

d) Meeting and moving with the ball.

e) Dribbling and "taking over" the ball.

Figure 234

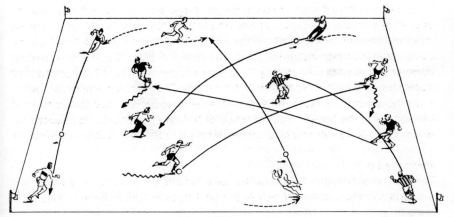

Figure 235

Movement tasks immediately you have *passed the ball* to your partner:

a) Adopt a squatting position (the heels stay on the ground, do *not* support your hands on your thighs).

b) From this squatting position, leap to head the ball straight in front of you, then to the side.
c) Press-ups (bend your arms).
d) As a sequence of movement: press-up – lie on your back – leap to head the ball – a short burst to take up a free position.

Note
Your partner should hold the ball and dribble with it until these movements tasks have been completed.

Figure 236

Following a short warming-up programme with technical-tactical objectives and a number of movement exercises, the training load is executed according to the interval principle. The period of load lasts 30 to 60 seconds according to the intensity of the load. The phases of rest should be used actively with tasks demanding concentration and extend to 60 seconds. Double this rest period in the case of youngsters and older players. The frequency of repetitions of a load task within a unit of time provides for a measurable comparison in order to detect an improvement within a training period. A training unit should comprise 10 to 16 load tasks with the corresponding active breaks.

The most effective improvement of speed and stamina as well as circulation capacity is arrived at through linking the interval method up to a continuous permanent load. This permanent load is enhanced through all games involving sides with their effective changes of pace, above all by matches involving a minority against superior numbers (3:5, 4:6, 5:7) and of course, competition itself. It is advisable, to keep a training diary in which the training forms, the load quantities and the results of medical examinations of the circulation which should be carried out periodically, are recorded.

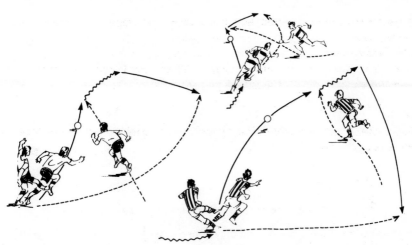

Figure 237 *Spurting at "running clear" pace*

A number of pairs link up with one another as they mill around. Use the marking lines as your target and make for them. A pass is called for by a sudden burst of speed into an empty space.

a) "Short" pass, b) pass over a considerable distance (meet and move with volleys).

During the break: Play the ball back and forward direct out of the air with the foot.

Figure 238 *Leaving and taking over the ball*

A and B run at high speed towards one another with and without the ball and leave the ball or take over the ball.

In the break: Play direct drop-kicks, one minute long.

241

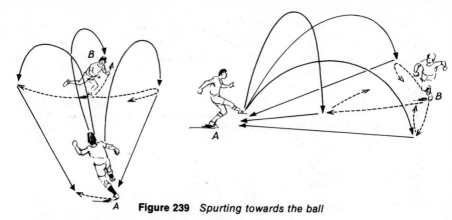

Figure 239 *Spurting towards the ball*

A begins (task during a break) and plays the ball high to B so that it either drops to the side of B or falls over his head. B should spurt to control the ball and play it back to A.

Each player continues for as long as he can with a maximum of 1 minute (It is the frequency that counts!).

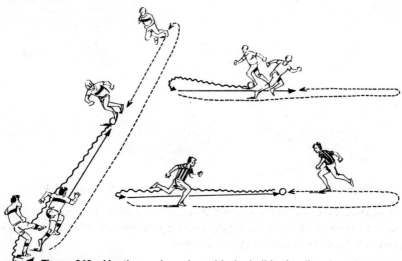

Figure 240 *Meeting and moving with the ball in the direction of running*

Stay 30 metres apart. Having passed the ball to partner B run at full speed towards his positions. B spurts towards the ball, meets it – without decreasing speed – and moves with it in the direction of running, dribbling with it until he reaches A's initial starting point. The most rapid possible turn, then B passes the ball and runs in the direction of A along with his pass. As many repetitions as possible within 1 minute. *In the break:* Direct heading of the ball.

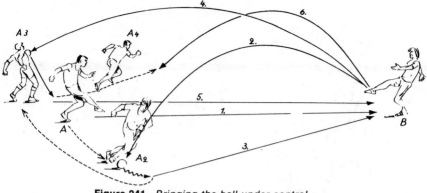

Figure 241 *Bringing the ball under control*

A passes the ball low to B. B lobs or lifts the ball in the air so that it drops to the side of A or beyond him so that A has to retrieve the ball at full speed, brings it under control and returns it low to B. Switch tasks after 1 minute.

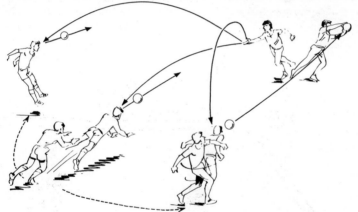

Figure 242 *Leaping to head the ball, "diving" header, volley-kick*

A throws the ball up in such a way that B can return it either by leaping to head it, by diving to head it or, if the ball is to the side, by means of a volley-kick. As many repeats as possible in the course of a minute.

Observe
Leap to head the ball using one leg only. When "diving" to head the ball, ensure that you break your fall by bending your arms!

Note
Each of these three movement tasks can also be executed individually during a minute of permanent load.

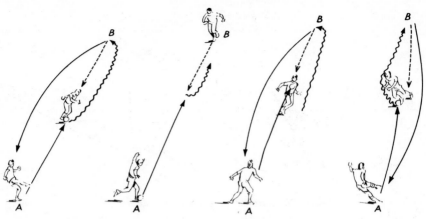

Figure 243 *Moving towards the man in possession*

A is in possession in the role of midfield player. B, 50 metres away as centre-forward, spurts towards A. A passes the ball hard (dose your pass according to the standard of performance) into B's path, who meets and moves with the ball while facing the opponent, then dribbles back to his starting position at speed. Then he passes the ball again to A. As many repeats as possible in a minute. Then switch around.

Figure 244 *Jumping from a squatting position*

From a squatting position, stretch yourself to jump over the ball and take up your squatting position once more. A and B alternate in jumping over the ball and attempt to repeat the exercise as often as possible within the course of a minute.

In the break: Passing the ball from out of the air with two touches.

Note
A and B should alternate jumping crosswise.

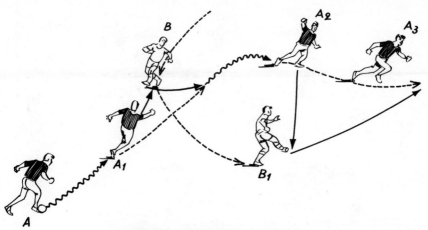

Figure 245 *"Playing and moving"*

A dribbles with the ball and uses B as the "wall". Together with his pass to B, A spurts into position and moves with the ball played direct from B in the direction of attack. Switch roles at the end of a minute.

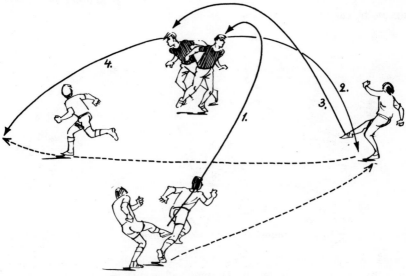

Figure 246 *Passing with the head*

Keep some 30 metres apart. A plays volleys to B and spurts into a position to the side along with his pass. B returns the ball to A using his head. Switch roles at the end of a minute.

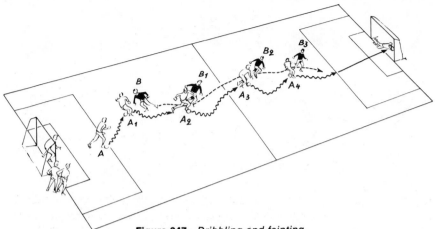

Figure 247 *Dribbling and feinting*

A dribbles the length of the pitch and attempts to pass B by means of feints. B drops back, barring his way, "delaying" him and as a result forces A to attempt new feints. A rounds off with a shot at goal, then B dribbles against A in the opposite direction.

In the break: Stand 2 metres apart, compel your partner to react as rapidly as possible by varying your passing.

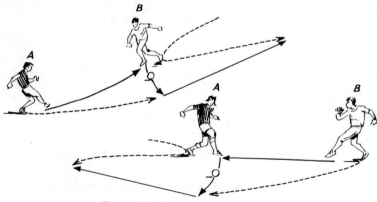

Figure 248 *One-two movements*

A puts B in possession with a pass and lends his support as "wall". B moves towards the ball, allows it to rebound (concealed pass) and spurts through in the direction of attack. A provides B, running through, with a direct pass. Then B initiates the one-two and sends off A.

In the break: Pass the ball high at close range. The other player meets the ball with his chest and returns it in the same manner out of the air.

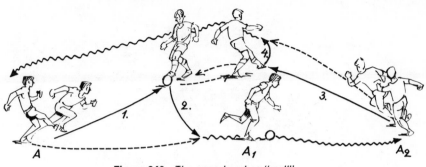

Figure 249 *The spearhead as "wall"*

A as midfield player passes to the spearhead and spurts together with his pass. B allows the ball to rebound (concealed pass). A gathers in the ball in his stride and moves with it in the direction of attack. As many repeats as possible within the space of a minute.

Figure 250 *One against one in the closest possible space*

The player in possession should attempt to assert himself on the ball.

Please observe
Get between your opponent and the ball! Feints: twist the shoulders, "left-right", pretend to execute the "Leo" trick, etc.

Note
This exercise is only really properly effective if the players tackle time and time again in the closest possible space.

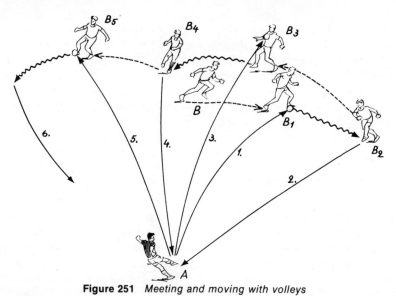

Figure 251 *Meeting and moving with volleys*

Keep a good distance apart: 30 to 50 metres. A volleys the ball into the path of B running clear at full speed. B meets the volleys and moves with the ball, returning it to A after dribbling rapidly. Change roles after a minute is up.

Note
A switch should be made to the rest exercise if top speed is no longer possible on account of dwindling strength. The object is to keep going for a whole minute at full pace.

Figure 252 *Two against two or one against one*

To round things off, the pairs play two against two. If there is an odd pair left over, then they should play one against one. Two against two or one against one should finally be played for as long over a minute until all technical-tactical actions of attacking and defending play have been played employing full strength and efficacy. In the process, the basic tactical objectives should be dribbling and running clear, securing the ball in a tackle and immediate pursuit of the opponent, the instant possession is lost.

9.2. CIRCUIT TRAINING FOR THE FOOTBALLER

In football, fitness training is largely carried out using the ball. In the multitude of technical-tactical training forms, all aspects of fitness can be interpreted as having the effect of achieving a direct improvement in the playing strength. For of course, all the speed, strength and stamina which is built up must be re-applied when on the ball. The circuit form of organisation must contain the features of this special fitness. Through the growing number of repetitions at each stage, the general increase in performance can be determined. It goes without saying though that no indication is provided about the improvement in the special playing qualities.

Load duration at each stage: 1 minute.

Break between the stages: 1 minute.

Equipment: footballs, medicine balls, ropes, "Deuser" belt.

1. a) Spurt into your partner's position along with your pass. Your partner spurts towards the ball, moves with it and dribbles into your position.

Then, face your partner once again, play and run.

b) Dribbling, your partner comes towards you and takes over the ball. Change positions.

2. a) Leap over a medicine ball from a squatting position. Two partners jump alternately. Begin in a squatting position and return to it.

b) Sweep the medicine ball to your partner using the full instep, do not kick the ball! Alternately left and right.

3. "Playing the wall", one-two movement with a change of positions as in Exercise 1. A passes hard to B and runs diagonally into position. B runs towards the ball and allows it to rebound into the path of A. B spurts on to take up position A, A dribbles to take up position B. Keep some 15 metres apart.

4. Skipping, a) normal left-right skipping, b) five left – five right,

c) take rope in one hand, skip in a crouched position.

5. a) Jump to head the ball. Throw the ball up yourself, leap to make contact and head it to your partner using the full forehead.

b) "Diving" headers with a soft landing, catching yourself with your arms. Serve the ball to yourself and throw yourself to meet it with a powerful leap.

6. a) Throw the ball in against the resistance of the "Deuser belt". Ensure regular, rhythmic pulling is carried out (cycle wheel tube).
b) Instep kicks against the resistance of the "Deuser belt".
7. A throws up the medicine ball and then adopts a prone position (press-up), B leaps high to catch the ball, squats down and throws the ball up again – press-up, etc.
8. Football: 1 against 1. Assert yourself on the ball, win back the ball if possession is lost.

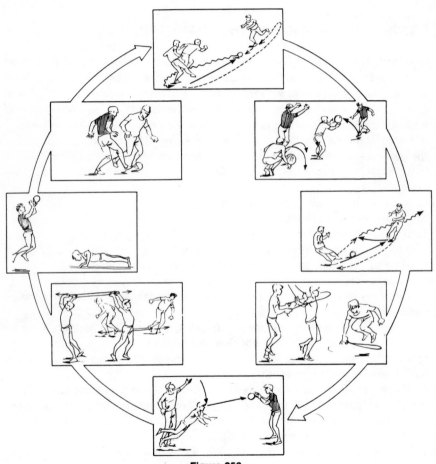

Figure 253